W9-BSE-113

RAISE A FIST,
TAKE A KNEE

ALSO BY JOHN FEINSTEIN

RAISE A FIST, TAKE A KNEE

RACE AND THE ILLUSION OF PROGRESS IN MODERN SPORTS

JOHN FEINSTEIN

LITTLE, BROWN AND COMPANY

New York Boston London

Little, Brown and Company
Hachette Book Group
1290 Avenue of the Americas, New York, NY 10104
littlebrown.com

First Edition: November 2021

Little, Brown and Company is a division of Hachette Book Group, Inc. The Little, Brown name and logo are trademarks of Hachette Book Group, Inc.

The publisher is not responsible for websites (or their content) that are not owned by the publisher.

The Hachette Speakers Bureau provides a wide range of authors for speaking events. To find out more, go to hachettespeakersbureau.com or call (866) 376-6591.

ISBN 9780316540933
LCCN 2021941972

Printing 1, 2021

LSC-C

Printed in the United States of America

For David Maraniss and Bob Woodward,
friends and mentors for more years than
any of us want to remember

Also, to the memory of John Robert Thompson Jr.,
who fought with me; taught me; and, finally,
inspired me to write this book

CONTENTS

Contents

PART III
Baseball and Other Pastimes

FOREWORD

By Doug Williams

I HAD TWO THOUGHTS WHEN John Feinstein told me he was planning to do research and write a book on race in sports. First, good luck corralling a topic that is so massive. And second, if anyone can pull it off, it's John. It isn't just that I respect him as a reporter, though I do, but it's this: he's white.

I know John would be the first one to tell you that he knows he can't possibly understand what it's like to wake up Black every morning and to go through life knowing there are people who are going to look at you as a Black man, not just a man.

I believe John has overcome the "disadvantage" of being white by talking to so many of us who have lived the Black experience. Plus, if this book were to be written by someone who is Black, a lot of people would shrug and say, "It's just another Black guy whining."

I've heard and read things like that all my life. We all get tired of hearing "Why are you always trying to make race an issue?" from white people who have no clue to the kinds of things we deal with on a daily basis.

Here's a fact: None of us are trying to make race an issue. Race *is* an issue.

In a sense, I was protected from racism as a boy growing up in Zachary, Louisiana, for a long time because I grew up in a segregated world. I had almost no contact with anyone white until I went to an integrated high school and played against integrated — or sometimes all-white — teams. That was when I first started to hear the word *nigger.* I was old enough to know what it meant, but at the time, it didn't seem like a big deal.

There's a lot of trash-talking in football — plenty of bad words get thrown around. You learn to laugh them off and keep playing. It wasn't as if we didn't notice; we just played through it.

Off the field was — and is — a different story. Every Black athlete, every Black person, can tell you a story about first hearing the word and coming to understand how ugly it is. I remember playing American Legion baseball after my first year in college. Sherman Floyd, a high school teammate of mine from Zachary, and I were the first two Black players in the league. We were standing in the outfield when we heard the word coming out of the opposing dugout. There was nothing going on, no one competing at that moment, and there it was. Since we were the only Black players in the league, we knew they were directing it at us.

How much did it affect me? Well, it was forty-five years ago, and I can still hear the word coming out of that dugout.

The word, which people nowadays often clean up as "the N-word," appears throughout this book. It might make you cringe; John told me he cringed every time he wrote it, but it is needed. Without it, you cannot fully understand the impact it has on people and how it makes people — Black and white — feel when they hear it or, in this case, read it.

You need to cringe sometimes to understand the real world.

When John and I first talked about this book, he told me he wanted to write it to try to explain how incredibly polarized the country was after the anthem protests of 2017. Both of us heard largely white crowds in NFL stadiums booing Black players who were kneeling for the national anthem.

They were called unpatriotic by, among others, the president of the United States. But as most people now understand, the protests had nothing to do with patriotism. Tragically, it took George Floyd's death for many people to figure that out. The video of Derek Chauvin killing Floyd made it impossible for the police to deny what had happened and made it clear that *this* was what Colin Kaepernick was talking about when he first sat—and then knelt—for the anthem in 2016.

John interviewed quite a few men who grew up in the Jim Crow South. He tells me that every Black person he spoke to had stories about being stopped for DWB—Driving While Black. That would include me. I thought Leonard Hamilton, the Florida State basketball coach, put it best when he talked about growing up with Jim Crow, which, in his hometown, included white-only water fountains and movie theaters and sitting in the back of buses, among other things.

"How can I possibly say there hasn't been progress?" Leonard said. Then he added, "But why, if we can land men on the moon, is it so hard for us to get along on earth?"

Amen to that.

As Ed Tapscott, the first Black CEO of an NBA team, puts it in these pages, "If you are Black, you have two jobs every day: one is your job; the other is to be Black." Arthur Ashe said something similar thirty years ago, talking about what it was like to be a Black tennis player growing up in Richmond, Virginia—once the capital of the Confederacy.

I know that every morning when I wake up, there are going to be people who will look at me skeptically for only one reason: I'm

Black. After my wife and I moved into a new house and a new neighborhood last summer, I suggested we take a walk to get to know our way around. She said, "Let's wait until we know more about the people around here."

In other words, how will people look at the new Black couple that just moved in? Fortunately, one of our new next-door neighbors came over the day after we arrived to welcome us and talk about his family—two kids at home, just like us—and tell us to be sure to ask if we had any questions or issues.

He's white. So far, so good.

It certainly helps that I'm still something of a celebrity in the Washington, D.C., area, where I played in the late 1980s for what is now the Washington Football Team. I was the starting quarterback on the team that won the Super Bowl in January 1988—Super Bowl XXII—making me the first Black quarterback to start and win a Super Bowl.

When I'm introduced at events around here, that's how I'm described: "the first Black quarterback to start and win a Super Bowl." Don't get me wrong: I'm very proud of that accomplishment and proud of being voted the MVP in that game. But perhaps someday, I'll just be a quarterback who started and won the Super Bowl. Not likely, but it would be nice to get to a point where we don't keep track of how many Black quarterbacks have won a Super Bowl. Right now, the number is three: Russell Wilson won one with Seattle in January 2014, and Patrick Mahomes won one with Kansas City in January 2020.

I suspect that this number will grow considerably in the next few years, given all the talented young Black quarterbacks currently in the NFL and given that Black quarterbacks are more likely to get a fair chance than they got years ago. Several Black players before me could have won Super Bowls or championships (before the Super

Bowl era) playing quarterback. But it was hard to do that since they weren't allowed to play the position after college.

I look forward to the day we stop counting.

Sadly, even in 2021, what Ozzie Newsome—the NFL's first Black general manager—said about his experience as a fourteen-year-old trying out for a Pop Warner team and his present feelings about it still apply. Ozzie said he *knew* in 1970 that there was no way he would be given a chance to play quarterback.

When Ozzie says that things have clearly improved in the last fifty-one years, he's right. Back then, no Black quarterback had ever played in the NFL. Only Marlin Briscoe, playing nine games for the AFL's Denver Broncos in 1968, quarterbacked a team that would eventually be part of the NFL. Marlin finished second in the rookie-of-the-year voting that year. And yet, he never took another snap as a quarterback.

Even now, Ozzie believes that a Black man has to be twice as good to get a job in the NFL as a general manager or head coach—and he suspects the same often holds in other sports that he doesn't follow as closely. Numbers, as you'll see in reading the book, back him up. Ozzie began running the Ravens in 1996, won a Super Bowl in January 2001, but still wasn't given the title of general manager until a year later. My pal James "Shack" Harris ran the Jacksonville Jaguars from 2003 to 2009 but was never given the GM title.

Of course, you'll say Briscoe's experience in Denver was fifty-three years ago. Well, Lamar Jackson came into the NFL fifty years after that—in 2018. He was barely mentioned at all as a quarterback in the five thousand mock drafts conducted before the actual draft. The TV pundits—including Hall of Fame general manager Bill Polian—kept insisting his best position would be wide receiver or, perhaps, running back.

If not for Ozzie and his top assistant Eric DeCosta (who has now succeeded Ozzie as the team's general manager), Lamar wouldn't have been drafted in the first round—he was the thirty-second and last pick—because he was insistent that he was a quarterback. He refused to run a 40-yard dash at the NFL scouting combine because he knew his speed would give the so-called experts another excuse to say he should switch positions.

You know who else was fast? Steve Young. So was Fran Tarkenton. *No one* ever suggested they change positions coming out of college. Both are in the Hall of Fame as quarterbacks. The difference is, they were white. Lamar will be in the Hall someday too—as he has already shown in his first three seasons in the league.

People like to point out the progress that's been made when it comes to race. No doubt, progress has been made. But many people don't want to accept that race is still a massive issue for all of us. Most of these people are white. They just don't want to hear about racism—they want to pretend it doesn't exist because it doesn't affect their lives.

In 2017, when John was working on his book on playing quarterback in the NFL, he asked me right after that year's NFL draft where I thought Patrick Mahomes and Deshaun Watson would have been drafted had they been white. Mahomes had been taken with the tenth pick by the Chiefs; Watson twelfth by the Texans.

I said, "Ahead of Mitchell Trubisky."

He said, "Trubisky went second."

I said, "Exactly."

The Chicago Bears traded up to the second pick and then took Trubisky, who had been a one-year starter at North Carolina. We all know what has happened since then: Mahomes has taken the Chiefs to two Super Bowls—winning one—and has been the league's MVP. Watson, his legal troubles notwithstanding, has been a franchise-type player in Houston.

Trubisky is now the backup quarterback in Buffalo after the Bears refused to pick up his fifth-year option.

When John quoted me in the book and in other places to make the point that it was still tough for some NFL scouts to look past color at the quarterback position, he was pilloried by people saying that Bears general manager Ryan Pace had just made an honest mistake. I'm sure it *was* an honest mistake, but how much was that mistake affected by Trubisky's *looking like* what was for years the stereotype of an NFL quarterback?

When Polian admitted in November 2019 that he had been wrong about Jackson, he said, "I was wrong because I used the old, traditional quarterback standard." He was referring to playing style. But to many, the old traditional NFL quarterback looks like Tom Brady—or Joe Namath or Joe Montana or John Elway or Johnny Unitas. And sounds like them too.

I doubt if Mahomes or Jackson receives the kind of hate mail I received when I played in Tampa Bay between 1978 and 1982. I doubt they ever opened an envelope and found a piece of rotting watermelon in it with a note that said "Throw this to your nigger friends."

But you can bet fans and media will be quick to jump on Mahomes or Jackson if and when they fail on any level. In 2019, the Ravens went 14–2, and Jackson was a unanimous choice for league MVP. Then they lost their first playoff game to the Tennessee Titans.

What comments did I keep reading and hearing? Jackson's very good, but he can't get it done in postseason. His postseason record at the time was 0–2. A year ago, the Ravens went on the road and won their first-round playoff game against the Titans. Then they lost on the road to the Buffalo Bills—who came within a play or two of beating the Chiefs in the conference finals.

Now the complaints are that Jackson can't throw the ball deep consistently. I would suggest that those people check the Ravens receivers in 2020 and list all who were legitimate deep threats.

Mahomes has plenty of receivers to throw to—short, middle, or long. That might help explain why his postseason record is 6–2, including those two Super Bowl trips. A great quarterback needs help. Dan Marino never won a Super Bowl. Anyone want to make the argument he wasn't a great quarterback? The same is true for Tarkenton and Sonny Jurgensen—among other greats.

If you look at the NFL today, most of the best young quarterbacks are Black: Mahomes, Jackson, Watson, Dak Prescott, Kyler Murray, and Wilson—who is the only one in the group who is over thirty. The jury is still out on Tua Tagovailoa and Jalen Hurts. Jordan Love is waiting his turn in Green Bay, Trey Lance was taken third in the spring 2021 draft by the 49ers, and Justin Fields went at number eleven—chosen by Pace, the general manager who passed on Mahomes and Watson to take Trubisky.

Lesson learned?

Tony Dungy, the first Black coach to win a Super Bowl (2007), astutely notes that it wasn't that long ago that most of these young stars would have been told they should change positions.

Not that long ago indeed. Ask Jackson.

RAISE A FIST,
TAKE A KNEE

INTRODUCTION

Not until I was on my way to see John Thompson in the fall of 2017 to talk about my idea to write a book about race in sports did I find myself thinking about what triggered my desire to understand more about the issue.

Thompson and I weren't always friends. Far from it. When I covered his great Georgetown basketball teams for the *Washington Post* in the 1980s, we fought often and argued constantly.

To me, it was a natural part of the adversarial relationship that often exists between reporters and the people they cover. I had a similar relationship with Maryland basketball coach Lefty Driesell when I covered his teams.

In fact, Driesell made a habit of calling me early in the morning, knowing I was single and not a morning person, whenever he didn't like something I'd written.

"Wake up, Faahnsteen," he'd say. "I gotta get on you."

Usually, by the time I went to practice that afternoon, Lefty had forgotten what had upset him so much that he felt the need to call me.

It was different with Thompson. For one thing, nothing short of a court order would get a reporter into a Georgetown practice most days. Once, in December 1983, before a game in Las Vegas, I was invited to practice. Even then, Georgetown's sports information director was instructed to sit with me.

"Miss Fenlon," the SID said, referring to Thompson's academic coordinator and alter ego, Mary Fenlon, "told me to keep an eye on you."

Maybe she was concerned I was going to steal a basketball. Or worse, speak to one of the players. When I asked Thompson why Fenlon felt someone needed to keep an eye on me, he laughed and said, "Mary doesn't trust the media. And she especially doesn't trust *you*."

Judge a man by his enemies, I suppose.

There was another important difference between my relationship with Thompson and my relationship with Driesell: I was white, and Thompson was Black. Anytime I criticized Thompson on any topic—whether it was his half-court offense or his refusal to play Maryland in the 1980s—there was always someone ready to call me a racist, usually someone from Georgetown.

One person who never saw our differences as having anything to do with race was Thompson. "My job is to protect these kids," he'd say to me, talking about his players. "Your job is to get them to talk to you even when I might think that isn't the best thing for them."

Thompson was often accused of playing the race card as he built his program. He frequently brought up the fact that he was Black and most of his players were Black, because he thought it was an important issue. In 1982, when he first coached Georgetown into the Final Four, he was asked during a press conference how he felt about being the first Black coach to reach the Final Four.

"I resent the hell out of that question," Thompson said, "because it implies that I'm the first Black coach *capable* of reaching the Final Four. I'm not. There have been plenty of men who came before me who were just as capable, if not more capable. I'm just the first one to get the opportunity who was lucky enough to make it here. They didn't have the same opportunity."

Thompson never shied away from bringing up race. That doesn't mean he played the race card. Many called him a racist because there were years in which all his players were Black. "I'm a Black coach," he said to me once. "Most of the best players, not all, but most, are Black. So, if I have an advantage going into a Black home to recruit a Black player, I'd be a fool not to recruit those players who see my blackness as a positive."

Sometimes, John got so angry with me that he wouldn't speak to me. There were also times when he did speak to me—even when Fenlon told him not to do so.

In 1984, after Georgetown had won the national championship, the *Washington Post Magazine* asked me to do a long profile on him. I called him at home and left a message. Calling his office was a waste of time; I knew he'd never get the message. He called me back at about 1 a.m., answering my sleepy hello with his usual, "What the hell do you want?"

I told him. To my surprise, he said he'd think about it. I had figured the answer would be no. A few nights later—again at about 1 a.m.—he called and said, "I'll meet you for breakfast next Monday at 9 a.m. at the Key Bridge Marriott."

We ended up having four sessions there, and as we walked out after the last one, I said, "I have two questions that have nothing to do with the story."

We were standing in the rain in the parking lot in the front of the hotel.

"Make it fast," he said. "I'm getting wet."

"Why did you give me all this time?" I said. "We spent most of last season fighting over everything. I almost got into a fistfight with one of your assistant coaches [Craig Esherick]. So why give me the time?"

He smiled. "Let me make one thing clear. It's not because I like you."

"Never thought it was."

"But I respect what you do. You and I disagree often."

"No, pretty much always."

He nodded. "Probably right. But I don't believe you've ever judged me for good or for bad as a Black man. You've judged me as a man—even when I thought you were wrong and you thought I was wrong. I respect that."

I was so touched—honored?—by the comment that I almost forgot my second question. He reminded me: "What was the other question?"

"Oh, right," I said. "Why did we meet here? Wouldn't it have been easier for you to have me come to your office?"

He nodded again. "Probably," he said. "But I didn't want Mary [Fenlon] to know I was talking to you. She can't stand you."

Once again, I was honored.

Fast-forward from October 1984 to October 2017. Thompson had retired in 1999. He had become host of a local radio show, and after a few years, I'd become a semiregular on the show.

We were, if nothing else, a unique pairing. Once, when the show was being broadcast from the site of a local golf tournament outside Washington, D.C., John asked me a series of questions on the basics of how the PGA Tour worked. After I'd answered the questions, he looked at me and said—on air—"John, you're so damn smart. Why are you such a jackass?"

I shrugged and said, "I've often wondered the same about you, John."

I'm not sure which of us laughed harder. I *am* certain that many listeners were shocked. By then, Thompson had iconic status in D.C., and the thought that anyone would speak to him that way—even jokingly—was no doubt unthinkable.

What I came to understand as the years went by was how fortunate I was to have had access to Thompson, whether as the subject of stories I wrote, as an adversary, as a friend, and—later—as a mentor. Thompson was a mentor to many people for one simple reason: he was smarter than the rest of us.

That's why I went to see him on that October day in 2017. In the back of my mind, I'd been thinking for years about doing a book on race in sports. As I drove into downtown D.C. thinking about what I wanted to ask Thompson, I thought back to the first time in my professional life that I'd come face-to-face with race as an issue.

It was in October 1975. I was a junior at Duke and had already decided I wanted a career in journalism when I graduated. Duke's football team was playing at West Point and, as the sports editor of the *Chronicle*—the student newspaper—I flew with the team to the game. It was a semi-homecoming for me. I'd grown up on the west side of Manhattan and arrived at Duke streetwise in many ways; naive in others.

I was certainly naive on the subject of race. My neighborhood was filled with white people (many of them Jewish), Black people, and Hispanic people. We played ball together in schoolyards and in the park. We never gave anyone's race or religion any thought. The only question was whether you could play.

Duke was different. One of my freshman roommates was Roger Golightly, an extremely good guy from Morganton, North

Carolina—the same town that produced Senator Sam Ervin, who at that moment was chairing the Senate's Watergate hearings. One night, Roger and I drove to Chapel Hill to hear Senator Ervin speak at the University of North Carolina.

"You know, I'm really glad we're roommates," Roger said on the drive over. "You're a good guy. I honestly didn't know what to expect because I'd never met a Jewish person before."

It was said without rancor, merely a statement of fact. But it occurred to me at that moment that I sure as hell wasn't in Manhattan anymore.

In October of my junior year, I was looking forward to Duke's game at West Point against Army for several reasons. Part of it was knowing I'd have time to go into New York on Friday and see some old friends. Just as important—perhaps more important—was that the *Durham Morning Herald* had assigned me to cover the game. Then, as now, Duke wasn't very good in football, and with both North Carolina and North Carolina State playing important games that weekend, the *Herald* decided not to staff the Duke–Army game.

That decision was a boon for me. I was already working as a stringer—a nonstaff writer who wrote occasional stories—for the *Herald* and the fact that they were trusting me to write both a lead and a sidebar on the game on deadline was a big deal. In return for writing two stories, the *Herald* would pay me $50—huge money as far as I was concerned.

In the second half, struggling on offense, Duke changed quarterbacks, bringing freshman Mike Dunn into the game. Dunn led a key touchdown drive, and Duke won, 21–10. In my lead, I wrote about Dunn's performance and how the defense shut Army down in the final two quarters. My sidebar focused on Dunn, who had been a star recruit and now appeared ready to take over for good as the starting quarterback.

I was very pleased with myself. I'd written two solid stories and made the deadline with time to spare. The next morning, I eagerly grabbed the newspaper and began reading what I'd written.

The stories hadn't been edited much at all, which made me happy. But when I got to the third paragraph in the lead, I froze. "The game turned around when Coach Mike McGee brought black freshman quarterback Mike Dunn into the game."

A "black freshman quarterback"? I was stunned. I went to the sidebar. There it was again. "For Duke's black freshman quarterback Mike Dunn, this was a coming-out party."

I couldn't believe it. Duke had a star freshman linebacker named Carl McGee. Nowhere was he identified as "Black freshman linebacker Carl McGee." Tony Benjamin, the starting fullback and Troy Slade, the team's best receiver, were never identified as Black.

Forty-five years later, I told the story to Doug Williams, the first African American quarterback to win a Super Bowl. He couldn't stop laughing. "Boy were you naive," he said. "Back then, a Black quarterback was a big deal—anywhere, anytime. One of the reasons I went to Grambling was because I wanted to go somewhere where they had no choice but to play a Black guy at quarterback— because everyone on the team was Black."

Doug was right. In fact, I'm not sure Bob Davis, the editor who added *black* to my stories that day, wasn't also right. Duke had Black linebackers and running backs and wide receivers in the past. It had never had a Black quarterback. I had just never thought of an athlete's race as being news. As Doug Williams said, boy, was I naive.

As the years went by, I couldn't help but notice a common theme to much of the racism I encountered in sports. Many, if not most, of those who saw color or stereotyped color were shocked to be called racist.

I remember sitting in 1992 with Al Campanis, who had been fired by the Dodgers in 1987 after he had said on ABC's *Nightline* that the reason so few African Americans had been given the chance to manage in the major leagues was because they "lacked the necessities" to lead a team. Campanis couldn't believe people thought him a racist. He'd been friends with Jackie Robinson when Robinson first came to the Dodgers.

"If Jack were still alive, he'd be outraged by what happened," Campanis said.

It was a version of the old cliché "But some of my best friends are Black." I still remember an Augusta member telling me proudly many years ago about the one day a year when all Augusta employees were allowed to play the golf course — including, of course, the many African Americans who worked there.

"We treat them like family," he said.

Just as Scarlett treated Mammy like family in *Gone with the Wind*.

Which is why it's fair to say I was extremely conscious of the issue when Washington quarterback Donovan McNabb had his blowup with Mike and Kyle Shanahan in the fall of 2010.

McNabb had played for the Philadelphia Eagles for eleven years before being traded to Washington in the spring of 2010.

The deal looked like a steal at the time. McNabb had been a solid, consistent quarterback and had taken the Eagles to the playoffs in eight of his ten seasons as a starter. He was thirty-three but still appeared to have plenty left in the tank, having been a Pro Bowl selection in 2009. The Eagles had gone 11–5 that year, although the season had ended with a thud: back-to-back losses to the Dallas Cowboys, in the season finale and then in a wild card playoff game in Dallas. It was the first time a McNabb-quarterbacked team had made the playoffs and failed to win at least one game.

Washington got him for two draft picks—a second and a fourth.

Mike Shanahan had been hired to coach Washington that season after Jim Zorn had gone 4–12 with Jason Campbell as his starting quarterback. The team had apparently upgraded at the two most important positions in pro football—coach and quarterback.

It didn't work out that way. Shanahan brought his son Kyle with him as his offensive coordinator. Kyle was thirty and viewed as a wunderkind offensive mind—especially by his father. The Shanahans and McNabb were oil and water almost from the start, especially McNabb and Kyle.

"Mike and I certainly had our differences," McNabb said. "Big ones in the end, but it was always professional. Kyle acted as if he should be in complete control. He had the job because of daddy; he was playing daddy-ball. There were times we were at each other's throats. It's really kind of amazing we never got into a fight."

The tension simmered for eight weeks, with Washington playing well enough to be 4–3, including a season-opening win against the Cowboys. Playing the Lions in Detroit, the team fell behind 31–25 with two minutes left after a touchdown pass thrown by rookie quarterback Matthew Stafford had given the Lions the lead.

Up until that moment, McNabb had taken every snap of every game for Washington. But when the offense took the field after the kickoff, Rex Grossman was the quarterback. On the first play, Grossman was sacked and fumbled. Ndamunkong Suh picked the ball up and ran seventeen yards into the end zone.

Ball game. The final was 37–25.

Naturally, Shanahan was asked about the decision to change quarterbacks—especially given the result.

The answer could have been easy: Shanahan had a gut feeling that Rex could get something done; Donovan wasn't having a great game; Shanahan thought a different look might be a good idea.

But that's not what Shanahan said. Instead, he responded, "I wasn't sure Donovan knew our two-minute offense well enough."

"I remember going to our PR guy and saying, 'What the hell is he talking about?'" McNabb said, his voice still filled with emotion ten years later. "He said he had no idea. We spent time on the two-minute offense every Wednesday. I was in my twelfth year in the league. How could I possibly not know the two-minute offense?"

Not surprisingly, Shanahan was asked the question again the next day. This time, he revised his answer. "I wasn't sure if Donovan was in good-enough shape to run back-to-back plays in the two-minute offense."

"That really upset me," McNabb said. "I had a hamstring tear dating to preseason, but I'd played through it. I always believed you couldn't win anything sitting in a tub rehabbing. I always said you can't help the club, sitting in a tub. So, I'd played, and I'd played well. Then he says that."

Washington had the next week off. That Sunday, during ESPN's pregame show, Chris Mortensen, a network "insider," reported that "sources" inside the team had told him that the Shanahans had been forced to cut their playbook in half for McNabb. This time, they had hidden behind anonymity in calling their quarterback dumb.

The cowardice of using Mortensen—an excellent and respected reporter—to legitimize their campaign to publicly humiliate McNabb infuriated me. For the record, I had never met or covered McNabb and had no reason to defend him. The issue for me wasn't McNabb versus the Shanahans; it was race.

The Shanahans were using racial coding, pushing the excuses that had been used in the 1960s and 1970s to keep Black players from getting the chance to play quarterback. Back then, the loud whispers always said the same thing: Black guys weren't smart enough to play quarterback; they didn't have the work ethic needed to play the position; and their speed — they were all fast, right? — was utilized best at positions like running back, wide receiver, and defensive back.

"When I was in the eighth grade in 1970," said Ozzie Newsome, the first African American general manager in National Football League (NFL) history, "I went to tryouts for Pop Warner football. When I'd played in the sandlot or schoolyard, I always played quarterback because I was the best player. It was automatic.

"At the tryouts, they told us to go to whatever position group we wanted to try out for. Quarterbacks were one place; receivers another; linebackers another. I started to jog over to the quarterbacks — that was my position. Everyone standing there was white. I stopped and thought, 'There's no way they're going to let me play quarterback.' I knew that Marlin Briscoe had played the position for the Broncos in the AFL [American Football League] a couple of years earlier. I also knew he'd played well and they'd made him a wide receiver the next season.

"I went to where the wide receivers were."

That was fifty-one years ago. The decision worked out just fine for Newsome, who is in the Pro Football Hall of Fame as a receiver — and should also be there for his work running the Baltimore Ravens from 1996 through 2018.

"I know we've come a long way since then," Newsome said. "But here it is, fifty years later, and I still feel as if you have to be twice as good if you're Black to be a quarterback, to be a head coach, to be a general manager. There's never been a Black general manager in the NFL who has been fired and gotten a second chance. Not one." He smiled. "Progress? Absolutely. But we're still a long way from where we need to go."

The incident with the Shanahans wasn't the first time that McNabb had been involved in a race-related dust-up that he hadn't started.

Coming out of Syracuse, he had been selected by Andy Reid and the Philadelphia Eagles with the number two pick in the 1999 NFL draft. Eagles fans in the draft audience booed the pick loudly. Angelo Cataldi, the extremely popular host of the morning-drive radio show on WIP, Philadelphia's all-sports station, had been campaigning all spring for the Eagles to draft Heisman Trophy–winning running back Ricky Williams from Texas.

Reid, who had been hired by the Eagles after the 1998 season, thought the team needed a quarterback who had greater potential than Doug Pederson, who he had signed as a free agent. Pederson would become a hero in Philadelphia in February 2018, when he led the Eagles to their first Super Bowl victory—as the head coach.

McNabb heard the boos and wasn't really bothered by them. "It just kind of made me want to say, 'Okay, I hear you, but I'm going to go out and prove you wrong,'" he said. "Look, Ricky was a Heisman Trophy winner, a very talented guy. And Angelo was very popular and respected in town. I honestly didn't see that as being racial, except maybe for a few people who would have preferred they take a white quarterback if they were going to draft a quarterback."

McNabb was one of five quarterbacks taken among the first twelve picks that year in what was considered a quarterback-rich draft. Tim Couch was taken by the Cleveland Browns with the first pick, Akili Smith was taken third by the Cincinnati Bengals, Daunte Culpepper went eleventh to Minnesota, and Cade McNown twelfth to Chicago.

It was supposed to be the most quarterback-rich draft since 1983, when Dan Marino was the *last* of six QBs taken in the first round. Yet, only McNabb and Culpepper ever made a Pro Bowl—Culpepper two, McNabb six. Only one—McNabb—ever took a team to the Super Bowl.

To me, Mike Shanahan's ability to get away with what he had said about McNabb and the negligence of a good reporter like Mortensen in allowing the Shanahans to hide behind anonymity in attacking McNabb's intelligence was outrageous.

So I said so—on a local TV show called *Washington Post Live.* I accused the Shanahans of racial coding. I argued that Shanahan had the absolute right to change quarterbacks when he wanted to—he was the coach, after all—but that the reasons he had given both publicly and then anonymously were inexcusable.

Did anyone in the media—national or local—back me up? Yes, one person. Michael Wilbon, my former *Washington Post* colleague who has since become rich and famous working for ESPN, supported me. The rest shook their heads and clucked or accused *me* of playing the race card. Rick Reilly, then of ESPN, and a friend of the Shanahans from his Denver days, wrote an entire column attacking me for calling Shanahan a racist for benching McNabb. He went on to cite, as proof that Shanahan wasn't racist, the fact that Shanahan had cried when two of his Black players in Denver had died.

No doubt Shanahan cried when his dog died too.

Reilly only had two things wrong: I never criticized Shanahan for benching McNabb, and I never called him a racist. It wasn't as if this was the first time I'd been attacked for something I'd written or said, but I'll admit the vitriol coming from my colleagues—whether it was in print, on TV, or on the radio—surprised me. Most of the media people who cover the NFL, especially on the print side, are white men. Their best sources—especially in front offices—tend to be white men. So, looking back, I shouldn't have been surprised. Thirty-five years after the Mike Dunn incident, I still had a naive streak in me.

A week later, on the day Washington was to host McNabb's former team, the Eagles, in a Monday night game, the team grandly announced it had signed McNabb to a $78 million contract extension. If you read the fine print, though, only $3.5 million was guaranteed.

In those days, I did a weekly hit on a local sports talk radio station with a guy named Steve Czaban, who is as far right as I am left. He began my appearance that week asking if I was ready to apologize to Shanahan in light of the new contract. Clearly, Czaban suggested, there was no way the team would sign the first-year savior of the franchise to such a lengthy and lucrative extension if there were a serious issue between McNabb and the coach.

"There's no extension," I said. "They've given him $3.5 million in hush money. I guarantee he won't be on the team next season."

As it turned out, Shanahan benched McNabb for good before season's end, claiming he wanted to see what Grossman could do as the team's starter. Grossman was thirty and had been in the NFL for eight years. He had been the Chicago Bears starting quarterback when they had gone to the Super Bowl four seasons earlier. Shanahan knew exactly what Grossman could and couldn't do.

McNabb never played another down in Washington after Grossman took over. He was traded to Minnesota during the off-season.

My accurate prediction about the contract and the hush money wasn't what stuck with me. What did was the anger directed at me because I had the audacity to say that Shanahan had been guilty of racial coding.

"Mike and I never really got along," McNabb said. "I didn't like the way he went out of his way to humiliate [Albert] Haynesworth because he reported to camp out of shape. I was shocked when I was told that Rex was going in during the Detroit game. But, hey, I've been benched before. That's fine.

"But then he and Kyle went out of their way to publicly insult my intelligence. That was what really upset me. You bet I was willing to take their money. I'd have been willing to come back and win the job the next year—if it had been a fair competition. I loved the DMV [D.C.-Maryland-Virginia] area. But there was no way it was going to happen. They went with Rex the next season because Mike has to always prove he's right."

In 2011, Washington was 5–11. Two years later, the Shanahans were fired.

The more I thought about the McNabb–Shanahan incident, the more I realized that race had been a part of my life and career for even longer than I'd realized.

I had never felt completely comfortable on the golf tour, in part because most players weren't just Republicans but were far enough to the right that when Donald Trump came on the political scene, they became some of his most loyal supporters.

It went beyond that, though; I'd covered politics early in my career, and some of my best sources had been Republicans. They were in the minority in the Maryland state legislature, and the minority party is always more willing to leak inside information than are those in the majority. These were men and women I respected. They were smart, they came to their conclusions after studying the issues, and they understood that compromise was part of the political process.

More and more, I found myself drawn to another minority— African American basketball coaches. Men like John Thompson, George Raveling, Tommy Amaker, Leonard Hamilton, Big House Gaines (who Thompson introduced me to), and Doc Rivers became my go-to guys when I was writing stories that weren't about jump shots and zone defenses.

At the Final Four, Thompson would frequently sit at a table in the hotel lobby restaurant holding court, surrounded by other African American coaches. I would walk over and ask if I could sit down. John would give me a dirty look, say something funny, and then tell me to pull up a chair. I always walked away from those sessions feeling smarter.

And then came Colin Kaepernick.

I wasn't all that surprised at the anger directed at him from white people who, like Trump, were angry and offended by his actions and who, like many others, suggested that if he didn't love America, then he should leave the country. Kaepernick protested because he *did* love America but wanted to see it get better.

He was pilloried throughout 2016, and I had no doubt he was going to be blackballed once the San Francisco 49ers released him in March 2017. There are legions of people who can't stand Kaepernick, and they will point out that Kaepernick asked for his release. He did, because he knew that new management wasn't going to give him a chance—any chance—to retain his starting job and would probably cut him. So he asked for the chance to look for a new job sooner rather than later.

He never had a chance. Throughout the 2017 season, stories

popped up constantly on internet sites quoting "unnamed NFL executives" who said Kaepernick hadn't been blackballed but just wasn't a very good player anymore. He was twenty-nine years old and had been the starter — albeit on a bad team — for the last eleven games of the 2016 season. And these sites were saying that he wasn't one of the best sixty-four quarterbacks out there. Seriously?

Early in that season, only a handful of players who had followed Kaepernick's example of kneeling for the national anthem continued to do so in protest during the anthem. On the third weekend in September, *six* players in the NFL knelt. The following Friday, Trump, during a campaign rally for a Senate candidate in Alabama, went into his rant, saying that NFL owners should fire anyone who didn't stand for the anthem. "Wouldn't you love to see one of those NFL owners when somebody disrespects our flag say, 'Get that sonofabitch off the field right now. Out! Out! He's fired!'"

Trump went on to claim that a drop in NFL ratings was due to attempts to make the game less violent, to eliminate helmet-to-helmet hits in an effort to make the game safer for the players. In short, who cares what happens to the players; they are there to entertain *me*. Sort of like the gladiators in Rome.

That Sunday, more than two hundred NFL players either knelt or stayed in the locker room during the playing of the anthem. The issue came roaring back — which may have been what Trump wanted: make white America angry at Black America.

A week later, when the Baltimore Ravens hosted the Pittsburgh Steelers, the entire Ravens team took a knee, holding hands, *before* the anthem began. Then they stood for the song. Many — if not most — in M+T Bank Stadium booed their team for this action. Most of those fans were white. Somehow, peaceful protest, even before the anthem began, wasn't acceptable.

At that moment, the country could not have been more divided on the issue of race. It was time for me to go see John Thompson. It was time to begin working on this book.

When I told John what I wanted to do, he laughed his deep-throated laugh and said, "John, you might as well try to explain the Holy Trinity."

Then, turning serious, he added, "Which is why you *must* do this book."

In doing my reporting, I was thrilled by the number of people I interviewed who were pleased — often more than pleased — I was doing the book. Kevin Blackistone, a *Washington Post* colleague who has written eloquently on racial issues for years, said to me, "If I write this book, it will be written off by a lot of people as a Black guy trying to create racial issues that aren't there. Some people are going to accuse you of being a white guy doing the same thing. But it *will* be different."

I believe it is different. George Raveling, the basketball Hall of Famer who was born in a segregated hospital in Washington, D.C., in 1937, said he was 100 percent in favor of my doing the book. But he also said this: "I know you'll talk to a lot of Black people and you'll learn a lot. But you can never know what it's like to walk in the shoes of a Black man. You just can't."

I understand this, and in fact, I think I understand Raveling's observation even more after doing more than a hundred interviews for this book. My friend Ed Tapscott, who was the first African American CEO of an NBA team, explained it this way: "If you are a Black man in this country, you wake up every morning with two jobs to do. One is your job, the one you get paid for every day. The other is being a Black man. It is a job in itself, every single day."

Ed added one more thing: "You're going to get attacked for doing this book. You'll get attacked from the right in the same way you got attacked on the McNabb–Shanahan story: 'How dare you bring this up; how dare you ask us to think about something we want to pretend doesn't exist.' And you'll get attacked by some Black folks, too, who are going to say, 'Who is this white guy claiming he knows what it's like to be Black?'"

I would never make that claim. I wish Kaepernick, sociology professor Harry Edwards, Kareem Abdul-Jabbar, and Spike Lee had been willing to talk to me. I know I would have learned from them. But I think those who did talk to me allowed me to have a much clearer understanding of the Black experience in sports—and in this country—than I had before I started this book.

I hope that after you read it, you will also have a better understanding. That was my goal when I went to see John Thompson that day in 2017. I only wish he were here to tell me if I succeeded.

PROLOGUE

THE ICONS:
Mexico City, 1968

T HEY ALL REMEMBER THE FIRST TIME they heard The Word. In almost every case, they remember not being sure what the word meant but sensing that it was meant to inflict pain.

"It was in fifth grade," Tommie Smith said. "Four of us were playing in the back field behind Central Union Elementary School. It was an integrated school. As soon as the bell rang, one of the kids jumped up and said, 'Last one in is a nigger baby.' I had no idea what that meant, but I made sure I finished first running inside. Then, later, I asked my parents what that meant."

Being told what the word means and why it might be directed at you was a slap in the face for all. "It's not a moment you ever forget," said Joel Ward, who grew up in Canada and was exposed to less racism than what most American kids experience. "I was about ten and I was playing hockey and got tangled with another kid, and he said,

'Get off of me, nigger.' I had no idea what it meant, but I knew it wasn't a compliment."

Years later, in 2012, when he had become a very solid player in the National Hockey League, Ward scored the winning goal for the Washington Capitals in game 7 of a playoff series in overtime against the Boston Bruins—in Boston. He was bombarded the next day with tweets that not only called him the N-word repeatedly but also suggested he "stick to basketball."

That stereotype is often repeated, even in today's supposedly more enlightened world. Cullen Jones, one of a handful of Black swimmers to succeed at the highest level of the sport—he won five Olympic medals as a sprint freestyler—remembers winning a close race as a teenager.

"I was standing with my parents after the race, and the mother of the kid who finished second walked over and said, 'Shouldn't you be playing basketball?' It was not a reference to my height. That was clear."

It is impossible for a white person like me to understand what it is like to be Black—especially a Black man, since so many people automatically fear them, including white authority figures.

"Every Black father has to sit down with his kids, especially the boys, at some point and give them The Talk," Pittsburgh Steelers coach Mike Tomlin said. "You have to explain to them that it is almost inevitable you are going to be stopped for DWB—Driving While Black. And you have to explain to them how they have to act when that happens. You can't be angry; you can't demand to know why you got pulled over. You have to be polite and completely non-threatening. That's the only way to guarantee you'll live through the experience."

When Tomlin's sons Michael Dean (now twenty-one) and

Mason (now nineteen) were approaching driving age, he sat them down for The Talk. "They both laughed at me," he said. "It was, 'Come on, Dad, we live in a safe neighborhood. That's not going to happen to us.'"

Tomlin paused. "It happened to Michael Dean three times in the first year. He stopped laughing."

The case can be made that Tommie Smith and John Carlos, his Olympic teammate in Mexico City forty-three years ago, started the Black Lives Matter movement forty-two years before anyone actually heard the term. Back then, it was called civil rights. Smith and Carlos, both graduates of San José State University, were mentored there by Professor Harry Edwards and competed in track and field events. They were among a group of Black athletes who considered boycotting those 1968 Olympic games for several reasons, including the potential participation of South Africa and Rhodesia. Another reason was the continued presence of Avery Brundage as chairman of the International Olympic Committee.

At a pre-Olympics meeting in Denver, shortly before the games were to begin, the athletes decided against a boycott.

"Instead," Smith said, "we decided that it was up to each of us to figure out how we wanted to make our voices heard. I knew if I did nothing, there would be no chance to make any progress. I couldn't do nothing."

Smith and Carlos had never been teammates; Carlos had transferred into San José State when Smith was a senior and had to sit out that season. But they knew each other, frequently trained together, and had often competed against each other. Smith had been the world record holder in the 200 meters until Carlos had unofficially broken his record earlier in 1968. Carlos's record wasn't officially recognized, because he was wearing a shoe that had not yet been approved for competition.

On the night of October 15, 1968, Smith pulled away from Carlos going around the turn in the 200 and sprinted to victory in a world record time of 19.83. Carlos was also passed in the final meters by Australian Peter Norman, who won the silver medal in 20.06—still the fastest time, even in 2021, ever run by an Australian. Carlos won the bronze medal.

What happened next has been the subject of books, documentaries, and debate for more than fifty-three years. While the three medalists waited for the medal ceremony to start, Smith pulled out two black gloves. The plan had been for each man to wear a pair of gloves, but Carlos had forgotten to bring his gloves. It was Norman who suggested each man wear one glove. Smith handed the left one to Carlos. "I wanted the right one because I'm right-handed," he said, laughing at the memory many years later.

He and Carlos took off their running shoes and put on black socks. The absence of shoes was to symbolize the poverty that so many Black people dealt with in the United States. The two men also placed buttons on their USA uniforms. The buttons read OPHR, which stood for Olympic Project for Human Rights.

The OPHR, the group that had considered the Olympic boycott, had made three demands before the Olympics: that Rhodesia and South Africa be barred from the games because of their apartheid (racial separation) policies; that Muhammad Ali's heavyweight title—stripped from him when he refused to be drafted—be restored; and that Avery Brundage step down as chairman of the International Olympic Committee (IOC) for decisions he had made in a previous era.

As chairman of what was then the American Olympic

Committee, in 1936, Brundage had given in to German "requests" that Jesse Owens, the four-time gold medalist, not be introduced to Adolf Hitler. Beyond that, Brundage had removed two Jewish sprinters from the US 4 × 100 relay team so as not to offend Hitler.

Rhodesia and South Africa were barred from the Mexico City games — although the IOC claimed that the decision had nothing to do with the demands of the OPHR but instead came about because the presence of the two countries would "inject politics" into the nonpolitical Olympics. Brundage remained in power, however, to the regret of Smith, Carlos, the OPHR movement, and, as it turned out, the entire Olympic movement.

While they waited to be called to the podium, Norman asked Smith and Carlos what the OPHR buttons were. When they told him, he asked if they had one he could wear. They didn't, but before the ceremony began, Norman found Paul Hoffman, the coxswain for the American eight-man rowing team, who was in the stadium. Hoffman had one of the buttons and happily gave one to Norman. Soon after, the three men walked back into the stadium for the medal ceremony. That act turned out to be as life-changing for Norman as it was for the two Americans.

The medals were presented. The three men turned in the direction of their country's flags as the "Star-Spangled Banner" was played. Smith and Carlos, each now gloved, bowed their heads and raised their arms to the sky, fists clenched. The photo of the two of them, with Norman standing in front of Smith, arms at his side, is one of the most iconic ever taken.

"It's been fifty-three years, and I feel like I'm still being asked to make the same argument over and over."

John Carlos was talking in short, almost breathless bursts. He's seventy-six now and doesn't give a lot of interviews — especially to people he knows nothing about. But he had agreed to get on the phone with me to hear why I wanted to talk with him for this book. The truth is, I never got to ask a question. Once I got through with my explanation, he began talking.

"Look at what just went on in Washington," he said — this was shortly after the attempted insurrection at the Capitol on January 6, 2021. "What do you think that was about? Race! What do you think would have happened if that had been a Black Lives Matter rally and it had turned into that kind of a riot and they had tried to attack the Capitol? You know what would have happened? There would have been hundreds dead and a lot of white people screaming they got what they deserved.

"This has been going on for more than four hundred years in this country, hasn't it? When Tommie and I did what we did, we were called every name in the book. We were thrown out of the Olympic movement. And you know what? There are still plenty of people out there who think we got what we deserved — just like there are people out there today who think that kid [Colin] Kaepernick got what he deserved.

"He sacrificed his career doing what he thought was right. He wasn't any different than Tommie and me. And the response wasn't all that different either, was it?"

Smith and Carlos were, in fact, banned from the Olympic movement and ordered to fly home from Mexico City by — you guessed it — Brundage. They were also ordered to return their medals.

"Never did it," Smith said. "They told me a time and place to go to, to surrender my medal. I just never went." Neither did Carlos.

The backlash against Smith and Carlos by white America, indeed by many in the mostly white media at the time, was perhaps best summed up by a column written by Brent Musburger, then a young columnist working for the *Chicago American.*

"Smith and Carlos looked like a couple of black-skinned storm troopers, holding aloft their black-gloved hands during the playing of the national anthem," Musburger wrote. "They sprinkled their protest with black track shoes and black scarfs and black power medals. It's destined to go down as one of the most unsubtle protests in the history of protests."

Smith and Carlos wore black socks—no shoes—on the medal stand. Their so-called black power medals were the OPHR pins— one of which was also worn by Norman. Musburger never did explain why a protest should not be "unsubtle."

"But you have to give Smith and Carlos credit for one thing," Musburger continued. "They knew how to deliver whatever it was they were trying to deliver on international television, thus ensuring maximum embarrassment for the country that is picking up the tab for their room and board here in Mexico City. One gets a little tired of the United States getting run down by athletes who are enjoying themselves at the expense of their country."

This was 1968, not 1858. Musburger could easily have been a plantation owner who couldn't understand why his "darkies" were complaining about working twelve hours a day in the cotton fields when, after all, he fed and housed them.

The US Olympic Committee (USOC) wasn't "picking up the tab" for the Olympic athletes—who in those days were paid nothing for competing—out of the goodness of its heart. It was picking up the tab in return for the athletes' bringing glory to the American flag by bringing home medals to the good old USA.

Musburger went on to become an iconic TV broadcaster, first

with CBS and then with ABC and ESPN, known mostly for his "You are looking live!" openings at games. He retired from ESPN in 2017 so that he and his son could run their own gambling business in Las Vegas, but he has continued to do radio work for the Las Vegas Raiders into his eighties.

In 2017, a year after Kaepernick had started the anthem protests, which had been continued by many of his former teammates in San Francisco, Musburger tweeted at one point: "Yo #49ers, since you instigated protest 2 wins and 19 losses. How about taking your next knee in the other team's end zone."

Musburger has never publicly apologized for the 1968 column even though there have been many stories urging him to do so. Carlos says he has no interest in even discussing Musburger other than to say, "He was proven wrong."

When I began conducting research for this book, I reached out to Musburger, who I've known for about thirty-five years. I sent him a text detailing the book and asking if he and I could speak about the column. He responded quickly, sending me a photo taken a few years ago in Las Vegas. It was a photo of him, Raiders owner Mark Davis, and Tommie Smith.

He offered no explanation of the photo other than to say that the three of them had eaten dinner together. I wrote back and said, "This makes me want to talk to you about this even more." He responded by saying how much he respected Smith's mother. He never responded to my request for an interview other than to say my bringing up the events of 1968 had made him think it was time for him to write his autobiography.

Later, when I spoke to Smith, I asked about the meeting and the photo.

"Mark Davis is a friend," he said, "and he asked if I would be willing to get together with him [Musburger] for dinner one night. I said, 'Sure, why not?' To be honest, I was curious what he might have to say. When I asked him what he was thinking when he wrote the column, he went on about how young he was [twenty-nine] and how he *had* to write the column that way because that was what his bosses wanted him to do.

"He said, 'I had to do it to protect my job, to take care of my family. I had to do it.' I waited for him to say 'I'm sorry.' Instead, he came over to me and started crying, put his arms around me and said, 'I had to do it, I had to do it.' He never actually apologized, but I still felt sorry for him at that moment. Not for what he did, but for the fact that he had to know how wrong he'd been. To me, the tears were his apology, but he never actually said 'I'm sorry.'

"He knew the column was racist; he had to know it. He just couldn't bring himself to say it."

While Musburger's column came to symbolize the reaction of much of the white media, there were columnists who defended Smith and Carlos and were outraged by Brundage's decision to throw them out of the so-called Olympic movement.

In a twist, the person who may have suffered the longest because of what happened that night was Norman—the Australian silver medalist. When Smith and Carlos told him what they planned to do, Norman, who had fought against the "White Australia" policy in his home country that had limited immigration by nonwhite people (sound familiar?) said he would support them in any way possible.

"When we told him [Norman] what we were going to do," Carlos said, "we thought we'd see fear. Instead, all we saw was love— and support."

That was when Norman found Hoffman. Later, the IOC

actually threatened to sanction Hoffman for giving Norman the pin that he had worn on the medal stand.

Because of that show of support for the two Americans by wearing an OPHR pin, Norman was pilloried in his home country for years. In 1972, even though he had bettered the required Olympic qualifying time in the 200 meters on thirteen occasions (and the qualifying time in the 100 meters five times), he was left off the Olympic team after finishing third in the 200 at the Australian Athletics championships. Running with an injury, Norman went 21.6—well above the qualifying time of 20.9 and considerably slower than the Australian record time of 20.06 he had run in Mexico City.

The Australian Olympic Committee had the option of adding Norman to the team because he had met the qualifying standard in both the 200 and the 100 multiple times. The committee opted not to send him to Munich. In 2000, when Sydney was the host city for the Olympics, Norman was not invited to the games by the committee. The excuse was that it would be too expensive to invite all Australian Olympians. Norman was given the opportunity to buy tickets. But the committee failed to mention that Norman wasn't just an Olympian; he was a silver medalist and still held the national record in the 200.

Instead, Norman went to Sydney as a guest of the USOC. Brundage, who died in 1975, no doubt rolled over angrily in his grave.

The three men who stood on the podium together in Mexico City remained friends until Norman died of a heart attack in 2006 at the age of sixty-four. Norman had flown to San José in 2005 to be part of the unveiling of a statue on the San José State campus honoring Smith and Carlos. The statue, twenty-two feet high, depicts Smith and Carlos with fists raised on the first- and third-place medal platforms. The second platform is empty. Norman asked that it be left empty so that visitors to the statue could stand on his empty spot to feel as if they had joined Smith and Carlos in their protest.

When Norman died, Smith and Carlos flew to Australia to eulogize him at the funeral and to be pallbearers.

"He was my brother," Carlos said at the time. The USOC declared the day of the funeral to be Peter Norman Day, the first time it had ever made such a declaration for a non-American athlete.

In his eulogy, Carlos said, "Peter Norman was a man who knew that right could never be wrong. Go and tell your children the story of Peter Norman."

Although the Australian Olympic Committee clung to the myth that Norman's actions in Mexico City had not been punished in any way, the Australian Parliament finally issued a formal posthumous apology to Norman and his family in 2012.

There were four items in the official statement.

This House recognizes the extraordinary athletic achievements of the late Peter Norman...

Acknowledges the bravery of Peter Norman in donning an Olympic Project for Human Rights badge on the podium, in solidarity with African-American athletes Tommie Smith and John Carlos who gave the "Black Power" salute.

Apologizes to Peter Norman for the treatment he received upon his return to Australia and the failure to recognize his inspirational role before his untimely death in 2006 and

...Belatedly recognizes the powerful role Peter Norman played in furthering racial equality.

To say that the apology was too little, too late is an understatement. Norman lived the last thirty-eight years of his life under a cloud in his home country because he had the courage to support Smith and Carlos. He had been dead for six years before the parliament got around to admitting the Olympic Committee had been lying for years about its treatment of Norman.

"The sad thing is I knew — *knew* — that wearing the button wasn't going to be a good thing for Peter that night," Smith said. "The way the world was then, a white guy standing up for two Black guys, two *scary* Black guys, wasn't going to turn out well. But I admired him for doing it. I loved him for doing it. Right then and there, he did a lot to bridge the gap between Black and white. I wish there were more people in our country willing to stand up the same way Peter did."

Smith and Carlos were the lead pallbearers at Norman's funeral; Carlos on the left, Smith on the right. "That was the heaviest coffin I ever carried," Smith said. "Physically and emotionally."

Norman didn't live long enough to hear the apology read in the Australian Parliament. Smith and Carlos have become heroes to many — if not most — in the United States. In addition to the statue at their alma mater, both have received honorary PhDs. And in 2019 — fifty-one years after Mexico City — they were inducted into the USOPC (US Olympic & Paralympic Committee) Hall of Fame. It took the USOPC even longer than it took the Australian Parliament to get around to trying to right the wrongs of men like Brundage and Musburger.

A year earlier, Smith and Carlos were asked by USA Track and Field to present the Jesse Owens Award for 2018 to sprinter Noah Lyles. They were introduced — via video — by Colin Kaepernick. The standing ovation was long and loud.

The torch had been passed.

PART ONE

FOOTBALL

CHAPTER ONE

The Pioneers

Aⁿʸ ʜɪsᴛᴏʀʏ ᴏꜰ ᴀꜰʀɪᴄᴀɴ ᴀᴍᴇʀɪᴄᴀɴ ǫᴜᴀʀᴛᴇʀʙᴀᴄᴋs playing in the National Football League has to start with Marlin Briscoe—who, technically, never played a down at quarterback in the NFL.

Although the NFL-AFL merger had already been announced when Briscoe played quarterback for the Denver Broncos in 1968, the leagues didn't actually unite until the 1970 season. That was the year the NFL created two conferences—the National and the American—and three NFL teams (the Baltimore Colts, Cleveland Browns, and Pittsburgh Steelers) moved to the American Conference so there would be thirteen teams in each conference.

Briscoe grew up in South Omaha, Nebraska, and started playing Pee Wee football when he was eight. In one of his first games, his team—sponsored by and named Phillips Department Store—played Roberts Dairy, a team from North Omaha. Roberts Dairy had a ten-year-old on the team named Gale Sayers.

"Gale was bigger than any of us, even then," Briscoe remembered. "He was already known for his ability to cut and get around tacklers without being touched. At one point, he ran wide and I was the only one with a chance to tackle him. I got ready for him to cut, and he decided not to bother—just ran right through me. I can still feel his cleats on my chest. I started to cry, not because it hurt but because I was embarrassed. I remember lying on my back thinking, 'What the heck just happened to me?'"

He laughed. "What happened was, Gale was bigger, stronger, *and* faster than the rest of us. Truth is, he inspired me. I knew I'd never be that big or strong, but I could make myself into a good player. Plus, I always had a strong arm, a very strong arm."

By the time he got to high school, Briscoe was five feet eleven and 165 pounds. He played quarterback at Omaha South High School and was a star. His combination of speed and arm strength earned him the nickname "Marlin the Magician."

"When I was a senior, a lot of the big schools recruited me," Briscoe said. "But not as a quarterback. I would have loved to have gone to Nebraska, but they recruited a quarterback named Bob Churchich. We'd played against each other in an all-star game. My team won, and I outplayed him. We were exactly the same size. But we weren't the same color. They offered him a scholarship to play quarterback.

"To go to any of the bigger schools, I would have had to change positions. Remember, this was 1963. Only a handful of the big-time schools had allowed Blacks to play quarterback. Finally, Al Coniglia, who was the coach at the University of Omaha, offered me the chance to play quarterback. He guaranteed me two things: an education and the chance to play quarterback. That was good enough for me."

Briscoe started for three years and led Omaha (now known as the University of Nebraska–Omaha) to a 27–11 record. His statistics were outstanding. The "Magician" nickname stuck. One of his teammates as a freshman was Roger Sayers, Gale's older brother, who was a running back and a wide receiver. Another Sayers brother, Ron, was the youngest of the three. He arrived at Omaha two years after Briscoe and was chosen in the second round of the 1969 draft by the San Diego Chargers. By the time Briscoe got to college, Gale Sayers was starring as a running back at Kansas. He would be drafted by the Chicago Bears in 1965 and go on to a Hall of Fame career in the NFL even though he only played five full seasons because of injuries.

"Talented family," Briscoe said with a laugh.

Briscoe led Omaha to the Central Intercollegiate Athletic Association conference title in his junior season and graduated with twenty-two school records as a quarterback. The 1968 draft was the second "common draft," held after the NFL and AFL had agreed to merge. The twenty-six teams would not compete with one another on the field (other than in the Super Bowl) until 1970, but they held one draft beginning in 1966.

The NFL rushed to conduct an AFL-NFL draft because it meant avoiding bidding wars between NFL and AFL teams. The merger had come together after New York Jets owner Sonny Werblin outbid the St. Louis Cardinals for Alabama quarterback Joe Namath by paying him a then-record $427,000 for three seasons, more than double what the Cardinals had offered. The merger was good for the owners; it stifled competition for the players.

Briscoe was not going to be the subject of a bidding war. He was drafted by the Denver Broncos in the fourteenth round of the draft—almost by accident.

"Truth is, I never thought about playing in the NFL until after my junior year in college," he said. "I loved watching the NFL as a kid. I had two heroes — Jim Brown and Johnny Unitas. I even wore high-tops to emulate Unitas. But I wasn't thinking about playing in the pros until I saw a couple of guys from my school — Jimmy Jones and Jerry Allen — make it. Then, I began to think maybe..."

During Briscoe's junior year, a Broncos scout named Stan Jones came to Omaha to watch Jones and Allen practice. Watching Briscoe, he asked one of the coaches, "Who is that little guy throwing the ball?"

Jones was intrigued enough by Briscoe's speed and quickness on the football field that he came to watch him play basketball. Briscoe, a three-year starter in basketball, scored 22 points that night.

"I need a defensive back," Jones told Briscoe. "I think you have what it takes to play DB in the pros."

The Broncos were up front with Briscoe after the draft. "They said they wanted me to be a cornerback," he said. "There was absolutely no talk of me playing quarterback. I told them I'd be willing to come to camp as a cornerback but only if they gave me a tryout at quarterback. I remember the reaction: what the hell is a fourteenth-round pick doing trying to dictate terms at all? I was being offered the *privilege* of playing in the NFL. That was their point of view."

The Broncos finally relented and allowed Briscoe to take part in a three-day open tryout for quarterbacks. He was one of eight QBs the Broncos brought in for evaluation that week. Briscoe was the only one who stood out — apparently. At least, he was the one the *Denver Post's* Dick Connor wrote about. This was back when NFL teams still sometimes let the media watch practices.

Briscoe was pleased with how he had performed but not at all surprised when he found himself at cornerback after the three-day trial ended.

The Broncos starting quarterback was Steve Tensi, who had spent two years as John Hadl's backup in San Diego before Denver had given up two number one draft choices to trade for him before the 1967 season. Coach Lou Saban wasn't thrilled with any of the candidates he had in camp to back up Tensi. He selected Joe DiVito for the role but apparently remembered enough of what he had seen from Briscoe to make him the team's emergency, third-string quarterback.

And so, just before the start of the regular season, Saban and Stan Jones showed up at Briscoe's locker one day before practice.

"Look in your locker, my friend," Saban said. "You've got a new uniform — number 15." (Briscoe had been wearing number 43.) "You're our backup quarterback if something happens to Tensi or DiVito."

It didn't take long for something to happen to Tensi. He had broken a collarbone in preseason, and on September 29, 1968, in the home opener in Denver against the Boston Patriots, he broke it again. On came DiVito, who completed 1 of 6 passes for 16 yards and never took another snap as an NFL quarterback.

With the Patriots leading 20–10 in the fourth quarter, Saban decided to give Briscoe a shot, making history when Briscoe became the first African American to quarterback an AFL or NFL team. Briscoe completed a 22-yard pass on his first play and led the Broncos on an 80-yard touchdown drive, scoring the touchdown himself on a 12-yard run.

"I really didn't know very many plays," Briscoe said. "I hadn't practiced at all at quarterback and hadn't gotten into any preseason games at quarterback. I just kind of went out and played sandlot ball, threw it to open guys, took off and ran when I saw an opening. I remember coming in and I could see the guys were jittery. I wasn't.

I was used to being the man. I was cool with it, and it showed in the way I played."

He played well enough to get the start a week later against the Bengals. The Broncos won 10–7, raising their record to 1–3. Tensi was in and out of the lineup the rest of the season, and whenever he was hurt, Briscoe replaced him. In all, Briscoe started five games and threw fourteen touchdown passes—four of them in a 34–32 victory over Buffalo in November. In that game, he threw for 335 yards, a Denver rookie record that stood until someone named John Elway broke it in 1983.

Briscoe finished second in the AFL's rookie-of-the-year voting, behind Cincinnati running back Paul Robinson. Given Tensi's tendency to get hurt, Briscoe figured he would have a chance to become the starter in 1969.

"At the very least, I figured I'd proven to them I could play the position," he said. "Turned out I was wrong about that."

Although the Broncos didn't draft a quarterback in the 1969 draft until the eleventh round—Maryland's Alan Pastrana—they signed Pete Liske, who had enjoyed a good deal of success in the Canadian Football League. Clearly, Saban had decided that if Tensi couldn't play, Liske was his next choice.

Briscoe was back in Omaha, finishing up work to get his degree in education, when he heard about the Liske signing. At the same time, he heard that Saban had scheduled a pre-training-camp quarterback camp. He had not been invited. He flew to Denver and showed up at the Broncos team headquarters.

He was told on arrival that Coach Saban was in a meeting.

"The secretary looked like she'd seen a ghost when I walked in," Briscoe said. "A few minutes later, I found out why."

When the door opened, Saban walked out. So did quarterbacks

coach Hunter Ennis, along with Steve Tensi, Pete Liske, and "a couple of guys I didn't recognize," Briscoe said. "Clearly, I'd walked in when they were in the middle of a quarterback meeting. No one would look me in the eye."

Saban had committed the second-string job to Liske, the third spot to Pastrana. Briscoe was out of the mix at quarterback.

"In those days," Briscoe said, "there really wasn't much you could do once a coach had made a decision. Plus, Saban was the general manager, so there was really nothing for me to do except ask for my release and look for a job. I really thought, given what I'd done the year before, someone would give me a chance."

To this day, Briscoe believes that Saban made sure he didn't get that chance. "When I asked for my release, he said I had to wait seven days. There was no reason to wait seven days. He just said that was what he was going to do. Initially, I heard a number of teams were interested in me. Hank Stram [in Kansas City] told me later he'd been interested. The Chargers were interested; I'd thrown three touchdown passes against them. I think Lou got on the phone and had me blackballed. It wasn't all that different than what happened to Colin Kaepernick almost fifty years later; it was just for a different reason. He didn't want me going somewhere and having success at quarterback, because it would make him look bad."

And yet, Briscoe doesn't label Saban as a racist. "Lou was quirky," he said. "I don't know if he was a racist—he did give me the chance to play quarterback, which no one else ever did. I think, to be honest, he was just plum crazy. Heck, he cut Floyd Little once." (Albeit briefly.)

The late Floyd Little, who died in early 2021, was arguably the greatest running back in Denver history. But late in a game against Buffalo (the game in which Briscoe threw four touchdown passes), he fumbled with the Broncos, trying to run out the clock. Saban told him he was done for the day.

But when the Bills got the ball back with time running down, Little was in the huddle. "Just throw it to me," he said to Briscoe. "I'll catch it."

Briscoe did as he was told, finding Little for a 50-yard gain that set up the winning field goal. Little had come back into the game against Saban's orders. "After the game, Lou told him he was going to cut him," Briscoe said, laughing. "Then he said he'd give him one more game. Of course, he never cut him."

When Saban finally released Briscoe, a number of teams were interested in signing him — but not as a quarterback. Briscoe decided to go home and work toward a master's degree in education. The Edmonton Eskimos, who had drafted him to play in the Canadian Football League a year earlier, called and offered him a chance to play quarterback for them.

"Canada had no problem with the idea of Black quarterbacks," Briscoe said. "That was the good news. The bad news was I didn't really like Canadian football. Plus, I had this notion in the back of my head that I belonged in the NFL."

He finally signed with the Buffalo Bills as a wide receiver, knowing he had no chance to play quarterback there, either. "They had Jack Kemp, Tom Flores, and Shack [James Harris], so I knew I wasn't going to play quarterback. But I also knew I could play wide receiver and have success. So I agreed to go there. I wanted to play in the NFL."

James Harris had been drafted by the Bills in the spring of 1969 in the eighth round. Unlike Briscoe, he was undeniably the physical prototype of an NFL-AFL quarterback. He was six feet four and 210 pounds and had a cannon for an arm. He had played for Eddie Robinson at Grambling during a time when the school was called the Black Notre Dame. This was back in the days when Notre Dame was still *the* Notre Dame. The last time Notre Dame won a national championship was in 1988. The quarterback was Tony Rice, who was Black.

If Harris had been white, he probably would have been a first-round pick. He had starred in high school growing up in Monroe, Louisiana. Living in a town that still posted White Only signs on things like water fountains and public restrooms, he attended segregated schools right through high school.

"Until I was recruited," he said, "I really didn't have any extended contact with white people. Where I came from, we lived in our world and they lived in theirs."

Harris did draw the attention of a number of Division 1 schools—mostly in the Big Ten. "The SEC was out of the question back then," he said, "especially if I wanted to play quarterback. But Wisconsin, Michigan, and Michigan State all were interested."

Duffy Daugherty, Michigan State's coach, was way ahead of most coaches when it came to recruiting Black players. He already had a Black quarterback—Jimmy Raye—on his team. Harris had met Raye at a football camp, and Raye hosted him when he visited the campus.

"I had a trick I did back then where I could catch a football with my right hand and, without bringing it down, throw it right back. I had big hands, good hands. I think when the coaches saw that, they started thinking about me as a receiver. Maybe later they might have moved me to quarterback, but not then. I wasn't sure what I wanted to do until I met Coach Rob."

"Coach Rob" is what all his players called Eddie Robinson, the legendary Grambling coach who won 409 games in fifty-six seasons at the school.

"The minute you met him, you knew you wanted to play for him," Harris said. "There was an absolute sincerity about him you could almost feel when he walked into a room. Once he promised my mother that I'd graduate and promised me I'd play quarterback, it was a done deal. There was no thought about going to a Big Ten school and hoping I'd get a chance to play quarterback. At Grambling, I knew I'd get a legitimate shot to play the position."

Harris starred at Grambling on great teams. He was injured for much of his senior season—1968—but was still looked at by pro scouts as someone who might be good enough to play at the next level.

A year earlier, Eldridge Dickey, after starring at Tennessee State, was also considered a Black quarterback with NFL-AFL potential. When he was taken in the first round—the twenty-fifth pick—by the Oakland Raiders, a breakthrough, or so it seemed, had been achieved.

That same afternoon, the Raiders used their second-round pick on a quarterback out of Alabama, a player named Ken Stabler.

According to the news reports of the day, Dickey played very well in training camp and probably should have been Daryle Lamonica's backup. But just before the season opener, Coach John Rauch decided to move Dickey to wide receiver. He never played a down at quarterback in the NFL and ended up with a total of five career catches.

"I saw Eldridge Dickey play," Harris said. "We played against his team my junior year, and he was a star. He was great. There was no doubt in my mind he was good enough to play in the NFL or the AFL—as a quarterback. Back then, though, we didn't get the chance. We were always moved to another position. If you refused to move, you were looked at as a problem.

"In those days, if you were Black and dreamed of playing quarterback in the pros, you woke up and realized you were having a nightmare."

After making it clear to pro teams that he didn't want to change positions, Harris wasn't drafted until the eighth round by the Buffalo Bills—with the 192nd pick. He was the eighth quarterback chosen in what was hardly a quarterback-rich draft. The first QB taken was Greg Cook—taken fifth in the first round by the Cincinnati Bengals. The second was Columbia's Marty Domres—four picks later. None of the quarterbacks selected before Harris ever made a Pro Bowl. The most successful were Domres and Bobby Douglass, who was taken in the second round by Chicago.

Harris wasn't even the first quarterback taken in that draft from a predominantly Black school—known now as HBCUs (Historically Black Colleges and Universities). Onree Jackson, from Alabama A&M, was drafted in the fifth round (110th pick) by the Boston Patriots. He was cut during training camp and never played a down in the NFL or AFL. In fact, the first African American quarterback to take a snap for the Patriots was Jacoby Brissett—in 2016.

Like Jackson, Harris arrived at his first training camp as a long-shot to make the team. In fact, he had been so discouraged and upset when he dropped to the eighth round that he briefly decided to quit football.

"Coach Rob had warned me before the draft that I might drop," he said. "He had talked to a number of teams who asked if I'd be willing to change positions. I wasn't going to do that. We ran a winged-T offense, but Coach Rob had spent off-season time with NFL coaches so he could teach me what running a pro-style offense would be like. He'd also talked to Howard Cosell about the fact that there were no Black quarterbacks in the pros.

"I knew what had happened to Marlin Briscoe—that he'd been given a chance in Denver, played well, and then they'd wanted him to change positions. I knew all of us who were Black and played quarterback faced long odds. I knew how good Eldridge Dickey was, and they wouldn't give him a fair chance. I knew about others who had gone to training camps, had a bad exhibition game, and been cut.

"Even after Coach Rob had warned me about teams wanting me to change positions, I didn't really think I'd drop that far. I had all the things they look for in a quarterback: height [six feet four]; arm strength; I'd made big plays in big games, and I'd played for a great coach who had sent multiple players to the pros. I just had two problems: the color of my skin and the position I played.

"After the draft, I decided to go home. All I had wanted before the draft was to get enough money for signing so I could pay my mother's bills. That wasn't going to happen. I decided I'd use my degree [in education] and teach. My mom called Coach Rob, and the two of them said I needed to go back to Grambling and talk it over with Coach Rob.

"Deep down, I knew I wanted to play football. Coach Rob knew it too. But before I left to go to training camp, he said one last thing to me: 'If you don't make it, don't come back here and tell me you didn't make it because you were Black. Just go and play.' "

Harris arrived in Buffalo to find that he was seventh on the Bills depth chart at quarterback. "What that basically meant was that one bad practice could get me cut," he said. "Fortunately, I played well."

In fact, on a team that included an aging Jack Kemp, Harris won the job in training camp and started the season opener against the defending Super Bowl champion New York Jets—how odd does that phrase sound? Kemp replaced him in the second quarter, and

Harris saw limited playing time after that, coming off the bench several times during the Bills 4–10 season but not getting another start.

The next season was more of the same: the Bills had drafted Dennis Shaw out of San Diego State. Kemp had retired, and the Bills opening day starter was Dan Darraugh. Yes, *the* Dan Darraugh. By week three, Shaw was the starter, and the Bills beat the Jets on a late Shaw touchdown pass—to Marlin Briscoe.

By then, Briscoe was established as one of the Bills better receivers. He had signed with the Bills to play the position after it became apparent that no one in the AFL or the NFL was going to give him another chance at quarterback.

Briscoe and Harris quickly became friends, bonded by their experiences trying to have success as Black quarterbacks in a very white world. "Funny thing is, I didn't even know Marlin was Black until I saw a picture of him when he was playing in Denver," Harris said. "When I realized what he'd done in Denver, he became a role model for me. He clearly deserved the chance to play quarterback again. If anything, one of the things working against him was that he was such a good wide receiver."

Lou Saban never had a winning record in four full seasons in Denver and was fired (allegedly he resigned) during the 1971 season, with a 2–6–1 record. Briscoe became a starter at wide receiver in Buffalo and was often a target for Harris when Harris got a chance to play—which was rare.

Harris got no starts in 1970 and two in 1971—playing in seven games in all. At the end of the season, the Bills cut him and he went looking for another job.

He found one in Los Angeles, where the Rams needed someone to back up John Hadl. Chuck Knox was the coach, and the Rams were good. In 1973, they went 12–2 but lost in the first round of the playoffs. Harris played only in mop-up situations that year.

The next season, the Rams started out at 3–2 but were struggling on offense. When Knox decided to give Harris a start—his first since the opening game of the 1969 season—he played superbly against the San Francisco 49ers, completing 12 of 15 passes for 276 yards and three touchdowns. He also rushed for a touchdown in a 37–14 rout.

Two days later, Knox traded Hadl to Green Bay. Suddenly, Harris was the team's quarterback. It was a bold move by Knox. Hadl had been the NFC (National Football Conference) player of the year in 1973. But Knox was able to get five draft picks: two first-rounders, two second-rounders, and a third-rounder in return for Hadl. It would be a massive haul for a player who, though highly respected, was thirty-four years old.

The move proved to be one of the great one-way trades in football history. The Packers went 7–15 with Hadl as their starter the next two seasons. Dan Devine resigned at the end of the 1974 season to take the Notre Dame job, and Bart Starr replaced him and went 4–10 in 1975.

Harris led the Rams to a 10–4 record that season and the Western Division title, going 7–2 after taking over the team. The Rams beat Washington in their first playoff game before losing 14–10 to the Minnesota Vikings in the conference title game. Harris became the first African American quarterback to take a team to the post-season, the first to win a playoff game, and the first to start a conference championship game. He was also selected for the Pro Bowl and won the game's MVP Award.

Impressive.

"Even after that season, I never felt completely secure that it was my job," Harris said. "I started in Buffalo feeling if I had a bad practice or a bad exhibition game, I might be cut. In LA, Coach Knox certainly showed faith in me when he traded Hadl. But it felt as if they kept bringing in guys to take my job. It wasn't Coach Knox; *he* had faith in me. But the organization never seemed to completely accept me as a quarterback rather than as a Black quarterback."

It wasn't a bad practice or a bad game that cost Harris his job. It was an injury. The Rams were 10–2 in 1975, when Harris went down hard on his throwing shoulder early in a game against the Packers. Ron Jaworski came in and led the Rams to a win that day and then a season-finale victory over the Steelers.

The Rams again reached the conference final after beating the St. Louis Cardinals in the opening round of the playoffs with Jaworski as the starter. With Harris healthy, Knox gave him the start in the conference championship game against the Cowboys. It didn't go well: the Cowboys jumped to a 21–0 lead. Although Knox then went to Jaworski, things didn't get any better, and the Cowboys won 37–7.

Harris played three more NFL seasons — one with the Rams and two with the San Diego Chargers — but he was never completely healthy again. Just when it seemed he was ready to play well, the shoulder would force him back to the sideline. Even so, he retired after the 1979 season as the role model for all African American quarterbacks who would follow.

The reason Harris was recruited by Michigan State in the mid-1960s was Coach Duffy Daugherty. Daugherty's "underground railroad," to recruit Black players from the South, was chronicled in Tom Shanahan's outstanding book *Raye of Light: Jimmy Raye, Duffy Daugherty, the Integration of College Football, and the 1965–66 Michigan State Spartans.*

The Big Ten was light-years ahead of the more Southern big-time conferences—Atlantic Coast (ACC), Southeastern (SEC), Big Eight, Southwest, and even the not-as-far-south Pacific-8—when it came to recruiting Black players in general and, more specifically, Black quarterbacks.

Michigan State had a Black quarterback—Willie Thrower—as far back as 1950, and Minnesota had won a national championship in 1960 with Sandy Stephens playing quarterback. Daugherty, who had been an assistant coach on the Michigan State team that won the national championship in 1952 (Thrower's senior season), had figured out that the South was full of talented Black athletes who wouldn't be recruited by Southern schools. He built a powerhouse team with players like George Webster, Bubba Smith, Gene Washington, and Clint Jones. In 1965, the Spartans were 10–1 and won a share of the national title. A year later, they were 10–0–1 after ending up in a 10–10 tie with Notre Dame in what was billed as the "Game of the Century."

The starting quarterback for Michigan State in that game was Jimmy Raye, who had grown up in Fayetteville, North Carolina, where he attended a segregated high school and played in a segregated football league.

The state had two all-star games at the time: one for the white kids and one for the Black kids. Raye played well enough in the Black East–West game to draw a good deal of attention from college coaches, notably Daugherty at Michigan State and Murray Warmath at Minnesota.

Raye was supposed to visit Michigan State the weekend the Spartans played Illinois. But when President John F. Kennedy was assassinated that Friday, the game, and Raye's trip, were postponed. Raye didn't get to visit until spring, when he was hosted during the weekend by Bubba Smith, George Webster, Gene Washington, and

Charlie Thornhill, a Black kid from Roanoke, Virginia, a town not that far from Fayetteville.

"I was comfortable there and confident I'd get a chance to play quarterback," Raye said. "To be honest, I didn't even give it a thought until I got home and my mother asked me if I thought I'd get to play quarterback. When I said I thought so, she called Coach Daugherty and asked him the question straight out. He said, 'He'll be a quarterback until he decides he's not a quarterback.'

"We both thought that was a little bit of a loaded answer, but by then my mind was made up. I was going."

Freshmen didn't play in the 1960s—they weren't eligible to play on the varsity, and there were no freshman teams. They did, however, scrimmage against the varsity. Raye was voted the outstanding freshman for the fall of 1964.

"But when I checked the depth chart at the start of spring practice, I was listed ninth among the quarterbacks," he said. "Several freshmen I had outplayed during the fall were ahead of me. Funny thing is, I started looking from the top—which was a mistake because I had to go a long way down to get to my name."

After not getting a single snap in the first two scrimmages, Raye began to work his way up, thanks to injuries and players quitting the team. When he did get on the field, he continued to move up because of his play.

By the time the season started, he was number two on the depth chart, behind only Steve Juday, a senior. The Spartans were loaded in 1965, especially on defense. Whenever the offense stalled, Daugherty would send Raye into the game to up the tempo and change things up. The Juday–Raye combination led Michigan State to a 10–0 record, including wins over Ohio State, Michigan, Penn State, and Notre Dame.

Back then, the most important final polls (Associated Press and United Press International) were conducted before the bowl games. Michigan State was voted number one. Then, in the Rose Bowl, UCLA had shut out Michigan State for fifty-four minutes, leading 14–0, before Daugherty finally put Raye into the game.

"He had said he was going to put me in at halftime," Raye remembered. "Then, as we were leaving the locker room, he said to me, 'I'm going to stick with Steve for the moment. You'll understand when you're a senior.'"

With Juday subbing near the goal line, Raye led two desperation touchdown drives, but the Spartans were stopped twice going for two-point conversions. "On the second one, coach told me to pitch it to Bob Apisa. He was our big Hawaiian fullback," Raye said. "He didn't think he could be stopped from two yards out. Problem was, he'd hurt his knee and he did get stopped."

A year later, Raye was the starter for most of the season, and the goal was to go undefeated—even though archaic Big Ten rules made it impossible for Michigan State to return to the Rose Bowl for a second straight season. The Spartans were 9–0 when they faced Notre Dame in the "Game of the Century." After the 10–10 tie, Notre Dame still had one game left—against a relatively down Southern Cal team. When it won in a rout, most of the polls picked the Irish as number one.

A year later, with four of the top eight picks in the NFL draft gone, the Spartans went 3–7. Raye was drafted in the seventeenth— and final—round by the Los Angeles Rams. He had thought about going to Canada to try to play quarterback, but the Rams offered a $2,500 signing bonus and the chance to play...safety.

"When [Elroy] 'Crazy Legs' Hirsch called me, his first sentence was, 'Welcome to the Rams; we think you can really help us at safety,'" Raye said, remembering his first conversation with the Rams general manager. "I had never played defense in my life. But for the chance to play in the NFL, I figured, what the heck."

He played for two years as a safety and a punt returner for the Rams and the Eagles. He did get a chance to play quarterback as a rookie during training camp because the veterans were on strike and the team's three quarterbacks (Roman Gabriel, Milt Plum, and Karl Sweetan) were absent. Once they returned, his days as a quarterback came to a screeching halt.

His playing days ended after two seasons, shortly after he broke his arm trying to tackle the Cowboys Calvin Hill on a toss-sweep. "I remember thinking, 'What am I doing here?'" he said with a laugh. "It was time."

Raye returned to Michigan State to get the twelve credits he needed for his degree in education and then earned a master's degree in education administration. In the meantime, Daugherty used him as a scout before assistant coach George Perles left to join the Philadelphia Eagles staff and Raye was hired to coach wide receivers.

When Daugherty retired in 1972, Denny Stolz was promoted to take over. He kept Raye on the staff. Three years later, Stolz was fired in the wake of a recruiting scandal, and Raye was without a job. Fred Akers had just been hired at Wyoming and offered Raye a job. But Raye had also been offered a place at San José State and wanted to go there. "Too cold in Laramie," he said.

Daugherty, still his mentor, told him to go work for Akers because the Wyoming coach was a rising star in the coaching profession. Wyoming won the Western Athletic Conference in 1974 and went to the Fiesta Bowl. After the Fiesta Bowl season, Akers was hired at Texas and took Raye with him. That spring, Raye met Ken Meyer, who was the offensive coordinator for the Seahawks, at a coaching clinic. The two men hit it off, and when Meyer was hired to coach the 49ers, he hired Raye.

That was the first of *ten* NFL teams that Raye worked for over the next thirty-six years. On seven occasions, he was the team's offensive coordinator. On two others, he had the title of senior offensive assistant.

He was interviewed for head coaching jobs several times, starting with the New Orleans Saints in the 1980s. "There were no Black head coaches back then," he said. "I would have been the first. Didn't happen. There were others later, the Chiefs, the Packers, the Jets. Each time, they hired someone else."

Raye worked for Marty Schottenheimer in Kansas City from 1992 through 1998. Another coach on that staff was Tony Dungy. When Schottenheimer left the Chiefs, Raye thought he had a great chance to succeed him. Instead, the job went to Gunther Cunningham. Two years later, when Cunningham was fired, Raye again thought he might get the job. This time it went to Dick Vermeil, who had retired for a second time after winning the Super Bowl in St. Louis a year earlier.

By then, Schottenheimer had taken the job as head coach in Washington, where he was promised full autonomy by Washington's control-freak owner Dan Snyder. Schottenheimer hired Raye as his offensive coordinator but was gone after one season, when Snyder reneged on his promise to allow him final say on all football decisions. From there, Raye went to work for Herm Edwards with the New York Jets.

"I got to a point where I realized it didn't do a bit of good to be pissed off," Raye said. "If I'd come along a little later, maybe I'd have gotten a shot. But I didn't. Somewhere along the line, people decided

I was good enough to play in the band but not good enough to lead the band. That was frustrating, but what's worse is now I see it happening to my son."

Jimmy Raye III, a wide receiver at San Diego State, played one NFL season with the Rams in 1991. He briefly followed his father into the coaching profession, working for the Chiefs for one season, but moved off the field when he was hired by the Chargers as a scout. After four years, he was promoted to director of college scouting and then, eight years later, was made director of player personnel. That is the identical route followed by Eric DeCosta, currently the general manager of the Baltimore Ravens.

In 2012, the younger Raye interviewed for the job as general manager of the Chicago Bears. The Bears ended up hiring Phil Emery, who lasted three years in the job before being succeeded by Ryan Pace, who in 2017 infamously drafted Mitchell Trubisky ahead of Patrick Mahomes and Deshaun Watson.

Raye has since worked as a senior personnel director — but never as the general manager — in Indianapolis, Houston, and Detroit. In the spring of 2021, after another unsuccessful Lions regime was swept out of town, the new general manager Brad Holmes (who is Black) and the new coach, Dan Campbell, decided to clean house in the front office, leaving Raye without work.

"I feel as if my son has gone through the same thing I went through, except in the executive suites," Raye said. "He's done all the work one should need to get an opportunity. He's fifty-two years old, and he's experienced. And yet... What's most annoying is when people say the reason there aren't more Black GMs is because there aren't enough qualified candidates. Really? Does anyone really believe that?"

*　　*　　*

Marlin Briscoe's professional career as a quarterback ended soon after Jimmy Raye's brief strike-created spell at quarterback with the Rams in 1968 came to a close. Briscoe never played quarterback again after the 1968 season. But he had an excellent NFL career. He led the Bills in touchdowns for three straight seasons and in catches for two of those years. At the end of the 1971 season, he was traded to the Miami Dolphins for a first-round draft pick. The pick turned out to be Joe Delamielleure, who went on to have a Hall of Fame career as an offensive guard.

Dolphins coach Don Shula was willing to give up a first-round pick for Briscoe because he wanted more speed opposite Hall of Fame receiver Paul Warfield. Briscoe was part of the undefeated Dolphins team (17–0) in 1972 and another Super Bowl winner a year later. During that season, he led the Dolphins in receiving, with 30 catches (1 more than Warfield) on a run-first team.

He played one more season with the Dolphins before moving on to Detroit and San Diego for a year and then New England for a year. While with the Patriots, he caught a touchdown pass from Steve Grogan in a rout of the Oakland Raiders. In doing so, he created a unique niche for himself, becoming the first player to be intercepted by a Patriot (during his season in Denver) and to then catch a touchdown pass as a Patriot.

He retired at the end of the 1976 season, having caught 224 passes for 3,537 yards and 30 touchdowns. Hall of Fame numbers? No. But a very solid career? Absolutely.

And yet Briscoe never completely got over what had happened to him after his one season as a quarterback in Denver.

"I came a long way going from being a fourteenth-round pick to being traded for a first-rounder," he said. "I had a crazy career, a great one, with the Dolphins. I went from coming into the league barely making ten thousand dollars a year to making a hundred thousand—which back then was a lot of money.

"But I've often thought about what might have been if I'd been given a chance to play quarterback after Denver. I know Hank Stram had interest in me and so did the Chargers, because I'd thrown six touchdown passes against them in two games. But I think [Lou] Saban made sure no one signed me as a quarterback. I always had confidence in myself as a quarterback—dating to high school. Whenever I got the chance to play the position, I played it well. Think about it. I didn't start '68 as the QB in Denver and ended up second in the rookie-of-the-year voting.

"Why wouldn't you want to build on that with a young player? But Saban brought in Pete Liske, and when I objected, I think he had me blackballed. Like I said, he gave me a chance, but then he turned on me. Was it race? Or was it just that he was a very strange guy? I wasn't the only player who had a strange experience with him. I had a good career, but I've never completely gotten over having to change positions to keep playing in the league. It really bothered me for a long time."

Briscoe moved to Los Angeles after retiring and made a lot of money buying and selling bonds. But in the 1980s, he fell prey to the cocaine madness that was hitting the city and the country. He ended up in rehab and eventually served time in jail—twice. That's where he was on January 31, 1988, when Super Bowl XXII was played in San Diego. On that evening, Doug Williams became the first Black quarterback to start—and win—a Super Bowl.

Williams threw four touchdown passes in the second quarter and for 340 yards in all. Washington beat the Denver Broncos 35–10, and Williams was named the game's MVP.

"I sat there overjoyed and with tears in my eyes," Briscoe said. "It was bittersweet. I felt as if I had a hand in him being there. I felt so proud of him and was so happy for him. There were some inmates and guards who knew who I was who congratulated me when they saw how emotional I was. What made me cry was looking around and seeing that my life had turned into cement and iron. I was thrilled for Doug and for all of us who had played the position and fought through all the stereotypes about Black quarterbacks. But I was very sad about where my life was at that moment. That's what made me cry."

Briscoe got out of jail a year later and has been clean now for more than thirty-one years. He remarried, went to work at a Boys and Girls Club, and helped out with his local high school football team in Long Beach. Five years ago, a production company approached him about doing a movie on his life. Gregory Allen Howard, who wrote the scripts for *Remember the Titans* and *Ali*, wrote a screenplay. Lyriq Bent, a well-known Canadian actor, was signed to play Briscoe. The title of the movie was easy: *The Magician.* There was just one holdup: the NFL. To make the film feel and look real, the producers needed the NFL to grant them licensing rights, to use team names and uniforms and stadium names. So far, the NFL hasn't granted those rights.

"I still think the film will get done," Briscoe said. "But it's pretty clear the league isn't eager to see those days relived in a movie."

Briscoe loves what he sees when he watches NFL games today: Patrick Mahomes, Lamar Jackson, Deshaun Watson, Russell Wilson, Dak Prescott, and Kyler Murray are at the very top of the list among the league's best and most exciting players. Wilson and Mahomes have both won Super Bowls; Mahomes and Jackson have both been MVPs.

"When Jackson was coming out of college," Briscoe said, "I got a call from ESPN wanting to know if Lamar should change positions the way I did, because I'd had success doing it. I said, 'Heck no, this kid can play quarterback. Just give him the chance I never got after '68.'

"All these guys who are starring at the position today probably would never have gotten the chance back in the sixties and seventies. Guys like me and then Shack [Harris], Warren Moon, Doug [Williams]—we had to prove to people that a Black man was smart enough, tough enough, and enough of a leader to play quarterback. Back then, we were all referred to in the media as *Black* quarterbacks. Nowadays, these guys are just quarterbacks.

"That's progress for sure. But we're still not there. Look at what they tried to do to Lamar."

Harris agrees. "I've said often that when I was a kid, if you were Black and you dreamed of being an NFL quarterback someday, you woke up and realized that reality was a nightmare," he said. "Now, it can be a dream—but it's still not an easy one to make happen. Not even close."

CHAPTER TWO

"The Scoreboard Doesn't Lie"

J AMES HARRIS'S OBSERVATION THAT BLACK quarterbacks now have a realistic chance of living the dream of playing in the National Football League is an important one. But Ozzie Newsome's point that they usually have to be twice as good as white quarterbacks is true not just for football but for almost any sports-related job that is most often associated with white people: head coach, general manager, Major League Baseball manager or general manager, quarterback, head coach at power-five colleges in football or in basketball.

Life outside the arena—or stadium—isn't always easy, either.

Ed Tapscott, now a scout for the Minnesota Timberwolves, was the first African American to be the CEO of a National Basketball Association team. He was hired as the first president of the Charlotte Bobcats in 2003 by Robert Johnson—who, not coincidentally, was the first African American to own a franchise in the NBA, NFL, National Hockey League, or MLB.

Tapscott, a graduate of Tufts, had been a successful college coach at American University—succeeding future Hall of Famer Gary Williams—before moving to the NBA, first as the top assistant for New York Knicks general manager Ernie Grunfeld and then as the Knicks general manager.

During his time with the Knicks, Tapscott had an apartment in tony Riverdale, in the Bronx, east of the George Washington Bridge, near the northern tip of Manhattan. Most nights, after a game at Madison Square Garden, Tapscott could make it home in fifteen to twenty minutes since the traffic was minimal at that hour.

But not always.

"Once or twice a year—at least—I'd get pulled over somewhere between the Garden and my apartment," he said. "I drove a nice car, not anything crazy, but a nice car. The closer I got to Riverdale, the more likely I was to get stopped."

Tapscott's crime? Speeding? No. Drinking and driving? Absolutely not. Broken taillight? Expired license plates? Highly unlikely.

No, Tapscott was pulled over for the catchall that most African American men—especially those who drive a high-priced car—experience at some point: DWB. Driving While Black.

"Believe me when I tell you, I wasn't just careful, I was extra careful," Tapscott said. "But if a cop caught a glimpse of me, there was a decent chance I was going to get stopped."

Almost without fail, Tapscott would have to wait while the cop ran a check on his plates and on his driver's license. Because he had maintained his residence in Northern Virginia, he was asked, "What are you doing in this neighborhood at this hour?" When he explained that he worked for the Knicks and kept an apartment in Riverdale, he would usually be asked to show some kind of Knicks ID.

One night, when the cop finally told him he could go, Tapscott couldn't resist asking, "Do you think this is fair?"

The cop shook his head and said, "No, it's not fair."

For the Black athletes and coaches I interviewed who are fathers, giving their children, especially their sons, The Talk—the discussion that Mike Tomlin had with his sons as teenagers—isn't just about the possibility of being stopped while doing nothing wrong. It is about how they *must* handle themselves when stopped— whether the stop was legitimate or not: hands on the dashboard as soon as the cop walks up, ask permission before making any move to get out a license or registration, stay in the car at all times unless told to get out, be polite—ultrapolite as in "Yes sir, no sir." This is true when dealing with any cop but even more so when dealing with a white one, especially a white male.

"You have to understand," Tapscott said. "Anyone who gets stopped is going to be anxious, nervous. But for most white people, the anxiety comes from concern about getting ticketed, maybe more so if you've been drinking. No one wants a DUI.

"But if you're Black, it goes beyond that. You're worried that you might *die*. When a white person tells me they don't believe that, I say, 'That's because you've never been Black.'"

Gary Williams, Maryland's Hall of Fame former basketball coach, remembers that the first thing he loved about sports as a kid growing up in Collingswood, New Jersey, was the scoreboard. Most of the time when Williams played basketball in the schoolyard, he was one of a handful of white kids playing—sometimes the only one. But it didn't matter—because of the scoreboard.

"The scoreboard, even when it's just being kept in your head in a schoolyard, doesn't lie," he said. "It doesn't see color. All it does is tell you who can play and who can't play. If you can play, no one cares what color you are."

That fact was driven home to Williams on March 19, 1966. He

was a junior at Maryland, and the national championship game between Kentucky and Texas Western was played that night at Cole Field House on the Maryland campus. The security guards at the back door of the building let Williams and several of his teammates into the game. To say that security was different in those days is like saying computers are more important in our lives now than they were back then. The building, which seated 14,500, wasn't overflowing with fans, and Williams and his teammates found good seats in one of the sections reserved for Kentucky's fans.

Texas Western won 72–65 in what is considered the most important college basketball game ever played, winning with five Black starters against an all-white Kentucky team. What Williams remembers most about that night — beyond the anger of those sitting around him — was what many said when the game was over: "We've got to get some of them." Not "get" as in *attack,* but "get" as in *recruit.*

Most of those people would have been extremely unlikely to invite a Black person to dinner, but they would willingly recruit "them" if they might help Kentucky win games and championships. That certainly wasn't unique to Kentucky. Most Southern schools were slow to recruit Black players in the late 1960s and early 1970s.

Kentucky recruited its first Black player, Tom Payne, in 1969. The university finally won another national title — after a twenty-year gap — in 1978. The star of the championship game was Jack Givens, who scored 41 points to key a 94–88 victory over Duke. Givens was one of "them." He remains a hero in Kentucky's basketball pantheon. The scoreboard doesn't lie.

Colleges in the South began regularly recruiting Black athletes in the 1970s. In 1971, a year after losing to Southern California, 41–21, in Birmingham, Alabama, football coach Paul "Bear" Bryant recruited the school's first two Black players, John Mitchell and

Wilbur Jackson. This move came after USC running back Sam "Bam" Cunningham rushed for 135 yards and two touchdowns as part of an all-Black USC backfield.

Alabama assistant coach Jerry Claiborne, who would go on to success as a head coach at Virginia Tech, Maryland, and Kentucky, said of that game: "Sam Cunningham did more to integrate Alabama in sixty minutes than Martin Luther King did in twenty years."

Hyperbole? Certainly. But there's little doubt that many Alabama fans had the same reaction to Cunningham and his teammates that the Kentucky fans had to Texas Western. "We've got to get some of *them*."

Which they did. That same year, Bryant also recruited Condredge Holloway, a talented quarterback from Huntsville, Alabama. Holloway was very interested in playing for Alabama and its legendary coach. Bryant wanted Holloway to play on his team — just not as a quarterback. Years later, Holloway remembered Bryant telling him that Alabama "wasn't ready" for a Black quarterback. Holloway went to Tennessee — as a quarterback. He was also a superb baseball player. In the three seasons that he was Tennessee's quarterback, the Volunteers went 25–9–2 and played in three bowl games.

Holloway was taken in the twelfth round of the 1975 NFL draft by the New England Patriots, who told him they planned on using him as a defensive back. Instead, he opted to play in the Canadian Football League. There, he was on two teams that won the Grey Cup (Canada's version of the Super Bowl) and was voted the league's outstanding player in 1982. He was voted into the Canadian Football Hall of Fame in 1999.

One wonders what he might have accomplished if he had been given a fair chance to play quarterback in the NFL.

In those days though, Black quarterbacks were almost always converted to play other positions—speed positions: running back, wide receiver, defensive back.

Doug Williams would be the first one to tell you that Marlin Briscoe and James Harris played important roles in his football career: Briscoe because of what he did in 1968 and what he wasn't allowed to do after that and Harris because he became an important mentor while Williams was in college.

"Shack [Harris] and I are like brothers," Williams likes to say. "He's the big brother; I'm the little brother. There's a very good chance I would never have played in the NFL if not for Shack. Three people made it possible for me to get to the NFL: Coach Rob [Eddie Robinson]; Shack, and Joe Gibbs."

It is difficult to think of Williams as a little anything. He is a huge man, six feet four and 230 pounds, though still clearly in shape at the age of sixty-six. Unlike Harris, who speaks so softly most of the time that one has to sit completely still and lean forward to hear him, Williams is as loud when he speaks as he is big, his accent still distinctively Southern, the product of growing up in Zachary, Louisiana.

"Funny thing is, I never wanted to play football," he said with a laugh. "I was too small when I got to high school. Plus, baseball was always my first love. I was small, but I always had a strong arm."

His first hero was Los Angeles Dodgers pitcher Don Drysdale. Williams's dad was a Dodgers fan in large part because of Don Newcombe and Jackie Robinson. The closest major league city to Zachary was Houston—about a 280-mile drive. When Doug was nine, his aunt Gladys took him to the brand-new Houston Astrodome to see Drysdale pitch against the Astros.

"Something happened and Drysdale got scratched," Williams said. "They moved Sandy Koufax up a day. I was very upset I had to watch Koufax pitch instead of Drysdale."

Williams was the sixth of eight children. His oldest brother, Robert, was fifteen years older than he was, and it was Robert who insisted—demanded—that Doug play football. Robert Williams had been a good-enough baseball player that he'd been in the Cleveland Indians camp in 1964 after graduating from Grambling. But he tore a rotator cuff, and, in those days, that was a career-ending injury.

Robert returned to Zachary to coach baseball but was also an assistant football coach. When his little brother told him he intended to play baseball and basketball in high school, Robert corrected him. "He said I had two choices," Doug said, laughing fifty years later. "I could play football or I could whip him in a fight. That actually left just one choice."

Doug had yet to hit his growth spurt as a freshman. He was five feet six but had a strong arm. So he played quarterback and free safety, though not for long. Williams went to Chaneyville High School—the Black school in Zachary. Early in the season, Chaneyville played Second Ward High School. Second Ward's quarterback was Terry Robiskie, who would go on to star as a running back at Louisiana State and play in the NFL for five years.

"Thing is, Terry was the same size then [six feet one, 215 pounds] as he was in college and the NFL," Williams said. "I came up to try to tackle him at one point, and he just ran through me. After that, I told Coach [Robert] Lucas that I was a one-way player."

Williams finally hit his growth spurt as a junior, sprouting to six four in a little more than a year. It took a while for his coordination to catch up, but when it did, he became a star and a hot college prospect.

"I was still playing basketball and baseball at that point," he said. "I still wanted to be Don Drysdale or, if not him, then Pete Maravich. LSU recruited me for baseball, but it was after I had committed to Coach Rob. Once I made that commitment, there was no going back. It was done."

Williams had a decorated career at Grambling. He followed Harris and Matthew Reed at quarterback. Reed didn't play in the NFL but did play for two years in the World Football League and for three years in Canada. In other words, Williams had big shoes to fill. He was supposed to be redshirted as a freshman, but the starter got hurt midway through the season.

Williams stepped in and put up remarkable statistics for the next three and a half years, throwing for more than 8,400 yards out of Robinson's winged-T offense. He was the prototype NFL quarterback: big, mobile, and with a cannon for an arm.

"Lots of scouts came to see us practice and play," he said. "You have to remember, this was the midseventies, when the SEC was just starting to integrate. We [Grambling] still got great players, which is why people called us the Black Notre Dame."

Grambling was 39–8 during Williams's four years in school. The school went 4–1 on the rare occasions when it got to play a Division 1 team.

Grambling graduate Buck Buchanan was scouting for the Saints by then. He told Williams during his senior season that New Orleans had him high on its board but wasn't likely to take him early, because they had Archie Manning as their starting quarterback.

"I thought I had what it took to be a first-round pick," Williams said. "But I knew no Black quarterback had ever been drafted in the first round. If it hadn't been for Joe Gibbs, I have no idea where I would have been drafted."

Gibbs was then the running backs coach, working for John McKay and the Tampa Bay Buccaneers. The Bucs were an expansion team that had gone 0–14 in 1976, denied the ignominy of 0–16 only because the NFL didn't start playing 16 games in a season until 1978. The starting Tampa Bay quarterback for most of 1977 had been Gary Huff. The Bucs started 0–12 that year, a record that made them 0–26 in their sad two-year history. They finally managed to win their final 2 games to finish 2–12.

It was then that McKay, known for his sardonic humor said, "Heck, three or four plane crashes, and we're in the playoffs."

Gibbs was the one scout who spent time with Williams rather than just watching him play and practice. "He came in and sat in on the class I was student-teaching," Williams said. "We spent hours talking football, talking how to run an offense and what I would need to work on when I got to the NFL. I have no doubt he was the guy who convinced Coach McKay that they should take me in the first round."

They did — with the seventeenth overall pick, making history by doing so. No African American quarterback had been selected in the first round of the draft before then. Tennessee State's Eldridge Dickey had been taken in the first round by the Oakland Raiders but never played a down at quarterback in the NFL. Like Briscoe and so many others, Dickey was converted to wide receiver.

Even though he was a first-round draft pick, the Buccaneers were reluctant to pay Williams what was then considered first-round money. He held out during the first week of training camp before signing a five-year deal for $565,000. "Still low," he said. "But better than what they had offered me initially."

In spite of the late start, Williams won the starting job in training camp. But on opening day, he took a hard hit from the Giants Gary Jeter as was he was being pushed out of bounds. He felt something pop inside his shoulder. Not wanting to come out of the game, he returned to the huddle, called a play, and went to the line of scrimmage. But as he crouched to take the snap, he felt a searing pain in his shoulder and fell over.

The stadium probably wasn't half full, and Williams vividly remembers hearing a woman's voice from the stands. "Oh, Lord," she screamed, "They done shot him."

The notion of anyone in Tampa's largely white fan base shooting Williams may have been far-fetched, but he received more than his share of hate mail. He learned not to open anything that didn't have a return address on it, especially after opening one large envelope that had some rotting watermelon in it. "Throw *this*," the attached note said, "to your nigger friends."

"Tampa," Williams told me, "was a *Southern* city."

He won over a large chunk of the fan base with his play. The Bucs were 4–4 when Williams went down for the season with a broken jaw that had to be wired shut for several weeks. With backup Mike Rae as quarterback, they went 1–7 the second half of the season, to finish 5–11. Even so, the progress was apparent to everyone. A year later, with Williams healthy all season and with a defense led by the Selmon brothers—Lee Roy and Dewey—the Bucs finished 10–6, won the Central Division title, and beat a Dick Vermeil– coached Philadelphia Eagles team 24–17 in the divisional playoffs. They lost the championship game 9–0 to the Los Angeles Rams after Williams had to leave the game with a torn biceps.

"Wouldn't have mattered if I had been able to play the whole game," Williams said, years later. "That defense was great."

Even so, the turnaround was remarkable: the Bucs had won a total of 7 games in their first three seasons. In their fourth season, they won 11.

Williams continued to be the Bucs starter for the next three seasons, and the Bucs reached the postseason twice more. At the conclusion of the 1982 season, Williams knew he was due a big raise. He had been paid an average $113,000 a year on his initial five-year contract. That made him the fifty-fourth-highest-paid quarterback in the twenty-six-team NFL. "Jimmy Rae, my backup, was making more money than I was making," Williams said.

No one had been a bigger supporter of Williams than John McKay. He had often railed at reporters who referred to Williams as "Tampa Bay's Black quarterback," as opposed to "Tampa Bay's quarterback." He told people that if Williams had been white, he would have been drafted much higher than seventeenth in the 1978 draft.

I experienced McKay's wrath firsthand in 1979, when the *Washington Post* sent me to Tampa to do a story on Williams, who was beginning to emerge as a star. During McKay's Monday morning press conference, McKay pointed a finger at me and said, "Who are you?"

I told him who I was.

"Why are you here?" he asked.

"I'm doing a story on Doug Williams," I said, pretty certain I was about to get yelled at by McKay.

McKay smiled and said, "You mean to tell me that the *Washington Post,* the paper of Woodward and Bernstein, just now figured out that we have a Black quarterback? Is that why you're here?"

I was trapped. That *was* why I was there. It wasn't because the *Post* had just discovered the Bucs had a Black quarterback; it was because that quarterback was having a good deal of success. When I tried to explain that to McKay, he waved me off and turned away.

"Next question," he said.

I hadn't actually asked a question but felt pretty humiliated nonetheless. Fortunately, McKay and Williams were good guys. When McKay finished his press conference, he pointed a finger at me again and said, "Hey, Washington Post, follow me."

He took me back to his office and apologized for embarrassing me. "I just get sick and tired of people not judging Doug as a quarterback but judging him as a Black quarterback." I told him I understood why he felt that way. Then I told him the story about the Durham paper's insisting on adding the word *black* to my description of Mike Dunn four years earlier and how much it had frustrated me at the time.

From that point on, he couldn't have been nicer or more open. He talked about how people wanted to assume Doug wasn't smart, partly because he was Black and partly because of his Southern accent. "They take one plus one and come up with twelve as the answer," he said. "Fortunately, Doug is both smart enough and mature enough to handle it."

Soon after, I found myself sitting alone with Williams, an interview set up for me by the Bucs PR staff. I started out by apologizing to Williams for some of the questions I was going to ask. "I'm sure you're as sick of the whole Black quarterback thing as Coach McKay," I said.

Doug grinned. "It's not a problem," he said with a smile. "I've been a Black quarterback my whole life."

Nine years later, when he became the first Black quarterback to start in a Super Bowl, a reporter asked Doug during a mass interview how long he'd been a Black quarterback. The reporter was pilloried for asking such a stupid question. One of his defenders was Doug Williams.

"What he was asking was how long I'd been playing quarterback," he said. "He was nervous. There were a lot of people there, and it came out wrong. I knew the guy and I understood the question. I wasn't offended. I just tried to give him a funny answer to lighten the tension."

Doug's answer was the same one he had given me nine years earlier: "All my life."

The contract situation in Tampa after the 1982 season wasn't funny. Williams had started every game for four seasons and thought he was entitled to a big raise.

He wasn't looking to break the bank. He was looking to move up to the middle ranks of starting quarterbacks. His ask was $600,000 a year for four years. "I still remember walking down a hallway with [general manager] Phil Krueger while he told me that Mr. C. [team owner Hugh Culverhouse] had told him not to make friends with *his* money. The message there was pretty clear."

The Bucs ended up offering Williams $375,000 a year plus another $25,000 in incentives. This was during the nascent days of NFL free agency. If a player signed with another team, the team he played for had the right to match the contract. More important, if it chose not to match the contract, it had to be compensated with draft picks. That meant the team still held almost all the cards.

Williams decided he'd had enough of being treated like a second- or third-class citizen. His wife, Janice, had just died of brain cancer, and he was left to raise Ashley, their infant daughter. He went home to Zachary and worked for a year as a substitute schoolteacher.

"I was getting paid fifty dollars a day," he said, laughing. "I liked the work, enjoyed it. But I didn't feel as if I was done with football. I was still only twenty-eight years old. When Mr. Tatham called, I was ready to listen."

Mr. Tatham was William A. Tatham Sr., who had just bought

the Oklahoma Outlaws, an expansion team in the United States Football League. Tatham wanted an established NFL quarterback for his team, and Williams was available—and willing. "The truth was, I missed playing," Williams said. "I got paid a lot less than I'd been making in the NFL, but it was a lot more than I was making teaching. And it got me back into football."

Williams played two years for the Outlaws, first in Oklahoma and then in Arizona. Early in 1986, the USFL, in a desperate attempt to stay afloat, filed an antitrust lawsuit against the NFL, all the while planning to move its season to the fall to compete directly against the NFL. In July, the USFL "won" the lawsuit. The jury awarded it $1 in damages, which automatically tripled under antitrust law to $3. Soon thereafter, the league folded.

Again, it was Joe Gibbs who stepped into Williams's life at a critical moment. Joe Theismann's career had ended suddenly in November 1985, when he suffered a horrific leg injury in a game against the New York Giants. Jay Schroeder had stepped in and played well, but Gibbs needed a reliable backup.

"Can you handle being a backup?" Gibbs asked Williams.

"When do you want me there?" Williams answered.

Schroeder and Williams didn't get along well, especially after the incident when Gibbs sent Williams in to replace an apparently injured Schroeder. "When I got out there," Williams said, "Jay waved me away as if I worked *for* him, not *with* him. He was disdainful. I never forgot that."

By the end of the 1987 season, Williams had supplanted Schroeder as the starter and Washington made it to the Super Bowl, rallying in frigid weather in Chicago to beat the Bears 21–17, then hanging on to beat the Vikings 17–10 in the NFC championship game.

The night before the Super Bowl (in San Diego), Williams needed emergency dental surgery for an abscessed tooth. "They could have taken every single tooth out of my mouth, and I was still playing," Williams said. "No way was I not playing in *that* game."

The next day, Williams became the first African American quarterback to start a Super Bowl. In the first quarter, trailing the Denver Broncos and John Elway 10–0, he was sacked and rolled his ankle. When he couldn't get up quickly, the training staff came onto the field, meaning Williams had to come out. Schroeder came in for one play, was sacked, and Washington punted.

That was when Gibbs asked Williams if he was okay. "I told him I was fine," Williams said. "I was in a lot of pain, but I wasn't coming out under any circumstances—especially if it meant Jay was going to take my place."

Gibbs wasn't entirely convinced. "I'll give you one series," he said. "If you're hobbling, you're coming out."

Washington scored the next five times it had the ball—Williams throwing four touchdown passes. It was 35–10 at halftime and the final was 42–10. Williams threw for a total of 340 yards and was voted the game's MVP. Schroeder never saw the field again.

After accepting the MVP trophy, Williams walked into the tunnel and found Eddie Robinson standing there. "He had tears in his eyes," Williams remembered. "He said, 'You know, I'm not proud of you because of that trophy. I'm proud of you because you got hurt and got back up and played through the pain.' That might have been the best moment of all."

Williams was finally paid a legitimate starting quarterback's salary for the 1988 season, signing a three-year contract worth $3.5 million. But Mark Rypien—who he liked a lot—beat him out for the starter's job in 1989, and he was released at the end of that season. He never got a call from another NFL team. "There was no Joe Gibbs to rescue me," he said. "So, that was that."

Like Williams, Warren Moon graduated from college in 1978. Playing for the University of Washington, he was the MVP of the Rose Bowl Game on New Year's Day. The Huskies beat Michigan, a 14-point favorite in that game, 27–20. Moon ran for two touchdowns and threw for another.

Getting to play quarterback at Washington hadn't been a simple process for Moon. He'd grown up in Los Angeles, and even though he starred at quarterback for Alexander Hamilton High School as a junior and a senior, his Division 1 offers were contingent on his willingness to change positions.

"The funny thing is, I wasn't a great athlete," he said. "I wasn't that fast or quick, but I had a very strong arm. I didn't fit the stereotype of the Black athletes."

Frank Kush, then the coach at Arizona State, finally offered Moon a scholarship to play quarterback, and Moon accepted. But Kush then recruited two white quarterbacks and told Moon that the scholarship offer was still on the table but only if he agreed to a position change.

"I knew my best position was quarterback," Moon said. "And I was convinced I was good enough to play it at the Division 1 level."

Moon turned Kush down and enrolled at West Los Angeles Junior College, where he was allowed to play quarterback. After his freshman season, the only four-year school that recruited him aggressively was the University of Washington, which had a new staff headed up by Don James. Dick Scesniak, the offensive coordinator, was enamored of Moon's arm strength and offered him the chance to compete for the quarterback's job as a sophomore.

Moon was a three-year starter at Washington, and in his senior year, after a 1–3 start, he led the Huskies to the Rose Bowl. There they beat a 10–1 Michigan team that believed it could win the national title if it won the Rose Bowl. Washington pulled the upset, and Moon, after running for two touchdowns and throwing for one, was voted the game's MVP.

"I honestly thought after that game, with all the attention it got, that someone would draft me or at the very least invite me to an NFL camp," Moon said. "Bring me in, and if I can't play, just cut me."

Even though he was playing for a big-time program, Moon didn't have a Joe Gibbs—who had been the only NFL coach to spend any extended time scouting Williams. With the twenty-eight teams in the draft knowing that Moon thought of himself as a quarterback and a quarterback only, he wasn't taken by any of them. In those days, there were twelve rounds and a total of 334 players were drafted.

Doug Williams—picked 17th—was the first quarterback drafted. The next two were Pittsburgh's Matt Cavanaugh, 50th, and Stanford's Guy Benjamin, 51st. The last quarterback taken was Bill Kenney, from Northern Colorado, who went 333rd, the second-to-last pick of the twelfth round. No one took Moon. He could have gotten an invite to an NFL camp as an undrafted free agent if he had agreed to change positions. He had no interest in doing that.

Instead, he went to Canada, as many Black quarterbacks had before him. Among them were Marlin Briscoe (briefly), Condredge Holloway, Chuck Ealey, and J. C. Watts, who never played in the NFL but did get elected to Congress. Canada was always years ahead of the NFL when it came to race relations. The first Black head coach in the CFL was Willie Wood—hired in Toronto in

1980 — nine years before the Oakland Raiders made Art Shell the NFL's first Black head coach. Jeffrey Orridge became the first Black commissioner of any major professional league when he took over the CFL in 2015.

Moon was recruited to play in Edmonton by coach Hugh Campbell, who came to Seattle to meet with him. Campbell promised not only to play him at quarterback but also to pay him about the same money that an NFL second-round draft pick would make.

The Moon–Campbell combination in Edmonton was hugely successful. The team won five straight Grey Cups — the Canadian equivalent of the Super Bowl — with Moon twice voted the MVP of the Grey Cup championship game. In 1982, Moon threw for exactly 5,000 yards — making him the first professional quarterback to throw for that many yards in a season.

By then, the NFL had changed its mind about Moon. Suddenly, scouts saw a six-three, 220-pound quarterback with a cannon for an arm — not a *Black* quarterback with a cannon for an arm.

Because he had one year left on his CFL contract, Moon couldn't sign with an NFL team until after the 1983 season. Seven teams bid for his services — the Houston Oilers winning out, in large part because their coach at the time was Hugh Campbell, the same Hugh Campbell who had brought Moon to Edmonton.

"I knew I was taking a chance signing a contract to play in the South," Moon said. "I had a wife and three children by then, and playing in Seattle or Minnesota might have been easier. But the money in Houston was good, and I liked the idea of playing for Hugh.

"It certainly wasn't easy. I learned to have someone else open my mail if the team wasn't playing well; actually, I always had someone else open my mail. I'd gotten booed in Canada — but it had been on the road, and most of the time, it was because we were winning. In Houston, there were times I got booed—and worse—at home."

Moon was hugely successful in Houston during his ten seasons there. After three losing seasons—the first two under Campbell, the third under Jerry Glanville—the Oilers made postseason seven years in a row. Moon was voted the league's MVP in 1990 and ended up making nine Pro Bowls. He went on to play for Minnesota, Seattle, and Kansas City before retiring in 2000.

In all, he threw for 49,325 yards in seventeen NFL seasons, meaning he trailed only Dan Marino and John Elway when he retired. Even today, with the NFL having become a pass-dominated league in the twenty-first century, he is still twelfth on the all-time list, not bad for someone who didn't throw a pass in the NFL until he was almost twenty-eight years old. In 2006, he was elected to the NFL Hall of Fame—the first African American quarterback to be enshrined and the first undrafted quarterback to be given one of Canton's gold jackets. He also became the first person elected to both the CFL and the NFL Halls of Fame, having been inducted in Canada five years earlier.

"I'm proud of all I accomplished, and I like to think what guys like Marlin and James and Doug and I accomplished has opened the doors for the guys who came after us," Moon said. "But I look at the league today, and I know we aren't there yet. Five of the best quarterbacks in football right now—Patrick Mahomes, Russell Wilson, Lamar Jackson, Deshaun Watson, and Kyler Murray—are Black. Cam Newton was an MVP until he got set back by all his injuries.

"But other than Murray, all the other guys were passed over for white quarterbacks. Mahomes and Deshaun went behind Mitchell Trubisky. Russell didn't go until the third round. Maybe if he'd been taller, he'd have gone sooner. If he'd been white, I guarantee he'd have gone sooner. All the scouts wanted Lamar to switch positions — I felt like it was 1978 again when I started hearing that. All he did was become the MVP in his second season."

Tony Dungy, who was a quarterback at Minnesota in the 1970s and had *no* chance of being drafted to play that position, put it this way: "All these great quarterbacks today who have elevated our game — you can go down the list — would probably have been told to change positions in my day. It makes you wonder how many potentially great coaches are being passed over today. Any notion that there aren't plenty of qualified candidates out there is just flat wrong."

There's also Dak Prescott, who was taken by Dallas in the fourth round — with the 135th pick — in the 2016 draft. That was the draft in which Jared Goff and Carson Wentz went with the top two picks. In all, six quarterbacks were taken before Prescott. The NFL rookie of the year that season? Dak Prescott.

Nowadays, the pundits love Mahomes, Jackson, Wilson, Watson, and Murray. Clearly, they believe that if they shower praise on these players now, people will forget how wrong the analysts were about them a while back.

Jackson, who may be the quietest of the current group, probably sums up what he — and others — have had to go through, even now, well into the twenty-first century, when he has a good game.

"Not bad for a running back," he will say with a wide smile, remembering all the experts who said he lacked the skills to be a successful NFL quarterback when he came out of college. He has yet to sit down and talk at length about how he felt hearing this pronouncement from so many so-called experts. Someday, he will talk — and he will have quite a story to tell.

*   *   *

Ryan Fitzpatrick, who has now played for nine teams in seventeen NFL seasons, often likes to clown around with outrageous outfits or jokes after a win. He is considered funny and smart—which he is. He's also white and a graduate of Harvard. Cam Newton, who has been the NFL's MVP in the past, is considered arrogant and cocky because he shows up for postgame interviews in outrageous outfits.

There is, without doubt, a double standard when it comes to what a star—Black or white—can get away with, as opposed to a nonstar. But there is also a double standard when it comes to what many (most?) white fans will accept from a Black player and from a white player.

This difference was never more evident than during the 2017 anthem protests, when most of those kneeling were African American. The complaint heard over and over again from white people—led by the bleatings of Donald Trump—was, "How dare they ruin my enjoyment of football."

Never once did any player protest during a game. Never once was a game delayed in any way by the protests. White people—most of them men—have no problem with paying Black athletes to entertain them. But ask these fans to think or rethink the way white police officers much too often treat Black people? How dare you. Get out there, entertain me, help my team win, and shut up.

"I get very tired," Dungy said, "when I bring up a racial issue—like the current coaching situation, among other things—of people saying that I'm creating a racial issue when there is none. The people saying that, without fail, are people who aren't touched by racial issues, who have never experienced racism, who have never been labeled or called a name because of the color of their skin.

"Where in the world do they come up with the notion that an

issue has nothing to do with race? What they should say is, 'This has nothing to do with *me*, so I don't care.' That would at least be honest."

The scoreboard never lies, which is why the majority of players in the NFL and NBA are Black, but when it comes to those in authority, the numbers are much, much lower.

As the reaction to the anthem protests made clear, many white Americans—quite a few of them NFL season ticket holders, love Black players who help their teams win games. But they have little if any interest in what these players think on any subject beyond the decision to go for it on fourth and one.

To these people, the players aren't all that different from the gladiators who entertained the Romans a couple of thousand years ago. The athletes are there to entertain and, if they're lucky, they get to live to see another day. Nowadays, they're paid very well for performing. But the principle isn't so different.

"When you are choosing players in almost any sport at any level, it is almost always a meritocracy," Mike Tomlin said. "Everyone wants the best players because they want to win games. But when it comes to giving people a chance to lead, a chance to be the decision maker, all of a sudden politics often come into play. A lot of people want to see us in uniform, want to see us perform but don't really want to hear what we have to say—on the field or off the field."

Or as that great American Laura Ingraham might say, "Shut up and dribble." Or block or tackle.

CHAPTER THREE

"Not Bad for a Running Back"

ALMOST FIFTY YEARS AFTER MARLIN BRISCOE became the first Black man to play quarterback in a major professional football league — the American Football League — Black quarterbacks still had to be, as Ozzie Newsome said, "twice as good as a white guy."

On April 26, 2018, Newsome would benefit greatly from being right about that.

People call the room where an NFL team conducts its annual draft of college football players a *war room*. While the term may sound overwrought, there is no doubting the tension is undeniably real, especially on opening night, when the first of the draft's seven rounds takes place.

The Baltimore Ravens war room is large, complete with a massive table and plenty of chairs pushed against the walls for overflow personnel. It also has a rarely used fireplace.

On the first night of the 2018 draft, the four key men in the room were team owner Steve Bisciotti, general manager Ozzie

Newsome, assistant general manager Eric DeCosta, and coach John Harbaugh.

The team's top scouts were also in the room, and other coaches and scouts drifted in and out—but only when there was a specific reason to be there. To say that the atmosphere was all business is a vast understatement. Some teams allow TV cameras into their war rooms at times. Not the Ravens. The only TV cameras allowed come from their in-house production company, which is only let in for a few minutes *after* a key pick is made, when no decision making or even discussion is going on.

The Ravens had finished the 2017 season with a 9–7 record, missing out on a playoff spot in the final seconds of their final game. It was only the fourth time in Harbaugh's ten years as coach that the Ravens had missed the postseason, but it was also the third straight season without a playoff appearance. The 9–7 mark meant the Ravens had the sixteenth pick in the first round.

Joe Flacco had been the Ravens quarterback throughout Harbaugh's ten seasons as coach—taken with the eighteenth pick in the 2008 draft. He had led the Ravens to a Super Bowl victory in January 2013 and had become an iconic figure in Baltimore. But he was now thirty-three, and although he was still a solid player, there was some thought that it was time to draft someone who could replace him in the next year or two.

"It was a quarterback-rich draft," Newsome said. "But we knew the quarterbacks who were most highly thought of were going to be gone by the time we drafted. We weren't willing to give up what we would have to give up to move up high enough to take one of them, especially since we didn't *need* a quarterback at that moment. We still had Joe."

There was, however, a source of extra pressure to consider a quarterback: Bisciotti, who had become the team's majority owner in 2003. He had let both Newsome and DeCosta know that he thought it was time to at least begin the search for Flacco's successor.

Bisciotti is not one of those owners who think that becoming a billionaire in business makes you an expert in football. He would never tell Newsome and DeCosta what to do any more than he would try to tell Harbaugh who to play and not play.

"I've always told Ozzie, 'Do me a favor before you make a major move and let me know before you do it so I don't get a call from one of my friends telling me what you've done,'" Bisciotti likes to say with a laugh. "'Just keep me informed.'"

Newsome never looked at it as quite that simple. "It's his team and his money," he said. "I want to have his input."

Newsome had run the Ravens draft room since 1996, the year that then owner Art Modell moved the team from Cleveland. Modell had decided to part ways with Bill Belichick, who had been both the coach and the team's de facto general manager. Newsome had been a Hall of Fame player for the Browns and had worked under Belichick both as a scout and as an assistant coach.

Modell put Newsome in charge of the front office after firing Belichick but didn't give him the title of general manager. Instead, he was named vice president of player personnel. It wasn't until 2002, when the Ravens had already won a Super Bowl with Newsome running the team, that Modell formally made him the NFL's first African American general manager.

But Newsome *was* in charge, title or no title. Before the 1996 draft, Modell wanted to use the number four pick to take Lawrence Phillips, a talented but troubled running back from Nebraska. Newsome felt the Ravens had two good running backs and needed to use the pick to fortify the offensive line. He took Jonathan Ogden, knowing full well that if Phillips became a star and Ogden didn't, Modell would be very unhappy.

Phillips, taken two picks later by St. Louis, played in a total of thirty-five NFL games for three teams and rushed for 1,453 yards. That number would represent a pretty good single season but not much of a career. He died by suicide while in prison in 2016. Ogden was voted to the Pro Bowl in eleven of his twelve seasons with the Ravens and was inducted into the Pro Football Hall of Fame in 2013.

The Ravens had a second first-round pick in that draft, at number twenty-six. Newsome used it to take Ray Lewis, who many scouts thought was too small to be an effective NFL linebacker. Lewis played for seventeen seasons, was part of two Super Bowl winners, was voted to the Pro Bowl thirteen times, and, like Ogden, was voted into the Hall of Fame the first year he was eligible — 2018.

By any measure, a pretty good first draft.

Newsome was finally named general manager in 2002, two years after the Ravens beat the New York Giants to win the Super Bowl. After the Ravens missed the playoffs in 2017, Bisciotti, not wanting to lose DeCosta — who had been courted by other teams — announced that 2018 would be Newsome's last as general manager. He would retain the title of executive vice president, but DeCosta would step into the general manager's position after the 2018 season.

That meant the 2018 draft would be Newsome's twenty-third — and last — as the man in charge in the Ravens draft room. Both he and DeCosta agreed that the sixteenth pick should be used on a tight end. Flacco had always enjoyed great success throwing to his tight ends, the best of whom, Dennis Pitta, had been forced to retire because of a serious hip injury the previous summer.

"Tight ends were always Joe's best friends on the field," DeCosta said. "There were three guys that we liked a lot: Calvin Ridley,

Hayden Hurst, and D. J. Moore. We would have been happy with any of those three."

The Ravens had also done their homework on the quarterback class. The four that NFL scouts and pundits were raving about were Oklahoma's Baker Mayfield (the previous fall's Heisman Trophy winner), Southern California's Sam Darnold, Wyoming's Josh Allen, and UCLA's Josh Rosen.

All were expected to be taken in the top ten — and they were. Mayfield went first, to Cleveland; Darnold, third, to the New York Jets; Allen, seventh, to Buffalo; and Rosen, tenth, to Arizona. The only real surprise was that Rosen lasted until the tenth spot, something he whined loudly about.

Starting the previous fall, Newsome and DeCosta had been discussing another quarterback: Lamar Jackson of Louisville. He had won the Heisman Trophy in 2016 as a sophomore and finished third behind Mayfield and Stanford running back Bryce Love in 2017. Yet he didn't fit the mold, as ESPN's Bill Polian would say later, because he "didn't fit the old traditional quarterback standard" of an NFL quarterback, as in tall, strong-armed, and white. He was six feet two — almost two inches taller than Mayfield, who Polian raved about — but Polian deemed Jackson too short. He had a solid arm but not a cannon. He was fast on his feet. And he was Black.

Polian was simply the best known (he's in the Pro Football Hall of Fame as a general manager) of a large group of pundits and scouts who believed Jackson should be a wide receiver or a running back in the NFL — the old cliché that refuses to die.

Jackson was fast and elusive. He was an effective passer, though he did not have a classic cannon arm. He was also African American, and anyone who didn't think his race affected how he was viewed was at best naive.

A year earlier, the Chicago Bears had traded up to the second spot in the draft so that they could draft... Mitchell Trubisky, who had started a grand total of thirteen games at North Carolina. They had passed on Texas Tech's Patrick Mahomes—who went tenth to Kansas City—and Clemson's Deshaun Watson, who went twelfth to Houston.

Both Mahomes and Watson had become starters as college freshmen. Watson had led Clemson to a win over archrival South Carolina while playing on a torn ACL (anterior cruciate ligament). In his final two seasons as the starter, Clemson went 28–2, losing the national title game to Alabama in 2015, then beating the Crimson Tide a year later in a championship rematch, thanks to a final-minute drive led by Watson. Mahomes didn't have that kind of won–lost record, but he broke about a million passing records while starting 29 games.

Both men could run, if necessary, and both could also pass extremely well. Both were Black—and were selected after Trubisky. Some observers still claim that Bears general manager Ryan Pace simply made a scouting mistake. Mistakes *do* happen all the time. But given that Mahomes and Watson were clearly worlds better than Trubisky—*before* the two men became NFL stars—it is impossible not to question the idea that, in Trubisky, Pace saw someone who looked like the "traditional" NFL quarterback.

Now, a year later, Newsome and DeCosta were intrigued by Jackson, and they thought there was a good chance he would still be on the board when their turn came to pick. "My guess was he'd go somewhere between twenty-five and fifty-five," DeCosta said. "Which meant we'd have a chance to get him."

Newsome told DeCosta to get more input from the Ravens coaches and scouts. DeCosta talked first to two experienced scouts—Milt Hendrickson and Dwaune Jones. "They were both enamored of him," DeCosta said.

Then he talked to the coaches, starting with Harbaugh before moving on to offensive coordinator Marty Morninhweg and quarterbacks coach James Urban.

"We had to be sure everyone was on board with the idea that we'd have to change our offense for Lamar," DeCosta said. "You don't spend a high draft pick on a backup quarterback. You draft someone that high with the idea that he's going to be a starter."

By season's end, DeCosta and Newsome had watched a lot of tape on Jackson. "I watched him live quite often," DeCosta said. "Louisville played at noon a lot—usually not a featured game. Ozzie and I talked back and forth a good deal. I remember one day I saw him make a throw against North Carolina and I called Ozzie and said, 'Did you see that throw he made?' Ozzie had seen it. We both wanted to know more at that point."

DeCosta called Louisville coach Bobby Petrino and his offensive assistants. All raved about how quickly Jackson picked things up— whether while a play was developing or in offensive meetings.

There was one issue—a sensitive one. Jackson grew up in Boynton Beach, Florida, and tended to speak softly, quickly, and with a Southern accent. At times, he could be difficult to understand in the huddle. There was a clear racial overtone to this "issue": Jackson spoke with what some would call a Black cadence, as compared to—for example—Robert Griffin III, who sounded like a practiced public speaker.

"People can mistake talking the way Lamar spoke for not being smart," DeCosta said. "In fact, in Lamar's case, the opposite's true. But it was a concern."

DeCosta called James Harris, who was the first African American quarterback to lead an NFL team (the Rams) to the playoffs in 1974.

Harris had worked for the Ravens as director of player personnel, and he and DeCosta were friends. Harris had grown up in Monroe, Louisiana, and, like Jackson, was soft-spoken and had a Southern accent.

"He told me that he actually practiced in front of a mirror, to try to make sure his diction was always clear," DeCosta said. "His point was that it was something you could work on like almost any other skill."

By draft night, Newsome and DeCosta had agreed that if there was a chance to draft Jackson, they needed to give it serious thought. They had made a point of keeping their interest in Jackson quiet. DeCosta didn't want someone else who might be thinking of drafting him in the second round to trade up to jump in front of the Ravens.

"We'd been burned a couple times in the past," he said. "When Brady Quinn was coming out [of Notre Dame], we liked him a lot. We thought we could get him late in the first. But Phil Savage [the Ravens former scouting director] was the general manager in Cleveland and still knew a lot of our people from the time he spent with us. He traded up so he could take him."

Quinn went twenty-second — the Ravens were picking twenty-ninth — but his career was a bust. The next year, the Ravens drafted Flacco. Sometimes, a bad break can become a good one.

Five years later, when Bruce Arians left the Ravens to become the coach in Indianapolis, he knew that Newsome and DeCosta liked wide receiver T. Y. Hilton. "Because Hilton played at a relatively small school [Florida International], not many people knew much about him," DeCosta said. "Bruce did. He jumped in front of us in the third round and took him."

Hilton was *not* a bust. He has played in four Pro Bowls and is still one of the league's better receivers.

DeCosta wanted to be certain that nothing similar would happen with Jackson. He threatened his scouting staff with severe recriminations if it leaked that the Ravens were seriously looking at Jackson. When Jackson visited the team's headquarters, the team did everything but bring him in under dark of night. Even so, Albert Breer of *Sports Illustrated* heard that Jackson was in the building and called DeCosta.

"I bluffed him," DeCosta said. "I said, 'You better not write it unless you've got a really good source, and I don't think you've got one.' He didn't write it."

The Ravens went into draft night hoping to add some picks before the first round was over. They had the sixteenth pick, but once they had figured out that at least one of the three tight ends they wanted would still be there, they traded back (with Buffalo) to twenty-second. Then, when all three were still there at twenty-two, they traded again—this time with Tennessee—back to twenty-fifth. They had added three picks and had picked Hurst at twenty-five. A good night.

But could they make it better?

Kevin Byrne, the team's longtime vice president for public relations, came into the war room. He wanted to know if Newsome, DeCosta, and Harbaugh were ready to come downstairs to talk to the media about Hurst and the trade-backs. That was the way it usually worked: once the team's first round was over, the three men in charge came down to talk to the media.

DeCosta looked at Newsome. Newsome looked at DeCosta. Finally, Newsome said, "Not yet, Kevin."

Byrne knew better than to ask why. He nodded and left the room.

"I think we should call the Eagles again," DeCosta said.

Both he and Newsome had talked to Eagles general manager Howie Roseman about the possibility of trading the Eagles pick—the thirty-second and last in the first round—for two picks: a fourth-round pick that year and a second-round pick in 2019. The

Eagles were the Super Bowl champions and thought they had their franchise quarterback in Carson Wentz, so adding a pick seemed to make sense for them.

When DeCosta reached Roseman, knowing that time was short and that the Ravens clearly had a specific player in mind, the Philly GM wanted Baltimore to sweeten the deal. He wanted the Ravens second-round pick the next day—meaning he'd move twenty picks back from thirty-two to fifty-two *and* the fourth-round pick *and* the Ravens number two the following year. It was a steep price to pay to move up for a player who *might* still be there for the Ravens at number fifty-two, if they stayed exactly where they were on the board.

DeCosta told Roseman he'd get back to him. A decision had to be made quickly. He and Newsome consulted again. Even at that late hour, they still hadn't told the rest of the room what they were thinking.

"We didn't want to take *any* chances it might get out in any way," Newsome said. "Bill [Belichick] was at thirty-one. You never know what he might do."

There was another factor: DeCosta had talked about Jackson with NFL Network analyst Mike Mayock—one of the few people he trusted with knowing that he and Newsome were looking at Jackson as a quarterback. Mayock, today the general manager of the Las Vegas Raiders, had told DeCosta he thought the New Orleans Saints might have interest in drafting Jackson as an eventual replacement for Drew Brees. When the Saints traded up to the fourteenth spot in the first round, DeCosta had a brief moment of panic, until the Saints used the pick on a defensive end named Marcus Davenport.

The Saints were next scheduled to pick fifty-ninth the next day in the second round—seven picks after the Ravens. But DeCosta had been burned before. If the Saints traded up in the second round and took Jackson, he'd probably never forgive himself.

It was still Newsome's call. The two men knew that many teams were going to pass on Jackson because they had scouts who believed Jackson should be converted into a wide receiver or a running back. Jackson had made it clear he had no intention of playing any position but quarterback. He had refused to run the 40-yard dash at the NFL's scouting combine in February because he didn't want scouts using his speed as an excuse to put him at a speed position. That refusal had no doubt turned some teams off. In the minds of some, players aren't supposed to think for themselves.

Newsome and DeCosta liked Jackson as a quarterback. They knew they would have to change their offense for him, but that was fine with them. "The best teams always build an offense around their quarterback's skills," Newsome said. "We'd done that with Joe [Flacco] for ten years. If Lamar became our quarterback, we would have to change. But there was nothing wrong with doing that."

Newsome told DeCosta to call Roseman back and tell him they would make the deal if their guy — they didn't name him — was still there when the Eagles went on the clock.

Newsome remembered making a deal during the second round of his first draft in 1996. "I wanted a tight end named Jason Dunn," he remembered. "So I traded up with Detroit to take him. Only problem was, the Eagles took him one pick before the pick we'd moved up to, so we couldn't get him." Newsome laughed. "I never did *that* gain. Now, if we're trading up, we don't commit to the deal until the team we're trading with is on the clock."

Once Belichick had taken running back Sony Michel with the thirty-first pick and the Eagles were on the clock, Newsome confirmed the deal with Roseman. That led to Commissioner Roger Goodell walking to the microphone just before midnight to announce the final pick of the night: "There has been a trade," he announced.

"The Philadelphia Eagles have traded their pick to the Baltimore Ravens." He paused. "With the thirty-second pick in the 2018 NFL draft, the Baltimore Ravens select" — another pause; Goodell loves being on stage — "Lamar Jackson, quarterback, Louisville."

There was a roar inside AT&T Stadium — Dallas Cowboys owner Jerry Jones's monument to himself — where the draft was being held. It was nothing compared with the roar that went up inside the Ravens headquarters.

"All the years I've done this," Newsome said, "I have never heard a roar like that in response to a pick. It felt as if the whole building shook. Everyone knew we'd done something special at that moment."

DeCosta agreed. "A chill went right through me," he said. "The place just erupted. Ozzie and I were the only ones who knew what was going on, so everyone was thrilled when Goodell made the announcement. Ozzie and I looked at each other and smiled. It was a remarkable moment."

Because DeCosta, on orders from Newsome, had consulted with several of the team's scouts and the offensive assistant coaches, everyone had known that there was at least the possibility of taking Jackson.

All had liked the idea. But once Hurst had been selected, everyone figured the team was finished doing business for the night. The maneuvering to trade with the Eagles came as a surprise inside the building — one that everyone was clearly thrilled to see happen.

Harbaugh walked out of the room to call Flacco, knowing his quarterback was going to be stunned that the Ravens had picked someone to replace him. Flacco had actually considered going to bed after the Hurst pick, but Pitta, who was in town trying to sell his house and was watching with him, convinced him to watch the rest of the round — stick it out for seven more picks.

"Hey, Joe," Harbaugh said when Flacco answered. "We got you a tight end."

Flacco started laughing. "John," he said, "you didn't call me at midnight to tell me you drafted a tight end."

Harbaugh quickly conceded that Hurst wasn't the reason for the call and then explained the team's thinking.

The next morning, when Flacco called his wife, Dana, who was at their home in New Jersey, she said to him, "What does this mean?"

"It means," Flacco answered, "that everything has changed."

He was right. When Flacco got hurt midway through the 2018 season, Jackson became the Ravens starter. Flacco became Wally Pipp to Jackson's Lou Gehrig. He never started again in Baltimore and was traded to Denver that off-season.

In 2019, in his second year in the league and first as a full-time starter, Jackson became the second player in the history of the NFL to be unanimously selected as the league's MVP. The first? Tom Brady in 2010.

As Jackson often says in his postgame press conferences after he has played well, "Not bad for a running back."

Notably, Brady wasn't taken until the sixth round of the 2000 draft—the 199th pick that year. There was one major difference between Brady and Jackson: no one ever suggested Brady change positions.

Fifty years after Briscoe's debut at quarterback for the Denver Broncos, a Black quarterback was still being asked to change positions. Briscoe's first game at quarterback came nine days after Tommie Smith and John Carlos staged their black-gloved salute seventeen hundred miles away, in Mexico City. The world has changed a lot since those historic moments.

Or has it?

CHAPTER FOUR

Still Climbing the Wall

Lovie smith vividly remembers the way the 2012 football season ended. His Chicago Bears beat the Detroit Lions to finish with a record of 10–6, tied for second place in the NFC North, one game behind the Green Bay Packers and tied with the Minnesota Vikings.

The Seattle Seahawks had clinched the first of the NFC's two wild card spots with an 11–5 record. That left the Vikings and Bears tied for the second spot. The Vikings advanced because their record within the division was 4–2. The Bears were 3–3, and since the teams had split their two games, that was the tiebreaker to make postseason.

"It was disappointing to say the least," Smith said while coaching at the University of Illinois in 2020. "There aren't a lot of teams that have gone ten and six and not made postseason."

In fact, in 2020, Washington's nameless football team made postseason with a record of 7–9 after winning the pathetically weak NFC East. The last time a 10–6 team hadn't made postseason in the NFC had been in 1996 — also Washington.

It happens—but not often. At that point, Smith had coached the Bears for nine seasons. In January 2007, he had become the first African American ever to coach a team to the Super Bowl, beating his mentor Tony Dungy to the promised land by a few hours on the day of the conference championship games. That team, quarterbacked by the great Rex Grossman, finished 15–4 after losing to Dungy's Indianapolis Colts in the Super Bowl. The Colts had Peyton Manning; the Bears, Grossman. Who would you pick to win the game?

The year before, with Grossman hurt, the Bears had gone 11–5 with the equally immortal Kyle Orton playing quarterback.

In 2010, the Bears went 11–5 again and lost the NFC championship game to the Packers—who went on to win the Super Bowl. The Bears dropped to 8–8 a year later, when their new quarterback, Jay Cutler, broke his thumb trying to make a tackle after throwing an interception in the fourth quarter of a game against the San Diego Chargers.

The Bears won that day to up their record to 7–3. But without Cutler, they lost 5 of their final 6 games to finish 8–8. A year later, they started fast at 7–1 but hit a wall in the second half of the season, dropping their record to 10–6.

Smith's record for nine seasons was 89–63. The Bears had gone 29–19 in his last three seasons and would no doubt have been better than that if not for Cutler's injury.

Smith reflected on his expectations at the end of the 2012 season and laughed. "After you go ten and six, playoffs or no playoffs, and when you've been pretty consistent for a while, you go into the general manager's office thinking you're going to talk contract extension. It didn't turn out that way."

The Bears had a new general manager that year, Phil Emery. Like many GMs, Emery wanted to put his own stamp on the team. Plus, there was undoubtedly pressure from above after the disappointing second half of the season. Not to mention the yammering on Chicago's *three* all-sports-talk radio stations.

Emery didn't offer Smith a contract extension. Instead, he fired him.

The list of NFL coaches who have been fired after going 10–6 is pretty short. Very short, in fact. Here it is: Lovie Smith. Marty Schottenheimer was fired in San Diego after going 14–2 in 2006, but that was the result of a dispute with his general manager, not his won–lost record. Dungy was fired in Tampa Bay in 2001 after going 9–7 and making the playoffs.

In the eight seasons since Smith's firing, the Bears have had one winning season and are currently on their third coach, Matt Nagy. In all, they are 55–73 and haven't won a postseason game since Smith's departure.

"Someday, maybe, I'll find out what really happened, why I got fired," Smith said. "I never really did get an explanation from anyone. But there isn't much doubt in my mind that if you are a Black coach, especially in the NFL, you are on a shorter leash than if you are a white coach."

There's no better example of that than Dungy's tenure in Tampa Bay. It was Dungy who had hired Smith as his linebackers coach in 1996 when he got the job in Tampa. The Bucs had been in a state of disarray when Dungy took over. They had last made the playoffs in 1982, Doug Williams's fifth and final year as their quarterback. They had reached the postseason three times in the four healthy seasons that Williams was their QB.

When Tampa Bay refused to give Williams even a reasonable raise after the 1982 season and he had walked away and gone home to teach school in Louisiana, the Bucs spiraled. For the next thirteen years, their *best* record was 7–9 (once). They went 2–14 three times and 3–13 once. Trying to save $100,000 a year and letting Williams leave didn't turn out to be such a smart decision.

Dungy was hired to try to put the pieces back together after six coaches had failed in the thirteen years since Williams's departure. After going 6–10 his first season — 1996 — Dungy took the Bucs to the playoffs in four of the next five seasons, compiling a 48–32 record. The team reached the NFC Championship game in 1999 before losing to the "Greatest Show on Turf," the St. Louis Rams. They lost wild card games to the Donovan McNabb–led Philadelphia Eagles the next two years.

Dungy was fired after the 2001 season because of, according to ownership, a "lack of playoff success." This remarkable claim came from an organization that had made it to postseason three times in twenty years before Dungy's arrival and then had reached it four times in five years with him. The same charge was leveled against Marvin Lewis years later, after he had revived the moribund Cincinnati Bengals and taken them to the playoffs seven times.

Lewis, though, was 0–7 in the playoffs. Dungy was 2–4. He was hired by the Indianapolis Colts about fifteen minutes after being fired in Tampa Bay and went to the playoffs seven times in seven seasons as the Colts coach. He won the Super Bowl in February 2007, beating his pupil and close friend Smith in rainy Miami to win the title. In only one season — his first — did Dungy fail to win at least 12 regular-season games. That team went 10–6.

In the meantime, the Bucs hired the very glamorous Jon Gruden and won the Super Bowl in 2002 with a team largely put together by Dungy. Clearly, Gruden was the playoff coach that Dungy wasn't. Except he never won another playoff game in Tampa, only reaching the postseason twice in the next six seasons before being fired after the 2008 season.

On January 12, 2009, Dungy, after going 12–4 in his final season, announced his retirement at age fifty-three. Four days later, the Bucs fired Gruden. Eleven years later, after signing Tom Brady, they made the postseason again and, as in 2002, found lightning in the postseason bottle and won the Super Bowl.

In all, Dungy made the postseason eleven times in thirteen seasons as a head coach. Even now, at sixty-five, he still encounters teams that would love to coax him out of retirement. But Dungy isn't like other coaches, most of whom live to be in the coaching arena. He has been approached about coaching again numerous times. The only time he even thought about it was when Martin Mayhew, then the general manager of the Detroit Lions, called him.

"I told him no right away," Dungy said. "He reminded me I'd grown up in Michigan and had been a Lions fan growing up. He said, 'Think about it for twenty-four hours before you say no.' I agreed to do that. I sat down and talked to Lauren [his wife], and she was adamant. She said, 'If they move the team to Tampa, you can think about it. Otherwise, forget it.' She was right."

Tony and Lauren have eleven children, eight of them adopted. Their oldest daughter is thirty-five; their youngest daughter is five.

"It's kept us pretty busy," Dungy said with a laugh, sitting in the dining room of his home in Tampa. He and his family live in the same gated community where Derek Jeter and Mariano Rivera live.

Dungy, an evangelical Christian, wrote a book in 2007. *Quiet Strength: The Principles, Practices and Priorities of a Winning Life* reached number one on the *New York Times* nonfiction bestseller list.

His outspoken views have gotten him into trouble on occasion.

When the St. Louis Rams drafted Michael Sam, an openly gay player from the University of Missouri, Dungy said he would not have drafted Sam. "It's not because I don't believe Michael Sam should have a chance to play, but I wouldn't want to deal with it all," he said then. He clarified his remarks later to say that all the media attention that would have been focused on Sam—who was drafted in the seventh and final round and was cut by the Cardinals in preseason—would have been a distraction to his team. As it turned out, Sam never played in an NFL game. He played one game in the CFL before retiring.

Since giving up coaching, Dungy has also mentored coaches and players, notably Michael Vick, the quarterback who went to jail for his involvement in a dog-fighting ring. It was Dungy and Donovan McNabb who convinced Eagles owner Jeffrey Lurie and Coach Andy Reid to give Vick another chance in 2009 after his two-year NFL suspension was lifted. A year later, the Eagles traded McNabb to Washington and made Vick their starting quarterback—a job he held for three seasons.

Dungy is part of the generation of Black football players who had, for all intents and purposes, no chance to play quarterback in the NFL. He grew up in Jackson, Michigan, and went to all-Black schools until he got to high school, when he went to an integrated school. His dad, Wilbur, who had been a member of the Tuskegee Airmen, taught biology and zoology at Hamilton Community College and, later, Delta Community College. His mom, Cleomae, taught high school English, specializing in Shakespeare.

When Tony was four, his parents moved to an integrated neighborhood in Jackson. "I made friends right away," he remembered. "Some were Black, some were white. I never really noticed the difference. But in the next year or so, some of my white friends disappeared. I couldn't understand it, so I asked my father, 'Where did Timmy and Joey go? Why aren't they here anymore?' He explained to me, as best you can explain it to someone that young, that there were some white people who weren't comfortable living around Black people. I had no idea what he was talking about."

A few years later, when he was eight, Tony found himself watching a man standing in a doorway declaring, "Segregation now, segregation tomorrow, segregation forever." The man was Alabama governor George C. Wallace, and the place was the University of Alabama.

"We were watching on a tiny little black-and-white TV," he said. "I could barely tell what was going on, that he was trying to keep [two] Black students from registering to go to school there. Again, my dad tried to explain it to me. Again, I didn't really understand."

By the time he went to integrated Parkside High School, Tony was old enough to understand. As a junior, he was the star quarterback for the football team and, to no one's surprise, was elected one of the team captains for the 1972 team.

"But the other captain they chose was white," Dungy said. "There were going to be seven Black seniors on the team, and everyone knew the captains were going to be me and Bob Burton because we were the two best players. Except the coaches apparently didn't want two Black captains.

"The seven of us got together and decided if we weren't both going to be captains, we were going to quit the team — and we did. My father had always said if you wanted to go out on a limb for a principle that was fine — but do it to accomplish something. Just before practice was supposed to start, I got a call from Leroy Roquemore, who had been the assistant principal of my junior high school and was someone I looked up to and respected. He said essentially the same things to me that my dad had been saying. He asked me who would be hurt most if we didn't play and the answer—of course—was us. My dad had said the exact same thing to me but would never order me to go back and play. When you're sixteen, you aren't inclined to listen to your father anyway. I was willing to listen to Mr. Roquemore."

Dungy and his teammates returned to the team, and Dungy was highly recruited as a quarterback. By then—1973—Big Ten schools were regularly recruiting Black quarterbacks. Willie Thrower had started for Michigan State as far back as 1950, and Jimmy Raye had been a star on championship teams there under Duffy Daugherty in the 1960s. Sandy Stevens had led Minnesota to a national championship in 1960. The biggest win for the Gophers that season was against Iowa—quarterbacked by Wilburn Hollis, who was also Black. During Dungy's senior year in high school, Michigan's quarterback was Dennis Franklin, who would end up being a three-year starter for Bo Schembechler.

Which is why Dungy chose Minnesota, knowing no one was going to try to convert him into a running back or a defensive back. His pal Burton ended up playing for four years at Central State, an HBCU in Ohio. Dungy started for Minnesota for two seasons and believed he would be drafted when he graduated in 1977.

"I knew being a Black quarterback would work against me to some extent," he said. "At that point in time, the only Black quarterback who had been a starter on an NFL team was James Harris. Eldridge Dickey had been drafted in the first round by the Oakland Raiders, but they made him into a wide receiver. I figured I'd go somewhere around the fifth round."

He was wrong. The NFL had a twelve-round draft back then, and Dungy went undrafted, much as Warren Moon would go undrafted a year later. Moon ended up going to Canada for six years. Dungy was signed as a free agent by the Pittsburgh Steelers, who made him a defensive back.

He played for the Steelers for two seasons — being part of a Super Bowl–winning team at the end of the 1978 season. He then played in San Francisco for a year and retired in 1980 after playing briefly in training camp for the New York Giants.

He did get to play quarterback in the NFL — for one quarter.

"Terry Bradshaw and Mike Kruczek both got hurt in a game against Houston my rookie year, and I was the emergency quarterback," he said. "I came in late and didn't feel as if I did much [three of eight for 43 yards], but I must not have been awful because the next day, [Coach] Chuck [Noll] told me that if Terry couldn't go the next Monday night, I was the quarterback — they already knew that Kruczek was out. That told me that given a chance and some time, I might be good enough to play quarterback at that level. At least that was the message I was getting from Chuck."

The chance never came. Bradshaw recovered in time to play, and Dungy returned to playing safety.

When the Giants cut him in August 1980, he returned to Minnesota, his alma mater, as a defensive backs coach. A year later, Noll hired him in Pittsburgh. "I was the first Black assistant on Chuck's staff," Dungy said. "In fact, when I got hired, there were a total of ten Black assistants in the entire league. Twenty-eight teams, ten Black assistants."

Dungy advanced rapidly as a coach. In 1984, when he was twenty-nine, Noll made him his defensive coordinator. Five years later, after a 5–11 season, team owner Dan Rooney insisted that Noll shake up his coaching staff — a shake-up that included demoting Dungy back to his old job coaching the defensive backs.

Rather than accept the demotion, Dungy took a job coaching the defensive backs in Kansas City under Marty Schottenheimer. It was while he was there that he had his most memorable DWB incident.

"We worked late a lot," he said. "I was driving home at about two a.m., and a cop started following me on I-435. I got off, drove to my neighborhood, and he continued to follow. Finally, he pulled me over — I was now near my house, which was in a nice neighborhood.

"He claimed I had failed to signal at a turn. I was so tired I supposed it was possible, but I'd been aware of him following me and had been very careful. I was annoyed, though, because he'd started following me with no reason at all to do so — and followed me for quite a while. I told him that, which got me a ticket for failing to turn on my signal — at two in the morning!"

More instructive than that, Dungy remembered, was when his son Eric was driving to high school football practice on a Saturday morning with two of his friends in the car. "He ran a red light because they were late," Dungy said. "Cop pulled them over and gave him a ticket — which he deserved. Eric told me later that his only thought while the cop was writing the ticket was, 'My dad's going to kill me for this.' He said he was still kind of a nervous wreck when he got to practice and was distracted when practice started.

"His two friends, who didn't live in our neighborhood but lived in a much tougher area, were so upset, they couldn't practice at all. Eric was upset worrying about me and my reaction. They were upset worrying about what the cop might do to them — for running a red light. They honestly thought they all might get killed.

"It's all about perception and experiences. Eric had never been involved in anything that caused him to have that sort of fear; his friends had been. You also wonder what the cop was thinking walking up to a car with three Black teenagers in it. Everyone has preconceived fears based on their experiences."

Dungy spent three years in Kansas City before Dennis Green hired him in Minnesota as his defensive coordinator. In 1993, the Vikings had the number one defense in the league. Five head coaching jobs opened. Dungy believed he was ready to take the next step. Whether any of the owners looking for a new coach had any clue about whether he was ready is impossible to say because no one bothered to interview him. This was ten years before the Rooney Rule, which required NFL teams to interview at least one minority candidate when they were searching for senior coaching, operations, or management positions, was passed. Had it existed, Dungy would probably have at least had an interview. But the rule didn't yet exist, and he never got a phone call.

Three years later, the woebegone Tampa Bay Buccaneers fired Sam Wyche, the most successful of the four coaches who had succeeded John McKay after he retired in 1984. Wyche had gone 23–41 in four seasons. Dungy became the NFL's fourth Black head coach in the modern era.

Fritz Pollard had been a player-coach in the early days of the NFL, until the owners banned him and the nine other Black players (they weren't coaches) who were playing in the league in 1926. Among them was the great singer Paul Robeson. There was no formal ban at that point; Pollard and the others were simply removed from team rosters. Black players appeared sporadically in the league for the next eight years before team owners, led by George Preston Marshall, the blatantly racist owner of the Boston/Washington franchise, banned them completely until after World War II.

In 1946, NFL teams slowly began to sign Black players again. In 1959, according to the website Blackhistory.com, the league was still only 12 percent Black. Today, it is almost 75 percent Black. Remarkably, Marshall remains in the Pro Football Hall of Fame.

Not until 1989 did Al Davis make Art Shell the first Black coach of the so-called modern era. Green became the second Black coach when the Vikings hired him in 1992, and Ray Rhodes was hired by the Philadelphia Eagles in 1995. Rhodes had two good seasons in Philadelphia: going 10–6 back-to-back and making the playoffs both seasons, then fading to 3–13 in his fourth season, a record that got him fired. He was hired in Green Bay, went 8–8, and was fired after one season. Bit of a short leash.

Dungy's run in Tampa Bay was impressive by any standard, but nonetheless, he was booted after five years.

"I was disappointed, certainly," Dungy said. "But at least they gave me an opportunity. I can agree or disagree with decisions that are made to fire coaches. Sometimes owners are impatient and make mistakes as a result."

History shows that mistakes tend to be made more quickly when the coach is Black. Art Shell had one losing record (7–9) in five full seasons with the Raiders and made the playoffs three times. Davis fired him after he went 9–7 in 1994. Later, Davis called that move a mistake. Steve Wilks was fired by the Arizona Cardinals in 2018 after going 3–13 in his one season.

"I just don't see how you can judge a coach—any coach—after one season," Dungy said. "I think they knew who they wanted to hire [former Texas Tech coach Kliff Kingsbury], so Wilks was probably going to get fired regardless of his record."

Lovie Smith was an example twice: first getting fired in Chicago after going 10–6, then getting fired in Tampa Bay after taking over a terrible team and going 2–14 and then 6–10. "If I had known that was going to be the deal, I'd have never taken the job," Smith said.

"The people I went to work for gave me the impression they understood it was going to take a while to make the team really competitive again. I thought we were on the right track. Then the track ended."

This time, Tampa's owners let it be known that they wanted Dirk Koetter to take over as head coach because he would be a good tutor for rookie Jameis Winston. Smith had gone to a Super Bowl with Rex Grossman as his quarterback — but apparently the coach wasn't a good-enough quarterback whisperer to work with Winston.

Dungy was unemployed for one week after being fired in Tampa. When the Colts hired him, he carved out a seven-year-record there that landed him in the Pro Football Hall of Fame in 2016: seven seasons, seven trips to the postseason, six seasons with at least 12 wins, a Super Bowl victory, and an overall record of 85–27. He retired after the 2008 season at a time when most coaches are in midcareer.

"There were a couple reasons I retired when I did," he said. "One was professional; one was personal. We had already decided that Jim Caldwell was going to succeed me, and I wanted to leave him with a chance to still have a good team — put him in charge when Peyton [Manning] was still at the top of his game and we weren't about to get decimated by salary cap cuts.

"The other reason was personal. I wanted to go home [to Tampa] and be more involved in my community and with my family."

Both decisions worked out. Caldwell took the Colts to the Super Bowl in his first season, going 16–3. The Colts lost to the New Orleans Saints in the Super Bowl, but they had gotten there — making Caldwell the fourth Black coach (behind Smith, Dungy, and Mike Tomlin) to make it that far.

The Colts were a playoff team again the next year, going 10–6, but when Manning missed the entire 2011 season following neck surgery, they fell off a cliff, going 2–14. Some coaches might have survived, given the circumstance of losing one of the greatest quarterbacks of all time. Caldwell did not.

"I knew I was in trouble when they brought Steve Spagnuolo in to interview for the job of defensive coordinator and I never saw him while he was in town," Caldwell said, laughing. "Spags called me and said, 'What's up with that?' A few days later, I found out what was up."

Caldwell was quickly hired by Baltimore coach John Harbaugh as the team's quarterbacks coach. Late in the season, after a disappointing loss to Washington, Harbaugh fired offensive coordinator Cam Cameron and offered the job to Caldwell.

"I really thought I should be about the fourth choice based on my knowledge of the offense," he said. "But John said to me that wasn't what it was about; it was about leadership. I called Tony [Dungy] and asked him what he thought. He said, 'If John and Ozzie [Newsome] and Steve [owner Bisciotti] think you should do it, you should do it.'"

Caldwell did it, and the Ravens went on to win the Super Bowl. Quarterback Joe Flacco had an extraordinary postseason. He had fourteen touchdown passes and threw one interception in four playoff games, leading the Ravens to the championship.

Two years later, the Lions hired Caldwell as their head coach. Detroit had been to the playoffs once in the previous fourteen seasons. The Lions' 11–5 record in Caldwell's first season was their best since 1991. Three seasons later, he was fired after going 9–7 in back-to-back seasons. Caldwell's 36–28 record was the best for a Lions coach since Buddy Parker, who coached the team from 1951 to 1956.

"That's the only job I've ever gone after in my life," Caldwell said. "I was a Lions fan as a kid. My dad was a UAW [United Auto Workers] guy for thirty-five years. They had a quarterback [Matthew Stafford] I thought I could really help. It felt like it was just right for me."

Caldwell still felt that way four years later. Then he was fired. Bob Quinn, who had been working in New England under Bill Belichick, had been hired as general manager before Caldwell's second season and was clearly itching to make a change. Caldwell later learned that Quinn had wanted to fire him after his first season in charge, but team owner Martha Firestone Ford told him he couldn't do it after the team had just made the playoffs for a second time in three years.

"I watched Mrs. Ford's press conference when they let Jim go," Dungy said. "She said that the record under Jim had been good, that the locker room was a better place than it had been, that the culture of the organization was better, and the city felt better about the Lions than it had in a long time. Jim was just a wonderful guy . . . but they were making a change.

"I sat there laughing and shaking my head at the same time. Why did they make a change? Because they had hired a general manager [Quinn] from New England, and he wanted to bring in one of his own guys."

That guy ended up being Patriots defensive coordinator Matt Patricia, and everyone knows what has happened to the Lions since then. Patricia and Quinn were both fired three days after Thanksgiving in 2020 following an embarrassing 41–25 Thanksgiving Day loss to a bad Houston Texans team that came into the game with a 3–7 record. Patricia's final record in Detroit was a sterling 13–29–1, making Caldwell, with his 36–28, look like Vince Lombardi.

Caldwell was interviewed at the end of the 2018 season for head coaching jobs in Green Bay, Cleveland, and New York for the Jets. The Browns hired Freddie Kitchens, who went 6–10 and was fired after one season. The Jets hired Adam Gase, who went 9–23 in two seasons before being fired. Only the Packers got it right, hiring Matt LaFleur, who has gone 26–6 in two seasons.

Caldwell was finally hired as assistant head coach by rookie head coach Brian Flores in Miami but, for health reasons, had to walk away before the 2019 season began. "I'm a type two diabetic," he said. "And it turned out I had calcium in the linings of my arteries, which caused my calcium scores to go sky-high. I changed my diet, and they changed my medication. I stopped eating meat completely and took all sugar out of my diet. Everything I eat now is plant-based. I've lost thirty-four pounds, and I feel great."

Caldwell was talking in the spring of 2021. He had just turned sixty-six — in January — and wanted to coach again. "I'm healthy now and I'm confident I can help a team. I just need someone to give me another chance."

Even though seven new coaches were hired at the end of the 2020 season, Caldwell still found himself without a job as training camp approached in 2021.

"I could have a job as an assistant coach tomorrow if I wanted it," he said. "But I'm not one of those guys who wants to coach in some form until I'm eighty. If someone wants to give me a shot at being a head coach, I'd love one more chance. I was interviewed for the Houston job, but they ended up going with [David] Culley. I'm realistic. The list of coaches, Black or white, who have gotten a third shot is pretty short. But my record is pretty darn good, I think."

In the meantime, Caldwell has begun mentoring young Black coaches, trying to prepare them for when their chance comes to move up — to be coordinators or head coaches.

Marvin Lewis, who had also been fired at the end of the 2018 season, does have a job—as an adviser to Arizona State coach Herman Edwards. Lewis's firing in Cincinnati was not the result of a short leash: he coached there for sixteen seasons, took the team to the playoffs seven times, and was the franchise's all-time winningest coach, with a record of 131–122–3. Given that he took over in 2003 with the Bengals coming off a 2–14 season and not having had a winning season since 1990, his turnaround of the franchise was remarkable.

Lewis had spent one season as the assistant head coach and defensive coordinator in Washington under Steve Spurrier before Mike Brown finally offered him the Bengals job. The year before, he'd been offered chances to be the head coach at Michigan State and at Cal–Berkeley. He turned both down. "I wanted to be an NFL head coach, not a college coach. After I turned down those two jobs, I called Ozzie [Newsome] and told him. He said, 'You better be careful. You might end up as coach of the Bengals.'"

There was no worse job in the NFL when Lewis took over, but he made the franchise respectable for a long time. Even in those last three Bengals seasons, their worst record was 6–10. In 2017, when ESPN's Adam Schefter put out an inaccurate report that Lewis was done with the Bengals at season's end, his players responded by winning their last two games, including knocking the Ravens out of the playoffs in the final minute of the final game. If nothing else, the players showed what they thought of their coach. He returned as coach in 2018.

In their forty-three years of existence, the Bengals have had ten coaches. Lewis was the third to leave with a winning record, the first since Forrest Gregg went 32–25, his tenure ending in 1983. In all, the Bengals have had eighteen winning seasons—seven of them under Lewis. But the number people bring up first when discussing him is zero, as in zero playoffs wins, a record of 0–7 in the postseason.

"Hey, I'd bring it up too," Lewis said with a laugh. "We had chances to win and didn't; other times, we just got beat. And a couple of times, we were just unlucky."

The most unlucky moment came in 2005, Lewis's third season. It was the first winning season for the Bengals and their first trip to the playoffs since 1990. Lewis had completely turned the Bengals around. Carson Palmer, who hadn't taken a snap in 2003 as a rookie, had become a star at quarterback in his second season as a starter. The Bengals went 11–5 and won the AFC North. In the first round of the postseason, they faced their archrivals, the Pittsburgh Steelers. On Cincinnati's first play from scrimmage, the Steelers Kimo von Oelhoffen appeared to dive at Palmer's knee. Palmer went down. He had to come out of the game and needed reconstructive knee surgery.

John Kitna took Palmer's place, and after leading 17–7, the Bengals lost 31–17. It isn't unfair to wonder what might have happened if Palmer hadn't been hurt.

Palmer left the team after the 2010 season, insisting he would rather retire than continue to play for the Bengals — largely because of frustration with owner Mike Brown. The team drafted Andy Dalton in the second round and, after trading Palmer to Oakland, made the playoffs five seasons in a row with Dalton playing quarterback. But the postseason bugaboo continued. Then came three straight losing seasons, and Lewis was fired after the 2018 season.

There was no doubt that injuries and personnel mistakes made by Brown played a role in the team's going 19–28–1 in the last three seasons that Lewis was in charge. But Lewis blames no one but himself for losing his job.

"Mike [Brown] was a guy who didn't see color," Lewis said. "He saw wins and losses. He was the one who hired me when a lot of other owners had passed over me for one reason or another. I would have liked the chance to turn things around, but I understood."

Lewis had been the defensive coordinator for the Baltimore Ravens when they won the Super Bowl in January 2001 with arguably the greatest defense in NFL history. The Ravens beat the New York Giants 34–7 in that Super Bowl, and the only Giants points came on a kickoff return.

A year later, after Dungy was fired by the Buccaneers, general manager Richie McKay wanted to hire Lewis to replace him. But the team owners, the Glazer family, overruled him. Supposedly, they didn't want another defensive-minded head coach. Or perhaps they didn't want another Black head coach?

As for the Bengals, after Lewis was let go, like many NFL owners in recent years, Mike Brown hired a young offensive coach. Zac Taylor was the LA Rams quarterbacks coach — not a coordinator. But every NFL owner seems to be looking nowadays for the next Sean McVay, who took over the Rams at the age of thirty and had instant success. Taylor was thirty-five but had the advantage of working for McVay when Brown was looking for a new coach.

In two seasons, Taylor has gone 2–14 and 4–11–1. The Bengals had the first pick in the 2020 NFL draft and took Heisman Trophy–winning quarterback Joe Burrow, who appears to be a future star. Even with Burrow playing remarkably well for a rookie, the Bengals were 2–7–1 in 2020, after he suffered a major knee injury in the team's tenth game at Washington. The jury is still out on Taylor — and Burrow — but there's little doubt the Bengals would not have had two seasons quite so miserable if Lewis had still been their coach.

Lewis is happy living in Arizona and working for and with his old friend Edwards — who coached in the NFL for eight years with the New York Jets and Kansas City Chiefs. At sixty-two, Lewis says he would be open to an offer from an NFL team. Given his record in Cincinnati, it is amazing that no one has talked to him during the past two off-seasons.

The fact that neither Lewis nor Caldwell nor any of the up-and-coming young Black coordinators can get a job frustrates Dungy. There is no one more glass-half-full than Dungy, but he readily admits that the last few years have been discouraging.

"Two of the last twenty head coaching hires in the NFL have been African Americans," he said. "That's not a good number. I understand that things go in cycles and people are enamored right now of young coaches who have coached on the offensive side of the ball. It's funny, though, because four of the five longest-tenured coaches right now came from the defensive side of the ball.

"But even if you want offensive coaches, why hasn't Eric Bieniemy gotten a chance yet? I think there is racism involved there. How can there not be, at this point? The claim made was he doesn't call plays in Kansas City, but Doug Pederson didn't call plays there before he got the Eagles job. And Matt Nagy didn't call plays there, either, before he got the Bears job. He works with the best quarterback in the game [Patrick Mahomes], who raves about him, and no one is hiring him.

"There are also younger guys like Byron Leftwich [offensive coordinator for the Super Bowl champion Buccaneers] or Pep Hamilton [passing game coordinator and quarterbacks coach in Houston] who clearly have the ability to be head coaches if given the chance. Todd Bowles is a defensive coach, but how great a job did he do as coordinator in Tampa last season? And how good have the Jets been since they fired him? How can he possibly not deserve another chance?

"There are lots of good coaches out there, Black and white. If you hire a white coach, there's a very good chance he'll succeed. But if you aren't looking at everyone, at *all* of the best possible people, there's a chance you will miss on someone who might be the right answer for your team."

Bieniemy laughs when the subject of his many nonhirings comes up. "I have to take the approach that those jobs were not supposed to be the job that I get," he said. "I know I'm going to get a job because I know if I keep working at what I do and we continue to have success, sooner or later someone is going to sit in a room with me and say, 'You're the guy.'

"I just have to remind myself to be patient."

Bieniemy has been beyond patient. He's fifty-two, and for the last three seasons, he has been the offensive coordinator for the Kansas City Chiefs. All the Chiefs have done during those three seasons is lose the AFC championship game in overtime to the Patriots, win the Super Bowl, and lose the Super Bowl. Both postseason losses were to teams quarterbacked by Tom Brady—the Patriots after the 2018 season, the Buccaneers after the 2020 season. Their record since Bieniemy became the coordinator, including postseason, is 44–12.

Bieniemy works closely with Mahomes, who had already won the league's MVP award and had been to two Super Bowls by the age of twenty-five. The offensive coordinator has heard the oft-repeated excuse for his failure to win a head coaching job: he doesn't call the plays; head coach Andy Reid does.

"Do you know who didn't call plays before he became a head coach?" Bieniemy said. "Coach Reid. Also, Jon Gruden."

Not to mention Bieniemy's two predecessors as Reid's offensive coordinator in Kansas City: Pederson, who won a Super Bowl coaching the Eagles, and Nagy, the head coach in Chicago now.

Bieniemy grew up understanding that being Black meant a different life experience from being white. "My parents told me that when I was very young," he said. "So did my grandparents. The George Floyd murder was part of something that's gone on for years and years. The number of people who have literally gotten away with murder in cases like this is endless. The heroes in this case were the people who filmed the video. I can't even imagine what that was like for them."

Bieniemy spent the first ten years of his life in New Orleans. Black and white students did little mingling either in school or in sports. He played Pop Warner football beginning when he was five, and he still remembers the post-practice chant that one coach would recite every day.

"You have to remember this was a time when drug use was rampant in the inner cities," Bieniemy said. "The coaches always wanted us to understand how dangerous drugs were and also what it meant to be Black. The chant went like this:

"Coach: What is dope?
"Players: Dope is a poison debt.
"Coach: Who's the man who uses dope?
"Players: A dead man.
"Coach: Who was Dr. King?
"Players: He was free to fight by nonviolent protest and movement to fight for our rights.
"Coach: Who was Malcolm X?
"Players: He was a Black man trying to make things better for Black people.
"Coach: How?
"Players: Educating. Making sure Black families were doing the right things.

"You have to remember," said Bieniemy, who can still recite the refrain word for word, "this was less than ten years after Dr. King was assassinated and about a dozen years after Malcolm X was murdered. The coaches wanted us to understand that they were leaders and that because they were leaders, they frightened some people enough that they were murdered."

King and Malcolm X took different approaches to making Black voices heard. Both men were thirty-nine when they died, and more than fifty years later, their messages still resonate, although in completely different ways. And Bieniemy hasn't forgotten what the coaches were trying to tell the young football players.

When Bieniemy was ten, his parents divorced and he moved to Southern California. The area was completely different from New Orleans.

"Everything was diverse," he said. "The schools I went to had Blacks and whites and Asians — people from all over the world. It was definitely an adjustment for me, but I learned a lot."

He also became a football star at Bishop Amat Memorial High School, located in La Puente, a suburb about twenty miles east of Los Angeles. With all the major schools recruiting him, his first instinct was to attend USC. But after deciding he didn't want to go to school so close to home and to the gang wars still going on in Los Angeles, he ended up at Colorado.

"I went to visit, and it was absolutely beautiful," he said. "What I didn't realize was that I was going to a school with about thirty thousand students — fewer than three hundred of them Black. That's less than one percent. I learned that if you were a Black athlete in Boulder, you were a hero in the daytime, but nighttime could be dangerous. You had to be careful whenever you went out. What you'd done on the football field that day didn't matter if you found any sort of trouble."

Bieniemy stayed out of trouble and finished third in the Heisman Trophy voting in 1990, when Colorado shared the national championship with Georgia Tech. The San Diego Chargers took him in the second round of the draft—the thirty-ninth pick. The only reason he didn't go sooner was his size: five feet seven and 207 pounds without blazing speed.

He played in the NFL for nine solid, if not spectacular, seasons, spending four years with the Chargers, four with the Bengals, and his final season, in 1999, with the Eagles. That was Andy Reid's first season as an NFL head coach, and it was Reid who encouraged Bieniemy to go back to Colorado to finish his degree in sociology.

During his last two seasons in Cincinnati, Bieniemy had gotten to know an assistant coach named Al Roberts. "He saw something in me, potentially, as a coach," Bieniemy said. "He would ask me what I'd do in leadership situations, in game situations, if I had to make decisions. That got me thinking that maybe I'd like to coach when I was done playing."

Reid encouraged him in that direction, recommending that Bieniemy get his degree if he wanted a chance at a college coaching job. After graduating, Bieniemy was hired to coach at Thomas Jefferson High School in Denver—less than an hour from Boulder. He spent the 2000 season frequently making the trip to Boulder to work as a volunteer for Colorado coach Gary Barnett whenever he had free time.

A year later, Barnett hired him as the running backs coach. Bieniemy went from there to UCLA and then got his first NFL job with the Vikings in 2005. After a stint as Colorado's offensive coordinator, he returned to the NFL when Reid took the Chiefs job in 2013 and offered him the job as running backs coach. Five years later, when Nagy left to coach the Bears, Reid promoted him to offensive coordinator.

His close relationship with Mahomes—and Mahomes's and the team's success—put him on the radar as a potential head coach in 2018, even more so in 2019, and then again in 2020.

And yet...

"Look, I've been in a lot of rooms interviewing for a lot of jobs," Bieniemy said. "I've had ten, maybe it's eleven, job interviews. I know when someone is hiring, they aren't just looking for talent necessarily or what's on your résumé. They want to feel comfortable with that person. I haven't been in too many interviews where the guy interviewing me has looked like me. Or, I guess you could say, where I looked like him."

Bieniemy has managed to keep a sense of humor through it all—perhaps as a means of self-preservation. Others don't find it nearly as amusing.

"I have no idea why Eric Bieniemy isn't a head coach," Mike Tomlin said. "None. We worked together on the same staff in Minnesota fifteen years ago. We sharpened our coaching swords together. You could see then that he was going to be a head coach someday. I never thought all these years later he still wouldn't have gotten a chance yet.

"It's unfathomable to me. It's also more proof that when Ozzie Newsome says you have to be twice as good to get a chance as a Black man in this sport, he's right. I've always tried to be an optimist about things, but there are times when it becomes difficult. Eric Bieniemy is an example of why I sometimes feel that way."

Bieniemy appreciates those who feel the way Tomlin does and the support he's gotten from plenty of coaches—including his boss, Reid, who has also expressed dismay that Bieniemy doesn't have a job yet.

"It means a lot to me that so many guys have spoken out for me," he said. "What does bother me sometimes is that when you get interviewed a lot and you don't get a job, you start to hear whispers that 'maybe he doesn't interview so well.'

"I've had interviews where I walked in and knew almost right away the guy was just fulfilling a Rooney Rule obligation. I've had others where I walked out thinking I'd knocked it out of the park and had a really good shot at the job. I know I'm better at interviewing now than I was a year ago, and next year I'll be better than I am now. Experience matters.

"On the other hand, I'm pretty sure there have been guys hired with much less coaching experience than me who probably weren't that great in their interviews but *looked* like what the team was looking for in a coach. Let's be honest. It happens."

Dungy isn't exactly the kind of person who jumps on tables and screams to make a point. He is, by nature, soft-spoken and gentle — different from the prototype for a successful NFL head coach (Bill Belichick notwithstanding). But when he does bring up race as an issue, he says, there is always some sort of backlash.

"The comment often is, 'Why do you have to make everything about race?'" he said, laughing. "The fact is, I don't make everything about race. But it is 2021, and I would say we still have a long way to go in this country and that a lot of the problems are people who don't see race as an issue because they don't *want* to see race as an issue.

"It's very much still an issue. I'm always an optimist. I see things getting better in some areas. We've certainly made progress at the quarterback position. Thirty or forty years ago, Mahomes, Deshaun Watson, Lamar Jackson, Russell Wilson, Dak Prescott, Kyler Murray — there's a good chance they all would have been asked to change positions."

Jackson *was* asked to change positions. "I know that," Dungy said. "I didn't say we're there yet. I said we're making progress. It's time, though, that we see that kind of progress in leadership positions — whether it's coaching or in the front office. I know Roger Goodell wants it to get better, I really do believe that. But he can't tell the owners what to do. They have to figure it out for themselves."

I brought up the comment Doug Williams had made when I asked him where Mahomes and Watson would have gone in the 2017 draft if they had been white.

"He said they would have gone ahead of Trubisky, who the Bears took at number two," I said.

"What you should have asked," Dungy answered, "is where Trubisky would have gone if he had been Black?"

Amen.

CHAPTER FIVE

The Younger Generation

M IKE TOMLIN STILL REMEMBERS THE FEELING. It dates to when he was five years old, living in an apartment complex in Hampton, Virginia.

"There was a playground right there where we all played," he said. "My first memories of playing there include knowing that if we saw a police car come down the street, we all hid someplace. It was SOP — you see the cops coming, you get out of there. It was ingrained in all of us from a very young age."

Tomlin is now forty-nine and has been the coach of the Pittsburgh Steelers for fourteen years. He is the third-longest-tenured coach in the NFL, trailing only Bill Belichick, who has coached the New England Patriots for twenty-one years, and Sean Payton, who arrived in New Orleans a year before Tomlin was hired in Pittsburgh.

In 2009, Tomlin became the youngest coach (at thirty-six) and the second Black coach — following Tony Dungy — to win a Super Bowl. He took the Steelers to a second Super Bowl two years later. He has never had a losing season, and his teams have won at least 10 games on nine occasions and have reached the playoffs nine times, including in 2020, when they were 12–4 before losing in the wild card round to the Cleveland Browns.

Even though he's not yet fifty, Tomlin already has a Hall of Fame résumé.

Tomlin was hired by the Steelers at the age of thirty-four, but his journey to stardom wasn't an easy one. The response to a police presence as a kid was only part of what it was like to grow up Black in southeastern Virginia.

"If you ask me when I was first aware of race or the fact that being Black was a very different experience than being white, you might as well ask me when I first learned to talk," he said. "It was just *there,* part of my upbringing."

Tomlin's father had played in the Canadian Football League, and his older brother, Eddie, was also a football player. His parents split when he was very young, and he saw little of his father — Ed — who died of a heart attack in 2012 at the age of sixty-three. His mother, Julia, remarried when Mike was six.

Unlike Eddie, whose focus was always football, Mike played everything until late in his high school career. It was then that he realized football was going to be his best chance to get a college scholarship. Eddie was playing at Hampton — where their father had played when it was still Hampton Institute. Mike was recruited by Hampton and Norfolk State but thought he could play at a higher level.

He actually received some interest from Maryland and Duke, but Steve Spurrier left Duke for Florida at season's end and Maryland didn't offer him a scholarship.

Tomlin ended up at William & Mary because he fell in love with Coach Jimmye Laycock and liked the fact that receivers saw the ball often in Laycock's offense. Plus, William & Mary was a very good school academically and played consistently good Division 1-AA (now Football Championship Subdivision, FCS) football. The Tribe was 31–14 during Tomlin's four years, reaching the NCAA 1-AA tournament his junior year before missing it in his last season, with an 8–3 record.

Tomlin was a three-year starter at wide receiver. He caught 106 passes for 2,054 yards and twenty touchdowns. He averaged 20.5 yards per catch (still a school record) and was team captain as a senior. He graduated in 1995 with a degree in sociology but knew he wanted to pursue football. His mom, who had worked in the Norfolk shipyards while Mike was growing up, graduated from college on the same day as her younger son.

"When I left home for college, she decided to get her degree," said Tomlin. "The graduation ceremonies for Christopher Newport and William & Mary were the same day. I think I can honestly say that I was more proud of what she'd done than what I'd done."

Tomlin had hopes of playing pro ball after graduating. But coaching was always his backup plan.

"I wanted to chase it for as long as I could as a player," he said. "But I knew if that didn't work out, I wanted to coach."

He wasn't drafted by an NFL team, so he went to training camp with the Canadian Football League's Baltimore franchise. That was during a brief two-year-period when the CFL had five teams based in the United States. When he didn't catch on in Baltimore, Laycock helped him get a job as a graduate assistant at Virginia Military Institute. From there, he moved to Memphis, Arkansas State, and Cincinnati. Still in his twenties, he had developed a reputation as a stellar recruiter to the point where he was being courted by Notre Dame coach Bob Davie at the end of the 2000 season.

"It bothered me that people thought of me as a recruiter," he said. "That's still a problem today. Black coaches are thought of first as recruiters; they're the ones who can go into Black homes and sell themselves and their schools. The problem often is that when it's time to move up—to become coordinators or even to take on more responsibility on the practice field—you're blocked. People love having you on staff—to recruit. But give you more responsibility beyond that, put you in a place where you need to make critical decisions? Put you on a headset on game day? Much more difficult."

Tomlin was on a recruiting trip for the University of Cincinnati, visiting a player at St. Ignatius High School in Cleveland, when his phone rang early one morning. In addition to Notre Dame, both Michigan and Michigan State had expressed interest in hiring him. Tomlin felt as if he needed to continue working his job for Cincinnati as aggressively as he possibly could until he had an actual offer from one of those schools. Notre Dame looked like his best bet.

"I'm on my way to see this kid one morning and my phone rings," he said, laughing at the memory. "I answered, and a woman said she was Tony Dungy's assistant, and did I have a minute to talk to him? I thought it was one of my buddies playing a prank. I told her I was busy and to tell Coach Dungy to call me back later. I was probably pretty rude.

"A couple of hours later, after my visit, my phone rang, and this time it was Tony. I recognized the voice right away. I was in the car by then, and I felt sick to my stomach—so much so I had to pull over. He said he was interested in hiring me to coach defensive backs, and could I come down to Tampa for an interview? I couldn't believe what I'd done.

"You have to understand, my two coaching heroes back then were Tony and Ray Rhodes [Rhodes had coached the Philadelphia Eagles for four seasons, and the Green Bay Packers for one], and here was one of them calling me about a job and I'd been rude. The funny thing is, coaching in the NFL had never crossed my mind. I was a college coach; I knew the college game and landscape. I'd never played in the NFL, knew very little about it."

That was one of the reasons why Dungy was interested in Tomlin. He and his coaches had discussed bringing in a college coach to work with the defensive backs, specifically to teach them Dungy's "Tampa-two" defense, which wasn't easy to learn. Dungy had first heard Tomlin's name during a discussion of Cincinnati players and coaches. Hearing that Notre Dame was interested in hiring him, Dungy decided to find out more about him.

"I'd asked several of our scouts who spent time on college campuses if they'd noticed anyone who stood out to them as a teacher during practices," Dungy said. "More than one of them brought up Mike's name. They liked what they saw when he worked with his DBs. I decided I needed to meet him."

Tomlin was one of twelve coaches interviewed for the job. But within minutes of meeting Tomlin, Dungy knew that he was going to hire him.

"He had a presence, a confidence, when he walked into the room," Dungy said. "He wasn't cocky, but he was confident. Within fifteen minutes, I'd decided he was the guy I was going to hire. I still went through the process with the other guys, but Mike was the guy I targeted right away."

While Dungy was going through the process, Davie offered Tomlin a job at Notre Dame. "It was a bird-in-the-hand thing," he said. "I didn't know what was happening in Tampa. Rod Marinelli [the Bucs defensive line coach] was my lifeline. He kept telling me to be patient.

"Now, though, I couldn't be patient anymore. I had my bag in the car and was on my way to a plane to talk to Bob about taking the job. I was twenty-five minutes from taking off when I got a call asking if I could come back to Tampa to talk to Tony again. I had to make a decision. Sometimes in life the road *not* taken is important. I went back to see Tony.

"Working for him, even just that one year, was probably the most important learning experience of my life. I don't think I've ever met anyone so completely secure about what he was doing. He just wore the whole thing well: the pressure, being a leader, being willing to delegate, and dealing with the inevitable extra pressure of being a Black coach. He never blinked—at anything.

"Sitting in the same room with him every day, watching him work, listening to him—it was like getting a PhD in coaching. He was so comfortable with everything that came with the job, including the inevitable criticism. My temperament is decidedly different than his, but I always try to remember how he handled adversity. Never saw anyone who was better at it."

Being a defensive coach and someone who had played defensive back in the NFL, Dungy wanted to be sure his new assistant coach could handle being in charge of a group that included Ronde Barber and John Lynch—both future Hall of Famers.

"First time he met with the DBs," Dungy said, "I sat in, just to get a sense of his ability to take control of the room. He was twenty-eight years old, basically the same age as most of his players. I walked out of the room thinking, 'He doesn't need *any* help from me. He's got this.' And he did."

The Bucs went 9–7 that season, losing in the playoffs to the Philadelphia Eagles. Two days after that loss, Dungy was fired after going to the postseason four times in five years. It took the Colts exactly a week to hire Dungy to replace Jim Mora, who had gone 6–10 in his fourth season with the team.

The Bucs then traded four draft picks—two in the first round and two in the second — plus cash to Oakland to hire Jon Gruden as their new head coach. One of Gruden's first moves was to ask Tomlin to stay on as defensive backs coach. With the team Dungy had built, Gruden led the Bucs to the Super Bowl, where they dominated Gruden's old team from Oakland, 48–21, thanks in large part to five interceptions, three returned for touchdowns.

Tomlin worked for Gruden for four seasons before Minnesota's Brad Childress offered him the job as his defensive coordinator. In six years, Tomlin had gone from being a defensive backs coach for the University of Cincinnati to a coordinator in the NFL.

A year later, the ride became even more dizzying when he was hired to replace Bill Cowher as the coach of the Steelers. Tomlin didn't expect to get the Steelers job. He was, after all, only thirty-four and had been a coordinator in the NFL for just one year.

This was three years after the initiation of the Rooney Rule, adopted by the league's diversity committee in 2003 and named after the committee chair and Steelers chairman Dan Rooney. The rule required that teams interview at least one minority candidate when they had an opening for a head coach or for senior operations jobs. The theory was that if teams had to interview minorities, one candidate might strike a chord and be hired. At the very least, the thinking went, being interviewed would be a good experience for a candidate even if the person didn't get a job during that hiring cycle.

The NFL has a broad definition of what makes someone a minority. If you believe NFL PR, there are currently five minority coaches in the NFL. Three are Black: Tomlin, Miami Dolphins coach Brian Flores, and newly hired Houston coach David Culley. Washington's coach Ron Rivera, who was born in Fort Ord, California, the son of a Puerto Rican commissioned officer in the US Army and a mother of Mexican descent, is also on the NFL's minority list. He lived in

Germany, Panama, and Washington, D.C., when he was young and eventually played high school football in California. When Rivera was hired in Washington, team owner Dan Snyder was still clinging to the team's racist name — they were the Redskins. If that bothered Rivera, he never said so.

The fifth name on the NFL's list is Robert Saleh, the new coach of the New York Jets, who was born and raised in Michigan and graduated from Northern Michigan University. He is of Lebanese descent and happens to be Muslim, which appears to be a racial minority in the NFL's strange thinking. One wonders if the league would list Sid Gillman and Marv Levy, both Jewish, as minority coaches if they were coaching in the NFL today.

How exactly the NFL decides what makes someone a minority is difficult to say. Commissioner Roger Goodell tends to only do interviews with people who will ask him softball questions. When I requested the chance to speak to him for this book, Brian McCarthy, the NFL's vice president for communications (is there anyone working for a bureaucracy these days who is *not* a vice president?) first told me it was unlikely Goodell would talk to me. McCarthy suggested I try again in a few weeks.

I did that and was told Goodell didn't have time to talk to me. This was, for the record, right around the time that he and some friends were spending a day playing Augusta National Golf Club (where Goodell is a member) and superprivate Pine Valley and Cypress Point, flying by private jet (of course) from one course to another.

I'm glad Goodell could fit a day like that into his schedule. Notably, Augusta National only started admitting Black members in 1990 after the Shoal Creek debacle, when the PGA of America almost had to move its championship from there after the club's founder publicly admitted that there was no way a Black person would be granted membership to the club. Hall Thompson, Shoal Creek's founder, also happened to be an Augusta member. At the last possible minute, Shoal Creek backed down and admitted a Black businessman from Birmingham as an "honorary member."

Having been outed, golf officials began scrambling. Augusta National admitted a Black member soon after Shoal Creek did, though it didn't get around to admitting any women until 2012. The PGA Tour declared that no course could host an event if it discriminated against anyone—Black people, women, Jews. One of the host clubs that gave up hosting a tour event at that point was Cypress Point.

Clearly, Goodell is comfortable at super-rich golf clubs whose memberships are almost all white men.

When I got back to McCarthy, he told me Goodell would "pass" on my request. When I asked for an official reason why he was passing, I received this in return: "The commissioner is focused on doing the work to make improvements in NFL policies and programs that will lead to more opportunities and better outcomes for diversity hires across all areas of the league and teams."

He also told me that under NFL guidelines, a Jewish coach would not be considered a minority.

I'm sure Eric Bieniemy would find McCarthy's answer very comforting. I translated Goodell's response—through McCarthy—to say this: "I have zero interest in talking to you about an issue that has been an embarrassment for the league."

One person who believes that Goodell is genuinely embarrassed and wants to do better is Tomlin. "I honestly believe Roger feels badly about what's gone on the last few years," he said. "He knows there should be more minority hiring among coaches and general managers. But he can't make owners do what they don't want to do. They're the ultimate decision makers. In that sense, I feel badly for him because he's the out-front guy taking hits for things he doesn't control."

Tomlin was interviewed by the Steelers — specifically by then team chairman Dan Rooney and his son, team president Art Rooney III — even though they had already fulfilled their Rooney Rule commitment by interviewing Rivera, who had been the Chicago Bears defensive coordinator the previous three seasons under Lovie Smith. According to Dan Rooney, Tomlin "blew us away" in the interview and that's why he was hired.

Rooney's description of Tomlin's interview was almost the same as Dungy's description of his interview with Tomlin.

Two years later, the Steelers won the Super Bowl. Tomlin is the third Steelers coach since 1969: Chuck Noll won four Super Bowls and is in the Hall of Fame; Bill Cowher won one and is in the Hall of Fame. Not yet fifty, Tomlin was already tied for twenty-first on the all-time wins list, with 145 going into the 2021 season — just 4 behind Cowher, who is twentieth — and would seem to be on track to join his two Pittsburgh predecessors in Canton.

In spite of all this, Tomlin isn't thrilled with the current trend in NFL hiring practices. When he came into the league in 2007, he was one of six Black head coaches — seven if you counted Emmitt Thomas, who coached the last three Falcons games after Bobby Petrino fled to take the Arkansas job.

During the 2020 off-season, the NFL made a big deal of supposedly expanding the Rooney rule. Teams were required to interview two minorities instead of one for head coaching and front-office positions. The NFL also added incentives for minority hiring. Any team that had a minority hired by another team received an extra third-round draft pick; the team making the hire moved up six spots in the third round. There were other incentives when it came to hiring coordinators.

The net result? Black head coaches went from three to…three. Anthony Lynn was fired by the Chargers even though his team won its last four games. David Culley was hired by the Texans to replace Bill O'Brien—after Romeo Crennel had taken over from him as interim coach for the second half of the season.

The NFL would claim that minority head coaches went from four (including Rivera) to five, thanks to Saleh. The general manager numbers were slightly better. The season began with two Black general managers: Chris Grier in Miami (who hired Brian Flores) and Andrew Berry in Cleveland. Early in 2021, the Detroit Lions hired Brad Holmes to try to clean up the mess left by Bob Quinn; the Falcons hired Terry Fontenot (*after* hiring their new coach, Arthur Smith); and Washington hired Martin Mayhew, giving a Black executive a rare second chance to be a general manager—sort of. Although Mayhew has the GM title, he reports to Rivera.

Washington had been without a general manager for several years. Rivera was given absolute power by owner Dan Snyder a year earlier—except, of course, when Snyder decides to step in, as he has done in the past, and take away that absolute power.

If you count Mayhew, five of the thirty-two GMs are Black, along with three of the thirty-two coaches. When *ProFootballTalk's* Mike Florio posted a story citing the "improvement" in the league's minority hiring—noting that a number of new coordinators had also been hired—many of those posting responses said things like this: "Why doesn't the NFL worry about the fact that the number of white players isn't reflective of the country's population?" The comments are both ignorant and reflective of the kind of racism that exists among many fans of the NFL.

The answer to the question is simple: When the issue is who is going to play, sports is a meritocracy. Teams want the best players possible, regardless of race, religion, or political beliefs. In contrast, when leadership roles are being decided, there is still a decided advantage to being white.

Hall of Fame college basketball coach Gary Williams grew up as one of a handful of white kids playing in his neighborhood's schoolyard in Camden, New Jersey, and likes to say, "What I always liked about basketball, about sports, is that the scoreboard never knew what color you were. Once you got out there, you could play or you couldn't play. That's all anyone cared about."

Unfortunately, it isn't quite as simple when it comes to coaching or leading a front office. And most of those deciding who is going to play quarterback for NFL teams or coach or manage them are still white men.

Marvin Lewis had great success in Cincinnati for sixteen years but hasn't sniffed another NFL job since being fired after the 2018 season. "When I was young," he said, "my dad always told me that if I wanted something, there was a good chance I had to be twice as good as a white person to get that job. I think that's something all of us understand."

Anthony Lynn coached the Los Angeles Chargers for four seasons. He went 9–7 and 12–4 the first two years, and the Chargers won in Baltimore in the first round of the 2018 playoffs before losing to New England in the divisional round. A year later, they dropped to 5–11, but in 2020, with rookie quarterback Justin Herbert and an awful start that included several last-second losses, the Chargers won their last four games to finish 7–9.

Not good enough. Lynn was fired, and the Chargers hired Brandon Staley to replace him. Staley is not one of the many young offensive coaches who have been hired in recent years. He has coached on the defensive side of the ball for his entire career. He also has a total of four years of coaching experience in the NFL, one—the 2020 season—as a coordinator. Being an assistant to Sean McVay with the LA Rams opens doors these days, and the Rams, led by Aaron Donald, arguably the league's best defensive player, finished first statistically in defense in 2020.

Staley's résumé is not unlike Tony Dungy's in 1993. Dungy didn't get a single interview for a head coaching job after that season. Staley was hired as a head coach.

With Donald hurt and only playing a limited number of snaps, the Rams lost to Green Bay 32–18 in the 2020 divisional playoffs. The next day, the Chargers announced that Staley would be their new head coach.

Working for McVay helped, and so did the Rams defensive stats. So did being white.

"I was disappointed when Anthony [Lynn] was fired," Dungy said. "I thought he'd done enough to at least get another year. But the way I look at it, at least he got a chance." He paused. "The question is, will he get another chance?"

Lynn's overall record with the Chargers was 33–31. Jim Caldwell was 36–28 in Detroit. Marvin Lewis was 131–122–3 in Cincinnati. Lewis took over what was then considered the NFL's worst franchise. Caldwell took over an almost-as-bad Lions team. The Chargers were 4–12 and 5–11 the two seasons before Lynn arrived. He is now the offensive coordinator in Detroit. He's only fifty-two.

Three coaches with winning records coaching teams with moribund histories. Will any get another chance? A better question is this: is there any way a white coach with those numbers would *not* get another chance?

Bill Belichick was 36–44 in five seasons in Cleveland. And yet both the New York Jets—for about fifteen minutes—and the New

England Patriots were willing to give him another chance. Clearly, they did the right thing. Pete Carroll was 33–31 in five seasons coaching the Jets and Patriots. He then won a lot of games at USC and got a third NFL chance in Seattle in 2010. Again, the right move. On the other hand, Adam Gase was 23–25 in Miami and was instantly hired by the Jets after he was fired. He went 9–23 coaching in New Jersey. Even so, chances are decent he'll get yet another crack at running a team.

In a twist that was impossible to miss, Chicago Bears general manager Ryan Pace—the man who passed on both Patrick Mahomes and Deshaun Watson to take Mitchell Trubisky with the number two pick in 2017—traded up in the first round of the 2021 NFL draft to draft Justin Fields—who is Black—from Ohio State.

Trubisky flamed out so badly with the Bears that they didn't even offer him the fifth-year contract that almost all number one picks are offered. He's now in Buffalo as a backup to Josh Allen.

Mahomes can laugh now about what happened on draft night four years ago because he certainly has had the last laugh.

"Look, I would have loved to have been the first player chosen in that draft," he said. "But when I wasn't the first player chosen [defensive end Myles Garrett was], I really liked the idea of going to the Chiefs. I knew about Coach Reid and the coaching staff and liked the way they ran their offense. I thought it would be a perfect place for me.

"But of course you keep track of the other players in your draft, and you want to prove you're the best. That was a goal of mine, regardless of where I got drafted."

After leading the Chiefs to their Super Bowl victory in February 2020, Mahomes signed a ten-year contract that will be worth a minimum of $450 million. In the spring of 2021, Trubisky signed a one-year deal in Buffalo worth $2.5 million. It's fair to say Mahomes made his point pretty clearly.

Mahomes admits he was completely baffled a year later when he heard scouts and so-called experts saying Lamar Jackson should move from quarterback to either wide receiver or running back.

"If you watched him at Louisville, there's no way you could think he wasn't going to be a successful quarterback in the NFL," he said. "I think, because he's so fast, people tended to focus on his ability to run the ball. But he threw thirty touchdown passes the year he won the Heisman and just a few less [twenty-seven] the next year. The guy can *throw* the ball, and he can throw it on the run. There was never any doubt in my mind about him becoming a really good NFL quarterback." He paused. "Guess I was wrong because he's a *great* NFL quarterback."

I asked Mahomes if he thought anyone in any way would have thought about asking Jackson to change positions if he had had the same skill set and was white. He paused again.

"No, I don't think so," he finally said. "I don't see that happening."

Mahomes says that growing up, he wasn't exposed to very much blatant racism. "But I heard stories from my dad [a former major league pitcher], which make me realize how lucky I've been," he said. "It's still very much out there. We've seen that in the last year, and I think it's up to all of us who have a platform to work as hard as we can to change things for our children and for their children. We need to work in our communities and we need to be outspoken.

"What we all saw with George Floyd was sickening. It's a good thing that a lot of people, including a lot of athletes, have spoken up and taken action since then. I know the better I play, the more of a platform I have, and it's going to be up to me to make sure I use it for good."

Mahomes is outspoken on the subject of Bieniemy, his offensive coordinator who is still waiting for his chance to be a head coach.

"Obviously, it should have already happened," Mahomes said. "Selfishly, it's great for us to still have him around. But I've worked with him and I know what kind of a head coach he's going to be and how lucky a team is going to be to get him. It will happen. I'm just glad that *he* has the patience to deal with it."

Mahomes has heard the excuse that the process has been slower for Bieniemy because Coach Andy Reid is the Chiefs primary play-caller.

"That's a lame excuse," he said. "Almost every team with an offensive head coach, he calls most of the plays. Coach B. is very involved in our game planning all week and during the game. A lot of guys with head coaching jobs in the NFL right now were never the primary play-caller. Like I said, his time will come and he'll be a great head coach."

Mahomes is very aware of the political climate in the country. I asked him about Laura Ingraham's "shut up and dribble" comment directed at LeBron James.

"She's like a lot of people — she didn't want to hear his opinions, because she didn't agree with them," Mahomes said. "One thing a lot of people don't want to understand is that before we [athletes] speak up on an issue, we try to make sure we know what we're talking about. Saying 'stick to sports' is just another way of saying 'I don't agree with you, so I don't want to hear what you have to say.' That's fine. But I don't think it's going to stop any of us from speaking up."

Having made the horrific mistake of using the second pick in the 2017 draft to take Trubisky, Ryan Pace had to give the New York Giants the twentieth pick and a fifth-round pick in 2021 and a first-round pick and a fourth-round pick in the 2022 draft so the Bears could move to the eleventh spot last spring. That was a lot to give up.

Justin Fields was available at number eleven because he had somehow dropped in the minds of the so-called experts even after outplaying Clemson's Trevor Lawrence in the College Football Play-off semifinals. Lawrence had been anointed the number one pick at birth and was taken there by Jacksonville; Brigham Young's Zach Wilson became the hot choice to go at number two to the New York Jets and did so. And, in the surprise of the first round, North Dakota State's Trey Lance went at number three to San Francisco. That left Fields and Alabama's Mac Jones still available at number eleven. Pace took Fields. Jones went to the Patriots at fifteen.

No one knows which of the newly drafted quarterbacks will become stars. But it is hardly surprising that the white guys went first and one of the Black guys (Fields) was whispered about from the night of his last college game until the night he was drafted. There has certainly been progress since Marlin Briscoe's debut. But just as surely, there are still football people looking for what Hall of Fame general manager Bill Polian called the "old traditional quarterback."

The "old traditional" quarterback looked like Johnny Unitas, Bart Starr, or Joe Namath. Or Mitchell Trubisky.

Fifty-two years ago, when Ozzie Newsome was in eighth grade, he knew he had no chance to play quarterback for a Pop Warner team. Today, Lamar Jackson is quarterback of the team Newsome led for twenty-three years in the front office. It took Newsome—a Black general manager—and a draft in which four white quarterbacks were chosen well ahead of Jackson—to get him there.

In 2019, his second season and his first as the Ravens full-time starter, Jackson became the second player in history to be unanimously voted the league's MVP. The first was Tom Brady.

Not bad for a running back.

PART TWO

BASKETBALL

CHAPTER SIX

Pathfinders

WHEN JOHN THOMPSON WAS HIRED to be the basketball coach at Georgetown University on March 13, 1972, the Reverend Robert J. Henle was the school's president. In basketball terms, Georgetown was a little-known eastern independent at the time. It had enjoyed one and only one moment of real glory, and that had come in 1943, when it reached the championship game of what was then the eight-team NCAA Tournament before losing to Wyoming.

In the almost thirty years since that brief brush with glory, it had twice reached the National Invitation Tournament (NIT) — in 1953 and 1970 — and had lost in the first round both times. Thompson was hired to replace Jack Magee, whose fortunes slid quickly after that 1970 NIT season, bottoming in 1972, when the Hoyas went 3–23.

Thompson was thirty years old. He had been born and raised in Northwest Washington, D.C., and had starred at Archbishop John Carroll High School, leading the school to a 48-game winning streak, including a 24–0 record in 1960, his senior season. He'd gone from there to Providence College, where he had played under

Coach Joe Mullaney and Assistant Coach Dave Gavitt. Chosen in the third round of the NBA draft by the Boston Celtics to back up Bill Russell at center, he played on two NBA championship teams, averaging 3.5 points and 3.5 rebounds per game. Although he played very little, he established lifelong friendships while in Boston with Russell and Celtics coach Red Auerbach.

In the spring of 1966, when the NBA added the Chicago Bulls as an expansion team, the Bulls selected Thompson in the expansion draft. Rather than go play for what would inevitably be a bad team—the Bulls first winning season came in their fifth year of existence—Thompson retired and took a job as the basketball coach and a guidance counselor at St. Anthony's High School, which wasn't far from where he'd grown up.

He quickly turned the school into a local power—going 122–28 in six seasons. Years later, when he talked about how he had built his program he said, "Of course I recruited. Everyone recruited, even though it was supposed to be against the rules. I told players, 'The difference between me and other coaches is I'll *admit* I recruited you.' I won't play any games and say, 'Oh, he just wanted to come here.'"

That comment was a not-so-indirect shot at Morgan Wootten, the Hall of Fame coach at DeMatha Catholic High School. Wootten always insisted he didn't recruit—that players wanted to come to DeMatha. By the time Thompson got to St. Anthony's, there was truth in what Wootten said: DeMatha was *the* program in the D.C. area, and Wootten was already an iconic figure. Players did want to go to DeMatha.

DeMatha and St. Anthony's never played while Thompson was the coach at St. Anthony's. Each coach blamed the other. In 1971, the two schools reached the final of the prestigious Jelleff League summer tournament. Thompson sent cheerleaders, managers, and football players to represent his team that night. "If he won't play me in the winter, I'm damn sure not playing him in the summer" was his explanation. To this day, the game is referred to by basketball people in D.C. as "the greatest high school game never played."

Many years later, when both men were retired and were in the Naismith Basketball Hall of Fame, Wootten would occasionally appear on Thompson's local radio show in Washington. The two men said there had never been any bad blood between them, that it had all been created by the media.

I know that this claim wasn't true. I once asked Thompson why he had never recruited one of Wootten's players—some of whom very much wanted to play at Georgetown. "There are some people on this earth you can live away from," Thompson answered. "Morgan is one of those people for me."

On the day that Georgetown hired Thompson, Henle's message to Thompson was simple: "Get us to the NIT every so often, and I'll be very happy," he told his new coach.

"I'll do my best, Father," Thompson answered.

Years later, Thompson would laugh telling the story. "Getting to the NIT was never my goal," he said. "I had bigger plans than that."

It didn't take long for Thompson to start turning his plans into reality. From the beginning, he used his contacts as a D.C. high school coach and the fact that he was a Black coach at a predominantly white school to his advantage.

"It was kind of pointless for me to whine and complain that certain white families didn't want me to recruit their sons because I was Black," he said. "The fact was—and is—the majority of the best players were Black. Were there some white players I wanted to recruit—and did recruit? Yes. But the fact is, being a Black coach was an advantage for me with a lot of players and their families. I could sit in their living rooms and say, 'I know what it's like to be Black at a school where most of the students are white. That was my college experience—at Providence. I know it won't be easy, but I will always be there to protect your son.'"

By Thompson's third season, Georgetown was good enough to make not the NIT but the far more important NCAA Tournament. By then, most of his players were Black—many of them from the local D.C. area. At one point, with the team struggling, someone hoisted a banner through a window at McDonough Arena that said "Thompson the nigger flop must go."

Probably a measure of the suspicion that many white people held for the self-described "big [six feet ten, 300 pounds], loud, and intimidating Black man" were some rumors that were then circulating claiming that Thompson himself had arranged for the banner, to take pressure off his program by making race, rather than his coaching, the issue.

"There aren't that many things that made me really angry," he said to me in the spring of 2020, just before the pandemic began and a few months before he died in August. "That accusation did. To begin with, we were getting better, especially that third season. Beyond that, I always wanted desperately to win, but take it that far? My children saw that banner. You have to be fucking kidding me."

Georgetown did, in fact, improve greatly during that third season. After going 12–14 and 13–13 in Thompson's first two seasons, the Hoyas went 18–10 and made the NCAA Tournament for the first time since that long-ago run in 1943. A year later, they made the tournament again.

By then, Thompson's recruiting was beginning to really lock in, although Georgetown finally met Father Henle's goal in both 1977 and 1978 when it failed to make the NCAA Tournament but made the NIT—reaching the semifinals the second year and finishing with a record of 23–8. The next year, led by juniors John "Bebe" Duren and Craig "Sky" Shelton and a freshman shooting whiz named Eric Floyd, Georgetown went 24–5 and returned to the NCAAs. That was the first of fourteen straight NCAA trips and eighteen appearances in nineteen seasons.

People outside Washington first began to take note of Thompson in 1980, when Georgetown reached the Elite Eight before losing to Iowa in overtime with a Final Four trip at stake.

What drew people's attention to Georgetown that season—other than the team's 26–6 record and winning the inaugural Big East championship—were two games against local rival Maryland. The Terrapins were coached by Lefty Driesell, one of basketball's true characters, and led by Albert King, Buck Williams, and Greg Manning. Maryland won the ACC regular-season title and lost to Duke in the ACC Tournament final on a controversial no-call at the end of the game.

In those days, Washington's local teams played one another regularly. That year, American University played Navy, and Georgetown played Maryland in an early December doubleheader in the old D.C. Armory—which was right across the street from RFK Stadium, then the home of Washington's NFL football team.

Midway through the second half of a tight game, Thompson began barking at the officials, walking to midcourt to do so. Back then, there were no coaches' boxes and coaches were free to roam up and down the sideline. As usual, Thompson's complaints included a raft of profanity. Years later, at an elegant dinner honoring him,

Thompson paused in the midst of a wave of profanities—mostly used as terms of endearment—and said to the semi-shocked audience, "You have to understand; I'm fluent in two languages—English and profanity."

Driesell, hearing what Thompson was saying, stalked to mid-court and screamed at the officials that they had to give Thompson a technical foul for his language. He and Thompson were face-to-face in what, at that moment, was a confrontation of two very large men: Driesell six feet five and Thompson six feet ten.

I report this firsthand, because I was sitting no more than ten feet away and could hear everything said quite clearly.

"That's a technical," Driesell bellowed, pointing at Thompson. "You have to give him a technical!"

"Shut the fuck up and mind your own damn business, mother-fucker!" Thompson yelled, using his favorite word.

At that moment, the officials' concern wasn't who did or did not deserve a technical foul. It was keeping the two large, angry men from lunging at each other.

Things calmed down and Georgetown went on to win the game. Afterwards, Driesell was furious. "I been coaching college basketball twenty years," he said. "And I ain't never had another coach speak to me that way."

Thompson wouldn't talk about the incident that night, but as luck would have it, both teams reached the NCAA Tournament's Sweet Sixteen in March—paired against one another in a game in Philadelphia's Spectrum.

On Monday of that week, Thompson held a rare press conference. He was asked about the December incident. "I owe Lefty an apology," he said. "It was heat of the moment, but there was no excuse for me speaking to him that way."

The next day, at his weekly press conference, Lefty was asked (by me) if he accepted Thompson's apology.

"'Course I do," he said. "Evabody knows, to err is human, to forgive divine, and aahm divine."

That seemed to cool things down, at least for the moment. Georgetown won the tournament game, 74–68, with no one cursing at anyone — at least not publicly. Two victories in a season over Maryland, including one in the NCAA Tournament with a spot in the Elite Eight at stake, made Georgetown the college hoops kings of D.C.

Which is why Maryland and Georgetown didn't play one another for the next fourteen years. Having supplanted Maryland and Driesell at the top of the D.C. basketball heap, Thompson simply refused to schedule Maryland or Georgetown's longtime archrival George Washington. He played American University for another few years, but after a shocking loss in December 1982 and a too-close-for-comfort game four seasons later, he told then AU coach Ed Tapscott during the postgame handshake, "That's it. We aren't playing you anymore."

"What you have to understand about John in those days is he was still looking at the world as an everybody-is-against-me proposition," said Tapscott, who later became general manager of the New York Knicks and then the first Black CEO of an NBA team — the expansion Charlotte Bobcats. "I looked up to him, literally and figuratively [Tapscott is about five ten] because of what he'd done at Georgetown. But in those days, he wasn't looking to mentor anybody; he was looking to build on what he'd already accomplished. That changed later, especially when he got out of coaching. But back then, I was no different than anybody else who might have gotten in his way by beating him in a basketball game."

Thompson's national profile—for good and for bad—went to a completely different level in 1981, when Patrick Ewing enrolled at Georgetown. Before that season began, Thompson was quick to point out that Georgetown had been to the NCAA Tournament three years in a row *before* Ewing arrived.

"We didn't get Patrick to get good," he said back then. "We got Patrick because we *are* good."

Ewing was anything but a gentle giant. He played with his elbows up and a scowl on his face. Thompson had always been protective of his players when it came to the media, but Ewing's presence took the protection—and the media's frustration with it—to a whole new level.

I first encountered Thompson's cloak of secrecy—and his temper—during the Elite Eight season of 1980. I was writing a feature story on the team's two senior stars, Craig Shelton and John Duren, and was given a rare chance to talk one-on-one to each in person. I liked them both. Routinely, as I always did, I asked them what their majors were and what they thought they might do when—someday—they finished being basketball players.

They were the same questions I had asked every college athlete I had ever interviewed, dating to my college days as a student reporter. Shelton and Duren answered the questions as routinely as I had asked them.

Late that night, I got a call from Thompson. He didn't even say hello. "How dare you ask those two boys what their major is!" he screamed. "How dare you ask them what they're going to do after basketball! It's none of your damn business what they're going to do when they finish playing basketball!"

"John, those are routine questions I always ask—"

"Are they routine questions you ask white kids?"

That question made me angry. "You're damn right they are," I said. "I just did a piece on Mike O'Koren at North Carolina. Call him. Ask him if I asked those questions."

The screaming stopped. His voice grew softer. "It's still none of your damn business," he said.

"I'm writing about people. I want to tell the reader more about them than their stats."

John, as I would learn through the years, never gave up on an argument without a fight.

"Why?" he said. "You're interviewing them because they play basketball. You have no idea what they went through to be seniors in college."

"And that's a story worth telling."

There was a long pause. "Did I wake you?" he asked.

"Yes."

"Good."

I heard a click.

For the next few years, we had a good relationship, even though I often chafed at the lack of access to the players — especially after Ewing's arrival turned their national profile up to Defcon 5.

The Big East had a rule that a team's locker room had to be open for fifteen minutes after each game. Thompson always went to the interview room at the exact moment when the locker room opened, forcing reporters to choose between listening to him or interviewing the players. Most reporters chose him — with good reason — because he was much more loquacious and quotable than any of his players.

If you did go into the locker room, you were shadowed by Thomson's two assistants, Mike Riley and Craig Esherick. The rule, we were told, was basketball questions only. Do *not* ask a player what his major is and expect an answer.

One night, Ewing rolled an ankle with about eight minutes left in a one-sided win over Boston College. Since he wasn't needed, he sat out the rest of the game. The question was, would he be ready to play that Saturday at Pittsburgh?

I was standing with a small gaggle of reporters when someone asked Ewing if he thought he would be okay for Saturday. Always careful, Ewing said, "I don't wish to discuss my injury."

"Why not, Patrick?" I asked. "If you don't know how serious it is, please just tell us that."

Before Ewing could answer, Esherick put his hand on my shoulder—he was standing directly behind me—and said, "Basketball questions only, John."

I turned around and said, "He got hurt playing basketball, Craig. How is that not a basketball question?"

Ewing didn't answer the question. He played that Saturday.

Thompson's most famous quote is often reported inaccurately. Stories written about him after his death (and his posthumously published autobiography) said that he had responded to a question about being the first Black coach to win a national championship by saying, "I resent the hell out of that question because it implies that I am the first Black coach *capable* of doing this."

Georgetown won the national championship in Seattle in 1984. Thompson's "I resent the hell out of that question" answer came earlier, in New Orleans in 1982. It was during the Friday press conference the day before the semifinals, the first time he and Georgetown reached the Final Four. He went on that day to talk about men like Clarence "Big House" Gaines and John McLendon. Gaines won 828 games at Winston-Salem State but never got a chance to coach at the Division 1 level. Wake Forest, a few miles down the road from Winston-Salem State, had seven coaches during Gaines's time there.

Gaines was never interviewed for the job. In fact, the school didn't hire a Black head coach until 2016 — eleven years after Gaines died.

McLendon had a three-year stint at Cleveland State before the school became a Division 1 program. He coached for most of his career at the North Carolina College for Negroes (now North Carolina Central) and Tennessee A&I (now Tennessee State) and had brief stints in the pros, first with the Cleveland Pipers of what was then the American Basketball League and then with the Denver Nuggets of the American Basketball Association (ABA).

Georgetown lost the national championship game to North Carolina in 1982 on Michael Jordan's famous shot and Fred Brown's infamous pass. Two years later, the Hoyas finally won the title with Ewing outplaying Houston's Hakeem Olajuwon in the championship game.

That victory made Thompson one of the big names in college coaching, along with Dean Smith (his mentor), Bob Knight, and Jim Valvano. Thompson, though, was different. He was, as he often said, "big, Black, and angry."

He was frequently labeled a racist by the media. One writer called him "the Idi Amin of college basketball." Most of the time, his team was all Black. In fact, Georgetown had become *the* school among Black teenagers. There were some who thought it was an HBCU. There was an HBCU in Washington, D.C. — Howard University. Thompson always liked that people thought Georgetown was an HBCU.

By the time Georgetown won the national title, I was very much in Thompson's doghouse. It had started when I was working on a lengthy piece on Ewing, who was then a junior. I had even been granted twenty minutes one-on-one with him. After talking to Ewing, I had some follow-up questions for Thompson. One night after a game, I waited for him to come out of the locker room to try to grab a few minutes with him to ask those questions. Worth noting, the two men were friends.

He walked out, as he always did, with his alter ego, Mary Fenlon. A former nun who had met Thompson at St. Anthony's, Fenlon had accompanied him to Georgetown as his academic coordinator. She was, unquestionably, the number two person in the pecking order at the school. She was even more of an us-against-them person than Thompson was, especially when it came to the media.

"John," I said as the two of them walked out of the locker room, "when you're finished in there [the interview room], I need to ask you a couple follow-up questions for my Ewing piece."

Before John could respond, Fenlon did. "He doesn't have time to talk to you," she said.

As I've mentioned before, Fenlon and I never got along. I was young and quick-tempered. (Now I'm old and quick-tempered.)

"You know what, Mary," I said. "I didn't think I was speaking to you. I could have sworn I was speaking to John."

Mistake. Thompson reared up to his full height, stood over me, and said, "If you talking to me, motherfucker, you talking to Mary. If you talking to Mary, you talking to me. If you fuck with Mary, you fuck with me. Do you want to fuck with me?"

As I said, I was young and quick-tempered. Also stupid.

In trying to learn more about Thompson, I had heard he was a soft player in high school and college. "Nothing but a pussy jump-shooter" was the way then UDC coach Wil Jones described him. The two men were friends, however. The point Jones and others were making was the irony of the soft player becoming the ultra-hard-nosed coach. Thompson wrote about this dichotomy in his autobiography, *I Came As a Shadow*, which was published not long after his death.

"Tell you what, John," I said. "Let's go outside. If what I've heard about you is true, I'll kick your ass. If not, you'll kick mine. Either way, I'll be famous."

Thompson stared at me in disbelief for a second, then burst out laughing. He put an arm around me and said, "You know something, motherfucker, I don't like you. I don't like you at all. But I respect your ass because you're fucking crazy. I'll talk to you when I'm finished."

The thing about Thompson was, when he did talk to you, he pretty much wrote your story for you. He was thoughtful and eloquent and never ducked a question, once you got the chance to ask one.

Later that season, I wrote a *Sporting News* piece in which I used the term "Hoya Paranoia" in explaining Thompson's secretive ways. Thompson was furious and so was Georgetown's president, the Reverend Timothy Healy. As luck would have it — bad luck for me — Healy often played tennis with Katharine Graham, the *Washington Post*'s publisher. He complained to her about the story and — surprise — labeled it racist.

Graham called George Solomon, the sports editor, to tell him what Healy had said. Solomon knew there was nothing racist about what I'd written and was, I suspect, embarrassed that the piece hadn't run in the *Post*. It hadn't, largely because Solomon was always afraid to criticize Thompson on any level. He called me into his office and demanded that I publicly apologize. I told him there was nothing in the piece I felt the need to apologize for, that the piece was both accurate and fair.

Solomon then invoked a technicality: I hadn't asked in writing for permission to write the piece. Back then, almost everyone on the staff routinely wrote for the *Sporting News*. I had been doing it for five years and had never asked for permission in writing. But Solomon was technically correct.

"If you don't apologize today, you're fired," he said. "You violated the union contract."

He was right about the contract. I still wasn't apologizing. I was rescued by Ken Denlinger and Tony Kornheiser, who went to Solomon and pointed out that he'd look foolish if he fired me for writing a story that almost everyone agreed was true.

"You willing to lose John because Father Healy got mad at him?" Tony said.

George eventually decided to suspend me (with pay) for a week, denying me the chance to go to scenic Pullman, Washington, to see Georgetown play during the first weekend of the NCAA Tournament. Heartbroken I was not. A week later, instead of sending me to Los Angeles to cover Georgetown in the West Regional, Solomon sent me to Atlanta, site of the East Regional.

As a result, I covered one of the greatest upsets in tournament history: Indiana's Round of 16 victory over North Carolina in what turned out to be Michael Jordan's last college game. It was the only time I ever saw Dean Smith cry during a postgame press conference.

Thank you, George.

Thompson didn't speak to me again until I sat down next to him during a practice at the Olympic Trials in May. At first, he wouldn't look at me. Finally, I said, "John, you want to be pissed off at me, that's fine. But you know the *Sporting News* piece had nothing to do with race. It had everything to do with your paranoia about the media."

In his autobiography, Thompson goes on at great length about media slights. In most cases, his anger was justified. But he *was* paranoid, and Fenlon (to whom he dedicated the book) often fed that paranoia. I liked and respected Thompson too much not to try to repair our relationship. But I wasn't going to back down from him.

As soon as I said the word *paranoia,* he started talking—loudly and angrily. "We just won the damn national championship. Who are you to criticize me?" he said.

"Did I criticize your coaching?"

"No. You aren't that dumb." He paused. "But you are pretty fucking dumb."

We went back and forth awhile until I finally said, "We can agree to disagree on the piece, but you *know* it had nothing to do with race. You didn't play the race card, but Father Healy did."

Silence. I stood up and put out my hand. He looked at me for a moment and then shook hands. "I still don't like you," he said. But he was smiling by then.

"Well, as it happens, I like you," I said. "But you really are a pain in the ass."

I tell those stories for a reason: in those days, you had to know Thompson, maybe had to fight with him, to understand him.

He was not, by any stretch, a racist. Not even close. Throughout Thompson's life, most of his closest friends, mentors, and advisers were white: Dave Gavitt, dating to when he was an assistant coach at Providence; Bill Stein, his Providence teammate who was his first assistant coach at Georgetown; Fenlon, who might have been his closest adviser and was his second in command for twenty-six years at Georgetown.

The coaches he looked to most for guidance were Red Auerbach, his coach in Boston, and Dean Smith, who selected him as one of his assistant coaches for the 1976 Olympic team. The other assistant on that Olympic team was Bill Guthridge, Smith's right-hand man at North Carolina, who also became a close friend. David Falk (unfortunately) was his agent. His closest friends in the media were Leonard Shapiro, Thomas Boswell, Ken Denlinger, Dave Kindred, Mark Asher, and Michael Wilbon. Bill Russell, his teammate in Boston, was a friend and mentor for more than fifty years. The only people on those lists who aren't white are Russell and Wilbon.

There are those who would argue that Thompson's three Final Four trips (1982, 1984, and 1985) all came with Ewing on the team and prove that Ewing was great and Thompson merely the beneficiary of having Ewing on his team. There's no question that Ewing was Thompson's greatest player and that the Hoyas were at their best with him playing center. But Georgetown also reached the Elite Eight in 1980, 1987, 1989, and 1996. In nineteen of his final twenty-three seasons, the Hoyas won at least 20 games — in three other seasons, they won 19 games. After his first two seasons, Thompson met Henle's request with four trips to the NIT in the next twenty-four years — each a consolation prize at the end of a down season. The other twenty years, Georgetown reached the NCAAs.

What might have been Thompson's greatest moment turned into his greatest failure. After winning the national title and reaching the Final Four three times in four years, he was named to succeed Bob Knight as the US Olympic coach for the 1988 games in Seoul, South Korea. This was a very big deal for Thompson: to be named to succeed Smith, Gavitt, and Knight as Olympic coach. Smith and Knight had led the United States to dominant gold medal performances; Gavitt never got to coach his team, because of the US Olympic boycott in 1980.

The 1988 Olympics were the last games in which the United States was represented by college players. Four years later, in Barcelona, the United States was represented by NBA players, the so-called

Dream Team, led by Michael Jordan, David Robinson, Charles Barkley, and Ewing.

In 1988, Thompson had Robinson, Danny Manning, Mitch Richmond, and Dan Majerle on his team. The United States was heavily favored to win the gold medal, but this was the last Olympics in which the Soviet Union sent a unified team before the country's breakup two years later. Thompson, always defense-obsessed, only picked one real shooter for the team: Bradley University's Hersey Hawkins. The rest of the role players were chosen for their defense.

But Hawkins hurt his ankle in a preliminary round game and was in street clothes for the semifinal against the Soviet Union. The Soviets won the game 82–76, the United States unable to hit a jump shot over the Soviets' sagging defense that cut off the inside while allowing the Americans to take jump shots — that were often off-target. The United States ended up with the bronze medal, the worst finish by an American basketball team in Olympic history.

Thompson was devastated by the loss. What was even more hurtful was hearing that his team's loss was the reason the United States decided to send pros to the 1992 Olympics. That observation, however, was urban myth. FIBA, the association that runs international basketball, had decided before the 1988 games to allow pros to play in the Olympics. That decision — surprise — was all about two things: TV ratings and marketing. Or, to boil it down to one word: money.

The formal announcement wasn't made until a year later, but the decision had been made before the Seoul Olympics. I know this because I reported the story for NBC (I was moonlighting as something NBC called a "Seoul searcher") during those Olympics.

Thompson had been criticized in the past for being overprotective of his players (by me, among others); for being a racist; for having a temper. He'd never been criticized for his coaching. Plus, deep down, he had to know that he had made mistakes picking the team. He had taken Stacy Augmon from Nevada–Las Vegas over Stacey King of Oklahoma. King was a bona fide scorer, Augmon a defensive special-ist who played for Jerry Tarkanian, Thompson's good friend and fel-low Nike employee. Thompson had left shooters like Arizona's Steve Kerr and Army's Kevin Houston off the team, and he had played J. R. Reid—who was playing at North Carolina for his mentor Smith—almost as many minutes as Robinson had played, even though Robinson was the better player by a wide margin.

Thompson was never quite the same after that Olympics. He still had some very good teams and reached the Elite Eight twice more. But he never made another Final Four. Georgetown, led by fresh-man center Alonzo Mourning and senior point guard Charles Smith, did win both the regular season and the tournament championships in the Big East in 1989. But the Hoyas—who had won six of the ten conference tournament titles in the 1980s—never won the con-ference tournament again under Thompson and never won the regular-season title outright, either, although they did share first place three times.

The last time I spoke to Thompson, just before COVID-19 hit and his health problems became serious, I asked him if losing the Olympics had changed him.

"Not really," he said. "It hurt to lose. It hurt to be given the chance to represent my country as the head coach and not win the gold medal. It hurt to hear people say I didn't do a good job.

"But what changed me more than anything was winning the national championship. I had been obsessed with doing that. We'd come so close in eighty-two, and then we got it done in eighty-four. I badly wanted it for Patrick [Ewing] because I didn't want people to say 'great player, but' about him the way they did about [Ralph] Sampson. But I also wanted it for myself. I wanted people to stop thinking a Black man couldn't win a national championship. I know there were people who thought that. Hell, even now, there are people who think white men are more apt to be great coaches than Black men. It's still harder to get a so-called big-time job if you're Black than if you're white. Look at the numbers. And this is twenty-damn-twenty."

As Thompson spoke, in March "twenty-damn-twenty," the numbers backed him up. In the so-called power-six conferences in college basketball: ACC, SEC, Big 10, Big 12, Pac-12, and the Big East, there were 75 jobs. Only 12 were held by Black coaches, 5 of those positions in Georgetown's conference, the Big East. The Pac-12 was 0 for 12. In total, 16 percent of those positions were filled by Black coaches, in a sport where more than 60 percent of the players in those leagues are Black. If you added in the AAC (American Athletic Conference) and the Atlantic-10, two leagues that regularly get multiple NCAA Tournament bids, the numbers got a little better: 6 of the 11 AAC jobs were held by Black men; 4 of the 14 coaches in the Atlantic-10 were African Americans. Add those numbers to the mix, and you get 22 out of 100.

In all, among the 353 Division 1 coaching jobs, 103 (29.17 percent) were held by Black men. That number, however, was somewhat deceiving since it included the 21 HBCUs that played in Division 1. Twenty of those coaches are Black. Take them out of the equation, and the number becomes 82 of 332, which is 24.1 percent. About 50 percent of those playing in all of Division 1 are Black.

"When I took the Georgetown job, it wasn't one that people were chasing after," Thompson said. "That's why they were willing and able to hire a Black high school coach. If you look at a lot of the jobs that Black coaches do get, they aren't exactly choice jobs, are they?"

Thompson took over a team that had gone 3–23 the year before he arrived.

Three Black coaches are notable exceptions to the rule that says Black coaches only rarely get the chance to take over programs that aren't struggling. Nolan Richardson succeeded Eddie Sutton at Arkansas in 1985 after Sutton had taken the Razorbacks to a Final Four in 1978 and had gone 22–13 in his final season—reaching the NCAA Tournament for a ninth straight time.

Tubby Smith took over at Kentucky in 1997 after Rick Pitino had led the Wildcats to three Final Fours in five years, winning a national title in 1996 and losing the national championship game in 1997.

Kevin Ollie succeeded his former coach and mentor Jim Calhoun at Connecticut in 2012. Having just been placed on academic probation by the NCAA, the Huskies couldn't play in the 2013 NCAA Tournament, but they were a year removed (2011) from the third of Calhoun's national titles.

As it turned out, Richardson, Smith, and Ollie had one other thing in common: each won a national title. They are the only three Black coaches since Thompson to win national championships. All three would no doubt say the same thing Thompson said all those years ago: There have been plenty of other Black coaches capable of winning a national championship. Only a handful have been given a realistic chance to do so.

CHAPTER SEVEN

Climbing the Mountain

N OWADAYS, THERE ARE REMARKABLE SUCCESS stories to tell about Black coaches, especially in basketball, which has always been a step — or two or twelve — ahead of other sports when it comes to being progressive.

Bill Russell was the first Black man to coach a major professional team when Red Auerbach turned the Boston Celtics over to him in 1966. In fact, at one point, the NBA had fourteen Black coaches — although that number has since gone down.

College basketball produced men like Big House Gaines and John McLendon, who never had the opportunities John Thompson referred to at the 1982 Final Four, but it has since produced men like Thompson, Nolan Smith, Tubby Smith, and Kevin Ollie — all national championship winners, not to mention George Raveling, John Chaney, Leonard Hamilton, and Tommy Amaker. All these men are an important part of the sport's history — not the sport's Black history, but the sport's history, period.

No story had more twists and turns, more moments of joy and moments of tragedy, than did Nolan Richardson's. In 1985, when he accepted the job at the University of Arkansas, Richardson knew he was taking over a program that had built a winning tradition under Eddie Sutton. Even so, he thought long and hard before accepting the offer from Athletic Director Frank Broyles — an iconic figure in Arkansas — to succeed Sutton.

"The fact is, I should have said no," he said in the spring of 2021. "It wasn't a good time in my life to start a new job — any new job."

Richardson had just finished his fifth season at the University of Tulsa. In 1980, he had taken over a program that had been through five straight losing seasons, including going 8–19 the year before he arrived. In Richardson's first season, Tulsa went 26–7 and won the NIT. This was before the NCAA had expanded to sixty-four teams and when winning the NIT was still a big deal in college basketball.

In five seasons at Tulsa, he went 119–37, including 50–12 his last two years. The Golden Hurricane reached the NCAA Tournament three times.

About 110 miles east of Tulsa, Frank Broyles needed a new basketball coach at Arkansas after Sutton had left to take the Kentucky job. It was almost impossible for Broyles not to notice what Richardson was doing at Tulsa. Broyles had been the Arkansas football coach for nineteen seasons, compiling a record of 144–58–5. That record included winning a share of the national championship in 1964 and losing 15–14 to Texas in one of college football's most famous games, the so-called Game of the Century, in 1969. (This "Game of the Century" came three years after the Notre Dame–Michigan State "Game of the Century." Not that sports is ever overhyped.)

By the time he gave up coaching in 1976, Broyles was also the athletic director at Arkansas. Instead of coaching, he added TV broadcasting to his résumé, working with Keith Jackson on ABC's top announce team for college football from 1977 to 1985. He also made sure he had free time for pilgrimages to play at Augusta National Golf Club, where he was a proud member of the club that hosted the Masters Tournament. In those days, Augusta National was all white and all male.

Broyles and Richardson could not possibly have been from more different backgrounds. Broyles had grown up in Georgia and starred as a quarterback at Georgia Tech. He had a pronounced patrician Southern drawl that was often imitated during his years at ABC.

Richardson was born in December 1941 — a few months after John Thompson. He grew up in El Paso, Texas, the second of three children. His father was rarely around, and after his mother died when Nolan was three, he and his siblings moved in with their grandmother, Rose Richardson — who Richardson always affectionately referred to as "Ol' Mama."

"It's impossible to explain how important she was in my life," Richardson said. "She was very smart and very tough. She never let me feel sorry for myself because of all the racism I faced growing up. She would say, 'Don't come back and tell me you couldn't do something because you were dealing with someone who was racist. All that means is you have to be better — *much* better — than the next guy.'

"That's really the way I've lived my life. I've always taken it for granted that I have to be way better than the next guy if I want to succeed at anything."

Richardson lived in the El Segundo Barrio of El Paso and could walk from his house across the nearby bridge into Juarez, Mexico. Many of his closest friends were Mexicans and Mexican Americans. In Jim Crow–segregated El Paso, Mexican Americans weren't subject to Jim Crow laws.

"I had two sets of friends," he remembered. "I had one group who could go into movie theaters, could go into swimming pools, could walk into any restaurant and get served. I had another group who—like me—couldn't do any of those things. Those aren't things you ever forget."

Richardson was often described in the media as someone who "coached with a chip on his shoulder."

He laughed at that description. "I didn't have a chip on my shoulder," he said. "It was more like a mountain. A boulder wouldn't be enough to describe it. I grew up hearing the word *nigger* for as long as I can remember. It was used by people all the time where I lived. I went to a small all-Black school. By small I mean this: the first grade and the second grade were all in one room. There wasn't enough space to give each grade its own classroom. I understood racism and what it entailed from the time I was very little. But Ol' Mama wasn't going to let me use that as an excuse not to succeed."

Like many kids from financially insecure backgrounds, Richardson used sports to escape. He was a three-sport athlete, excellent in football and basketball but probably best at baseball. After the US Supreme Court outlawed segregation in schools in 1954 with its *Brown v. Board of Education* decision, he enrolled as a high school freshman at Bowie High School.

He was the only Black kid on the school's athletic teams. The fact that almost all his teammates were Mexican Americans wasn't a problem for Richardson, because he had grown up speaking Spanish. If John Thompson was bilingual because he spoke English and profanity, Richardson was truly bilingual.

Richardson was recruited by several schools for baseball and basketball. But low board scores meant he had to spend a year at a junior college in Arizona before transferring back to his hometown to play basketball at what was then Texas Western College.

He arrived at Texas Western in 1960 and played for Harold Davis as a sophomore. Richardson enjoyed playing for Davis, whose style was wide open and who gave him the green light to shoot whenever he had the ball. But the young man soured forever on the coach when Texas Western was invited to play in a three-day tournament at Centenary University in Louisiana.

"He told me no Blacks were allowed to play," Richardson said. "He left me home. I thought he should have refused to go and forfeited the games. He didn't. We lost all three games."

Davis left at the end of the season to work in his family's thriving oil business. The school hired a thirty-one-year-old high school coach named Don Haskins in his place. Richardson was never thrilled playing for Haskins, largely because the coach liked to play half-court basketball and Richardson like to play up-tempo — as he would prove during his coaching career.

He went from averaging 21 points per game as a sophomore to 13.6 per game as a junior and 10.5 as a senior. But because Haskins left him little choice, he learned to play defense.

Haskins's way worked. The Miners were 37–13 during Richardson's junior and senior seasons, making the NCAA Tournament for the first time in school history, in 1963 — Richardson's senior year. Three years after Richardson graduated, they were 28–1 and beat Kentucky in the national championship game, 72–65, in what became college basketball's most famous game because Texas Western started five Black players against all-white Kentucky.

In later years, Haskins always insisted that he wasn't trying to make any kind of political statement by starting five Black players. "I was just trying to get the best players possible on the court to try to win the game," he often said.

It wasn't quite that simple. According to Rus Bradburd's excellent biography of Richardson — *Forty Minutes of Hell* — Texas

Western pulled into a hotel in Abilene, the same hotel where Richardson hadn't been allowed to stay several years earlier during a high school baseball tournament. When the manager told Haskins, "No coloreds here," the coach took his entire team to another hotel. He did the same thing in Utah at another hotel that would not allow the (then) four Black members of the team to register. Haskins may not have wanted to be cast as some kind of political reformer, but he did know racism when he saw it, and he stood up to it.

Richardson was a father by the time he graduated from college, having married his childhood sweetheart during his junior college year in Arizona. He and his wife, Helen, eventually had three children.

Soon after graduating, he took a job at Bowie High School, his alma mater. He taught English, social studies, history, and physical education. He also coached the JV football, basketball, and baseball teams. All for the princely sum, according to Bradburd, of $4,500.

In 1967, Richardson was drafted by the Dallas Chaparrals of the ABA and went to training camp briefly before a leg injury sent him back home to El Paso. His old job was gone, but he was offered the job of varsity basketball coach.

And so, a Hall of Fame career was launched.

"At that point in time, being a college coach never crossed my mind," Richardson said. "There weren't any Black coaches at major colleges. I don't mean only a few; I mean zero. So why would I be thinking I'd get a chance someday?"

Richardson built an excellent program at Bowie, but, thinking he had no chance ever to get a college job, he resigned at the end of the 1977 season. As luck would have it, Western Texas Junior College was looking for a coach. Rob Evans, then an assistant coach at Texas Tech, was recruiting one of Richardson's players at Bowie and recommended Richardson. The school was integrated but had never had a Black coach. Richardson went 101–13 in three seasons, including 37–0 his last season, when Western Texas won the National Junior College national championship.

His success led to the Tulsa job, which, five years later, led Frank Broyles to offer the Arkansas job.

Richardson knew he would be the first Black coach in the Southwest Conference. At that time, the ACC, the SEC, and the Big Eight had never hired a Black head coach. In 1970, Will Robinson had become the first Black head coach in Division 1 when he was hired to coach at Illinois State. He went 78–51 in five seasons and coached future Hall of Famer Doug Collins. Robinson left Illinois State in 1975 to take a scouting job with the Detroit Pistons.

The move from Tulsa to Arkansas would be a step up for Richardson, putting him at a school that had a legitimate chance to compete for a national championship. It would also put him at a place where some people might think, if not say aloud, "Why did we hire a nigger coach?"

Richardson knew all that. But that wasn't why he told Broyles he didn't want the job. His daughter, Yvonne, was dying of leukemia. She had been diagnosed two years earlier and was receiving treatment in Tulsa from doctors Richardson and his wife Rose felt comfortable with. Richardson and his first wife, Helen, divorced while Richardson was coaching at Bowie High School. Several years later, Richardson met and married Rose. Yvonne was born in 1972.

When Richardson told Broyles he couldn't take the job, because Yvonne needed to be near her doctors, Broyles told him there were also very good doctors in Fayetteville. Richardson thanked him for the offer and went home to tell Rose and Yvonne of his decision.

Yvonne Richardson was thirteen. As her father told the story, she said, "Papi, you're going."

Under orders from his daughter, Richardson went back to Broyles and took the job. He spent most of the next eighteen months making the 113-mile drive from Fayetteville to Tulsa to spend time with Yvonne.

"I never should have taken the job," Richardson said thirty-six years later. "I was trying to put in a completely different system than the one Eddie [Sutton] had run, and I was completely distracted. I thought Frank would understand, but he didn't. He'd gone out on a limb to hire a Black coach, and now all his fans and boosters were telling him he'd made a mistake. I told him I was trying, but I knew he thought it wasn't good enough. It was my fault. My daughter was dying. I shouldn't have been coaching."

Arkansas was 12–16 that season. The following season, Yvonne died in January at the age of fifteen. Arkansas improved to 19–14 and made the NIT, still well below the standard set by Sutton. Richardson believes to this day that Broyles was ready to fire him if the Razorbacks hadn't rallied to win their first-round NIT game against Arkansas State.

A year later, Richardson's recruiting began to kick in. He brought in players who could play his super-aggressive, attacking, forty-minutes-of-hell style. Arkansas went 21–9 and reached the NCAA Tournament's second round. It was the first of nine straight NCAA appearances—and thirteen in fourteen years.

In 1990, Arkansas made the Final Four, losing to Duke. Four years later, it won the national title—beating Duke in the championship game and making Richardson the second Black coach to win the NCAA title. A year later, the Razorbacks made it back to the final before losing to UCLA. That made three Final Four trips in six years.

Richardson was now officially a star in the coaching profession and, along with Thompson, John Chaney, and George Raveling, one of the leading spokesmen for Black coaches. They were at the heart of the Black Coaches Association when it was formed in 1988. They also led the fight against the NCAA when it passed Proposition 42, which would have made it impossible for athletes who failed to meet academic minimums — SAT scores and high school GPAs — to receive scholarships as first-year students. An earlier rule, Proposition 48, made athletes who didn't meet academic minimums ineligible to play their first year but allowed them to be on scholarship while they worked to improve their academic standing.

Thompson made himself the self-appointed leader in the fight against Prop 42, twice boycotting games his team was playing — the first time melodramatically stalking off the bench after the lineups had been introduced and the second time not showing up at all. But Richardson, Chaney, and Raveling were right behind him in full-throated support. Soon after, the NCAA abandoned the rule.

Thompson, having won a national championship and having been the US Olympic coach in 1988, had the most job security. That was why it was decided he would be the one to boycott the games and take the issue public.

Arkansas never again climbed the heights it reached between 1990 and 1995, but it continued to make the NCAA Tournament almost every year. The Razorbacks slipped to 18–14 in 1997 and settled for an NIT bid. In 2000, after going 7–9 in Southeastern Conference play, they had to win the SEC Tournament to get a bid — which they did, winning four games, including upsets of higher-seeds Kentucky, LSU, and Auburn.

Two years later, the Razorbacks took a drastic fall and went into the penultimate weekend of the regular season with a record of 13–12, 5–8 in the SEC. Even though Richardson had a six-year contract and had missed the NCAA Tournament *once* dating to 1988, there were whispers about his job status as his team limped through February.

After Arkansas lost at Kentucky on the last Saturday afternoon in February, Richardson was asked postgame about his job status. "If they go ahead and pay me my money, they can take this job tomorrow," he said in response to the question.

He also asserted that there was no way a white coach with his record would be asked about his job status, because it would never be in question. Richardson was entitled, he believed, to one bad season.

"The funny thing is, I'd made the comment about them taking my job before," he said, nineteen years after that fateful day in Kentucky. "My point was, if my bosses didn't think I was doing my job, they could take the job away from me at any time. I thought that was true of anyone not doing their job."

In essence, that's what Arkansas did. Richardson was allowed to coach one more game—at Mississippi State—and then was fired before the regular-season finale against Vanderbilt. He met with Broyles and Arkansas chancellor John White the day after the Mississippi State game. The meeting had initially been scheduled for Monday, but Broyles had a golf outing at Augusta National that day and he refused to cancel.

As a result, Richardson held his normal Monday press conference. He did not talk about the Kentucky loss or the impending Mississippi State game.

Instead, he talked about race.

"My great-great-grandfather came over on the ship," he said. "I did not come over on that ship. So I expect to be treated a little bit different."

There was more. Richardson noted that he was the only Black

head coach among the twenty-one coaches in the Arkansas athletic department. "I know for a fact that I do not play on the same level as the other coaches around this school play on. I know that. You know it. And people of my color know that. And that angers me."

Then he pointed at the media members in the room. "When I look at all of you people in this room, I see no one who looks like me, talks like me, or acts like me. Now, why don't you recruit? Why don't the editors recruit like I'm recruiting?"

He then added, "I've earned the right to have the kind of season I'm having."

There was more. He accused the media in Arkansas of wanting him fired, and he threatened to cut himself off from the media. No big-time coach had been more open with the media than Richardson had been. He was the anti–John Thompson. His practices were open, and he and his players were almost always available for interviews.

Arkansas went to Mississippi State two days later and lost. The next day, with Broyles back from Augusta, the coach met with the athletic director and Chancellor White. They asked him to resign. He refused, telling them, "You'll have to fire me if you want me gone."

They fired him.

A few days later, Mitch Barnhart, then the athletic director at Oregon State (he's now at Kentucky) called Richardson and asked if he'd be willing to meet him to discuss becoming the coach in Corvallis.

"It was just too soon," Richardson said. "I wasn't ready to throw myself into another job that quickly. A year later—maybe. But not then. I was still reeling."

Nor was he finished with Arkansas. He filed a lawsuit against the school, Broyles, and White, alleging he had been fired because of racism and that his First Amendment rights had been violated because the firing was due to the comments he had made about race in his final two press conferences.

The trial took place in May 2004. It revealed some shocking facts. Two members of the Arkansas Board of Trustees testified that they did, in fact, tell "nigger jokes" during board meetings—one member was the board's chairman. Witnesses brought up an incident that had taken place in 2000, when Richardson had gotten into a heated argument with local columnist Wally Hall and had called Hall a redneck. Hall's column reported that Richardson had called Arkansas fans "redneck SOBs."

The "redneck" comment had led to a letter written to a longtime member of the board of trustees calling for Richardson's firing for using the word *redneck*. According to Broyles, the board member, Jim Lindsey, had called to tell him about the letter. That night, at the annual Arkansas football banquet, Broyles walked over to the media table and told the all-white, all-male table that they should write that a Black man using the term *redneck* was no different from a white man using the word *n——*.

None of them did. But they also failed to report Broyles's attempt to make the two words equivalent.

William Wilson, the judge in Richardson's case, wrote extensively in his decision about the legitimacy of Richardson's claims of racism at Arkansas. In the end, though, he ruled that the school was within its rights to fire him because of his "take this job tomorrow" comment. He had, Wilson wrote, effectively resigned when he made that comment in public.

"When I read the decision, it felt like the judge was saying, 'He's right, he's right, he's right, he should win,' and then...I lost," Richardson said, able to laugh about it years later.

In English, the judge's ruling was direct: there was no doubt that

Richardson was the victim of racism, but he had given the school the legal right to fire him — racist or not — with his comments after the Kentucky game. Neither board member who admitted to telling the "nigger jokes" was removed.

Richardson was sixty when he was fired. He would later coach national teams from Panama and Mexico — his fluent Spanish helped — and briefly coached a WNBA team. But he was never offered a major college coaching job again.

"I got hit with the blackball," he said, laughing. "I know people said if I was hired I'd bring a lot of luggage with me; a lot of issues about race would come up. That scared athletic directors off. Some of the HBCU schools were interested early on, but I was still being paid by Arkansas, and any money they paid me would be deducted from what Arkansas was paying me [about $500,000 a year]. I'd have been working for nothing at schools that had no chance to win a national championship. I'd been spoiled by my success at Arkansas."

The greatest irony in Richardson's firing was that many in the media criticized him for the comments he made in his final two press conferences. *Sports Illustrated* described it as a "self-immolation." An *Arkansas Democrat-Gazette* editorial claimed he had "made a public ass of himself." Most of the media critics were white men who couldn't believe that someone who had made as much money as Richardson had and who had been placed on a pedestal for winning numerous games and championships could still be complaining about racism in 2002.

Those comments remind us of George Raveling's observation that a white person cannot possibly have a clear understanding about what it is like to be Black. "It gets back to so many of them thinking we should be *grateful* when we're finally treated as equals," he said. "As if they are *allowing* us to be equals. Gee, thanks for that."

Or, as Duke coach Mike Krzyzewski put it: "*They* achieve, in most cases, overcome racism to achieve, and then they're supposed to say thank you? Are you kidding me?"

Richardson was also often criticized because none of the Black players on his Final Four teams from 1990 and 1994 had graduated. In those days, if a player transferred and graduated, it still counted against the school where he had started. Junior college players weren't counted, and anyone leaving for the NBA early was counted as a nongraduate. The rules have since been changed to allow schools to have higher graduation rates — an NCAA public relations move.

"I always told my players, if you *want* to graduate, I will help any way I can," Richardson said. "I also told them if they didn't want to graduate — if they were convinced they were going to make money playing basketball — I understood that. The funny thing is, every one of those kids went back to school later and graduated. Every one of them."

Richardson is now retired and living on the farm he bought outside Fayetteville while coaching at Arkansas. In October 2019, more than seventeen years after his firing, the court at Bud Walton Arena was finally named Nolan Richardson Court.

"I'm completely comfortable with my career and my legacy," he said. "I know I went through a lot to get to Arkansas and to succeed at Arkansas. I also know that if I someday get to the Kingdom of Heaven, I won't be asked how many games I won. I'll be asked how many lives I touched and if I spoke up about injustices I saw. I know how many lives I touched, and I know I spoke up. And I'll keep speaking up as long as I have a voice."

Kentucky's coach on the afternoon of Nolan Richardson's second-to-last loss at Arkansas was Tubby Smith. His presence on the

Kentucky bench was proof that Richardson had gotten one thing wrong earlier in his career.

"I said there would be a Martian in the White House before Kentucky hired a Black basketball coach," he said. "I had that one wrong."

Like Richardson, Smith was part of a very small club: a Black coach hired at a power school that was not foundering at the time.

Smith got the Kentucky job when the Wildcats were coming off back-to-back appearances in the national championship game in 1996 (a win) and 1997 (a loss). He was already coaching in the SEC, at Georgia, and was recommended by Rick Pitino, the coach who had led Kentucky to those two championship game appearances. More important, Pitino convinced Smith—who had been his top assistant before being hired at Georgia—to take the job.

"I wasn't really sure if I wanted it," Smith said. "We were doing well at Georgia [45–19 with two NCAA bids in two seasons], and I had one son already there and another one coming. I was comfortable. But Rick said to me, 'It's Kentucky. It's one of *the* programs in college basketball history. You have to do it.'"

It was also a chance to be the first Black coach at a school most famous for playing in what was arguably the most important game in college basketball history, the 1966 national championship game when Texas Western had prevailed 72–65 over the Wildcats, at a time when Texas Western had five Black starters and when all Kentucky's players were white.

Four years later, Kentucky coach Adolph Rupp recruited his first Black player—Tom Payne, a seven-foot two-inch center. When Kentucky broke its twenty-year drought and won its fifth national championship in 1978, Jack Givens was the team's leading scorer and had 41 points in the championship game victory over Duke.

James Lee and Truman Claytor were the team's fourth and sixth leading scorers. All three were Black.

Having been one of Pitino's assistants at Kentucky, Smith had the advantage of knowing the school and understanding what he was getting into when he took the job. He also had the good fortune to have C. M. Newton as his athletic director. As the coach at Alabama in the early 1970s, Newton had recruited the school's first Black basketball players.

Still, there may not be anything that can prepare any person — Black or white — for the pressures that come with coaching Kentucky, a place where most fans view winning not as a privilege but a right. Winning SEC championships was nice, but it certainly wasn't the goal each season. Going to the Final Four was fine, but the goal — the expectation — in most seasons was to win the national championship.

Smith knew about the expectations; he especially understood the atmosphere after Pitino had reached three Final Fours in five seasons and come within an overtime loss of winning back-to-back titles in 1996 and 1997. But Smith couldn't resist the challenge — not just the challenge of coaching Kentucky but being the first Black man to coach the school.

Orlando Smith was born in 1951 in southern Maryland, the sixth of Guffrie and Parthenia Smith's seventeen children. He got his lifelong nickname when he was very young because he enjoyed the bathtub so much and, in his words, "because, back then, I *was* a little bit tubby."

His parents were sharecroppers and his father drove a school bus to make extra money. Segregation was a way of life. "I never took much notice of whites-only fountains or bathrooms," he said. "My parents told me early on that this was the way it was, that you didn't challenge what was the law back then. There were protocols, and you didn't challenge them, because if you did, it would mean trouble. I went to an all-Black elementary school and junior high school and didn't have very much contact with white people until I was fourteen."

Two important things happened when he was a high school freshman: Jim Crow—the law that made segregation legal—was finally outlawed, and Smith's all-Black George Washington Carver High School was consolidated with all-white Great Mills High School. By then, Smith was a pretty good basketball player—allowed to play by his father only if he continued to get good grades in school and got his chores done around the farm.

And then, in March 1966, Texas Western played Kentucky in the national championship game. "It was the first basketball game I ever saw on television," Smith said. "We had an antenna outside that we had to keep adjusting so the picture would keep coming in. But I remember watching that game and thinking, 'All those guys got to go to college to play basketball. I wonder if I can do that too someday?'"

Life at a consolidated high school wasn't always easy. The Black athletes and the white athletes clashed often. Smith's high school basketball coach was Gene Wood, who had played at Frostburg State in western Maryland.

It was a coach named Cecil Short who first convinced Smith to try out for the basketball team at George Washington Carver. "He saw me playing at lunchtime and came and asked me to try out for the JV team," Smith remembered. "At first my dad said no because I was supposed to come back to the farm every day to help out. Finally, he gave in when I promised I'd get all my work done at school and around the farm."

The next year, the two schools consolidated. "It wasn't easy for anyone," Smith said. "Remember, this was six years before *Remember the Titans*." That was the movie based on the 1971 T. C. Williams football team that was also integrated because of consolidation. "A lot of what happened there happened to us," he said. "The white kids weren't used to dealing with us, and we weren't used to dealing with them. It was all new. Plus, only a few of our teachers from Carver came over, and that didn't make it any easier.

"There were confrontations. Only about four of us went out for the football team, and that was uncomfortable too. By my junior year, I was pretty sure that my best chance to get to college was going to be basketball."

Wood wanted him to go to Frostburg State and took him to see the campus. Other mid-majors were interested, and so was the University of Maryland, which, several years earlier, had been the first ACC school to recruit Black players. Williams would have loved to have gone to Maryland, but when Frank Fellows was fired at the end of the season in 1969, the school hired a new coach with high ambitions: Lefty Driesell.

"Lefty was honest with me," Smith said. "He told me he wanted to go out and recruit his own guys. I understood that. No hard feelings."

Smith ended up at High Point College (now High Point University) in North Carolina, where he played for three coaches. Most importantly, one of them was J. D. Barnett, who later went on to coach at Virginia Commonwealth.

After graduation, Smith went home and coached Great Mills, his alma mater, for four years before moving on to Hoke High School. Two years later, Barnett was hired at Virginia Commonwealth and offered Smith a job as an assistant coach. Smith stayed for seven years before going to work for George Felton at South Carolina and, finally, Pitino at Kentucky.

While he was at South Carolina, he was offered his first chance to be a head coach — at the University of Maryland–Baltimore County. The athletic director there was Rick Hartzell, who spent forty years moonlighting as an elite college referee. He and Smith had crossed paths when Hartzell officiated. Hartzell thought Smith was one of the brighter young coaches he'd met and offered Smith the job.

Smith took it — for thirty-six hours.

"In the end, Donna [Smith's wife] didn't want to move," Smith said. "We had two boys in high school and, even though it was tempting to go back to Maryland, the timing wasn't right. I had to go back to Rick and tell him I couldn't take the job."

Years later, when Smith had become a star in coaching and Hartzell worked one of his games, the referee/athletic director liked to remind Smith that he had discovered him first.

Two years later, in 1988, Pitino and Smith arrived in Lexington in the midst of a two-year sanction hung on the school for recruiting violations during Eddie Sutton's tenure. In 1991, when the team came off probation, the Wildcats reached the Elite Eight of the NCAA Tournament before losing 104–103 in overtime to Duke in one of college basketball's most memorable games.

Kentucky's success helped Smith get his second job — the first one where he actually stayed long enough to coach a game — as a college head coach, this time at the University of Tulsa — the same school that had launched Nolan Richardson.

He was 49–23 in four seasons, and in his last two seasons, Tulsa reached the Sweet Sixteen of the NCAAs. His accomplishments led to his being hired at Georgia — making him the school's first Black basketball coach. He was also the third Black man hired as a head coach in the Southeastern Conference. Tennessee had hired Wade

Houston in 1989, and Arkansas, under Richardson, had joined the league in 1991.

Smith went 45–19 in two seasons at Georgia, reaching the NCAA Tournament both years and the Sweet Sixteen in 1996 after upsetting top-seeded Purdue in the second round. When Pitino left Kentucky to take over the Boston Celtics after going to the national championship game in back-to-back seasons, Smith put aside his doubts and took the job.

"It was, in the end, a challenge I couldn't resist," he said. "I knew Kentucky's history, but I had enjoyed working there with Rick as an assistant. I knew being the head coach would be *way* different, but I trusted C.M. [Newton]. Plus, Rick had ratcheted expectations back up with the success he'd had."

The story that might best explain what it's like to coach at Kentucky is the one about the caller to Smith's radio show in early March of his first season. The caller's opening comment was this: "Coach, I just want you to know I haven't given up on this team yet."

Smith never forgot that call. "Remember, the guy was being *nice*," he said, laughing. "He was trying to tell me he still supported us in spite of our awful record."

Kentucky was 25–4 at that moment. It was a good thing the caller didn't give up on the team. The Wildcats won the SEC Tournament, came from 17 points down in the regional final against (still) hated Duke, and beat Stanford and Utah in the Final Four to become national champions and finish 35–4.

Kentucky continued to be very good during the next nine years. It reached the Elite Eight three times and the Sweet Sixteen on two other occasions. Its *worst* record was 22–13. In 2003, the Wildcats were 32–3 before being upset in the Elite Eight by a Dwyane Wade–led Marquette team.

At most schools, that sort of record would probably have led to the court being named after the coach. But Kentucky is not most schools. There was considerable grumbling among members of the so-called Big Blue Nation. If fans were almost ready to give up on the team at 25–4, one can only imagine what they thought about a 22–13 record or back-to-back seasons when Kentucky lost in (gasp!) the second round of the NCAA Tournament.

"They started calling me 'Ten-Loss Tubby,'" Smith said. "We'd lost ten games a couple times and then twelve and thirteen. That's when the For Sale signs started showing up on my lawn."

When defenders of Smith's 263–83 record point out that he did win a national championship, the response heard frequently from the Big Blue Nation blue bloods is, "Yeah, but he did it with Rick's players." When Pitino won the national championship in 1996, there were nine future NBA players on the roster. Only three of those players were still around when Smith took over the Kentucky program—none a star.

To Kentucky fans, that was irrelevant. Nine years without a Final Four! Impossible. Double-digit losses! Two straight seasons without a trip to the Sweet Sixteen! The year before those two seasons, Kentucky was 28–6 and lost a classic double-overtime game to Michigan State in the Elite Eight.

None of that mattered. Smith understood that the only way to win back the spoiled denizens of the Big Blue Nation was to win another national championship. That, of course, is easier said than done. Since Smith's departure from Kentucky in 2007, the Wildcats have won a national title—but only one.

Smith knew that Marta McMackin, his executive assistant (who had worked for Adolph Rupp's successor, Joe B. Hall, and every coach since Hall), was protecting him from angry calls and emails directed at him. But it was Donna who finally convinced him that enough was enough.

"She said she could see the frustration on my face every day," he said. "I was unhappy and not enjoying my job. I always enjoyed my job. I loved to coach; I loved basketball. But I was unhappy. I was losing my hair. Donna said I didn't even realize how stressed I was. She was right."

Smith didn't think the pressure had very much to do with race. But he believed that he might have been cut a little more slack if he'd been white.

"Bottom line at Kentucky is the bottom line," he said. "When I first got there, C.M. told me one number mattered and one color mattered there: wins and green — as in dollars. I know that was true of him. But I long ago accepted the fact that if you're Black, there are going to be things that happen that you can't control. You can't be angry about them all the time. It's a fact of life, and you have to deal with it."

As it turned out, the man Kentucky hired to replace Smith, Billy Clyde Gillispie, went 18–13 in his first season and 22–14 in his second. In retrospect, "Ten-Loss Tubby" suddenly looked a good deal better. Smith had gone to the NCAA Tournament and won at least one game there in ten seasons out of ten. Gillispie never won an NCAA Tournament game: Kentucky lost in the first round of the tournament his first season and lost in the NIT quarterfinals in his second.

He was succeeded by John Calipari, a superb coach who had taken the University of Massachusetts to the Final Four in 1996 and Memphis to the national championship game in 2008. Both performances were vacated by the NCAA, but that didn't matter to Kentucky: Calipari could *coach,* and that was all that mattered. Wins and green.

In his first six seasons, Calipari took Kentucky to four Final Fours, winning a national championship in 2012. That was a remarkable run. Since 2015, Kentucky hasn't been to the Final Four a single time, and in 2021 — in the midst of the pandemic — the Wildcats finished an unthinkable 9–16. No one has put any For Sale signs on Calipari's lawn. Yet.

When Smith finally decided he'd had enough of the "I haven't given up on this team yet" crowd and accepted the job at the University of Minnesota in 2007, most of his coaching colleagues understood. I still remember standing in the lobby of the coaches' hotel in Atlanta at that year's Final Four watching Smith walk through on his way to a meeting. It looked to me as if every coach he encountered stopped Smith to congratulate him on his new job.

And for escaping his old one.

Today, after stints at Minnesota, Texas Tech, and Memphis, Smith has come full circle: he's the coach at High Point, his alma mater. He was fired after two seasons at Memphis because the school was enamored of the idea of bringing back Penny Hardaway, who had starred at the school in the early 1990s and was coaching a high-powered high school program in Memphis. Memphis wanted Hardaway to bring back the school's past glories. Of course, *glory* is a subjective word. The Tigers reached the Final Four in 1985 and again in 2008. Both those appearances were later vacated by the NCAA for recruiting violations.

Smith won 40 games in his two seasons at Memphis. Hardaway, after bringing in highly touted recruiting classes, won 43 in his first two years. His third team won the NIT. No doubt John Thompson's old boss at Georgetown, Father Henle, would have been proud.

Smith was almost sixty-seven when Memphis fired him. He had won 597 games, taken five schools to the NCAA Tournament (one of two coaches to do that) a total of eighteen times, and won a national championship. A career certainly worthy of Hall of Fame consideration. He was ready to retire.

But Nido Qubein, the president of High Point, was looking for a coach after firing Scott Cherry, who had been the school's most successful Division 1 coach during his ten seasons at the school. Cherry, however, hadn't been able to break through the glass ceiling of reaching the NCAA Tournament.

Qubein liked the idea of bringing in an alumnus — one who, along with his wife, Donna, had donated $1 million to help build a new basketball arena. The idea was even better if the alumnus had Smith's résumé.

But Smith wasn't sure. He called his friend Cliff Ellis, who had gone from the big-time (Clemson and Auburn) to the not-so-big-time at Coastal Carolina.

"The question is simple," Ellis told Smith. "Do you still love to coach? If you do, then High Point is no different than Kentucky: there's a gym, there are players you want to help get better, and there's competition."

Smith decided Ellis was right. During his first season at High Point, he sat in his locker room before a game at Longwood and pointed out that Ellis had been wrong about one thing. "Everywhere I've been a head coach before this, we traveled on charter airplanes. Here, we travel on chartered buses." He smiled. "But once you get to the arena, it's still coaching, plane or bus."

Four Black men have won national championships in Division 1 college basketball. Only one is still coaching college ball. He's doing it because he still loves it.

CHAPTER EIGHT

Dreamers

G EORGE RAVELING IS A HISTORIC FIGURE in the sport of basketball. He is in the Naismith Basketball Hall of Fame and the
College Basketball Hall of Fame. He was the first Black head coach
hired by a school in what was then the Pacific-8 (now the Pacific-12)
when Washington State made him the coach in 1972 at the age of
thirty-four. He took the school to its first two NCAA Tournaments
since 1941 — the third year the then eight-team tournament was
held — and then went on to success at Iowa and the University of
Southern California.

Being elected to the two Halls of Fame might be at the top of
Raveling's résumé, and his being one of the first Black coaches hired
at a power-five school is also right near the top of that résumé. But
the thing he is likely to be most remembered for has nothing to do
with basketball.

Among Raveling's many treasured possessions is one that stands
out from the rest: he owns the typewritten notes from Martin Luther
King's "I Have a Dream" speech, arguably the most famous and
important speech of the twentieth century.

King gave the speech on August 28, 1963, as part of a massive March on Washington for Jobs and Freedom rally that had been organized to show support for civil rights legislation introduced by President John F. Kennedy.

Raveling had grown up in Washington, D.C., and had driven down that Sunday morning with some friends from Philadelphia, where he was working as an assistant basketball coach at Villanova—his alma mater.

"We were walking around on the mall a few hours before the speech," he said. "Several people working for Dr. King came up to us and said they were looking for some guys willing to volunteer to provide extra security for him. I was six foot four by then, and my friends were big guys too, so I guess that's what they were looking for. Of course, we said we'd do it. Next thing I know, a few hours later, I'm standing behind Dr. King on the steps of the [Lincoln] Memorial while he's speaking to 250,000 people."

Nowhere in the typed version of the speech do the words "I have a dream" appear. King began the speech by referring to the fact that Abraham Lincoln had signed the Emancipation Proclamation almost exactly one hundred years earlier and then said, "One hundred years later, the Negro is still not free."

It was not until later in the speech—which lasted about seventeen minutes—after famed gospel singer Mahalia Jackson yelled, "Tell them about the dream, Martin!" that King began to say, "I have a dream," which became the words that defined the speech, the day, and the Civil Rights Movement.

Initially, he said, "Even though we face the difficulties of today and tomorrow, I still have a dream." He then repeated the words "I have a dream" eight more times.

"I still get chills almost sixty years later thinking about that moment," Raveling said. "A few minutes later, he finished, and when he turned to leave, I noticed he'd left the notes behind. I grabbed them, followed him and said, 'Dr. King, do you want your notes?'

"He turned around and said, 'You can have them if you want.'"

Several years ago, Raveling was offered $3 million for the notes. He turned it down.

Years ago, Raveling was approached by a lawyer from the Martin Luther King Museum in Atlanta. The lawyer wanted Raveling to donate the notes to the museum. Raveling, who wants the notes to eventually pass on to his children, offered to loan the notes to the museum for an indefinite period, asking only that the museum acknowledge that the notes were on loan.

The museum said no.

More recently, the African American Museum of History and Culture in Washington asked if Raveling would lend it the notes. Raveling said yes. The notes aren't on display yet, largely because they are so valuable that the paperwork involved is endless.

"I never would have thought almost sixty years ago, I would own something that is so much a part of our history," Raveling said. "It amazes me every single day."

Raveling was born in 1937 in Northwest Washington, D.C., in Garfield Hospital, which was located about two miles from the site of King's famous speech. Like the rest of Washington, the hospital was segregated.

"If you were Black, you had to go in the back door, and all the rooms were in the basement," Raveling said. "White patients went in the front door and had the other three floors in the building. The first breaths I took were of segregated air."

Raveling's father died when he was nine, and his mother was

taken to St. Elizabeth's Hospital when he was twelve, when she experienced a mental-health crisis. He went to live with his grand-mother on the second floor of a building that was divided into three apartments—with one bathroom for all three units. His grand-mother worked as a cleaning woman for a client whose daughter was the head of Catholic Charities in Washington. It was the daughter who suggested that George enroll in a boarding school in Hoban Heights, Pennsylvania, so that he could escape the city. At St. Michael's, he could get a better education than he was getting in the D.C. public schools.

"Where I grew up," Raveling said, "if you were Black, there wasn't much chance to dream. It was all about survival. There were certain things you knew you could do or not do. You didn't go into Georgetown at night. Dangerous if you were Black. If you saw a white woman on the street, you dropped your head. You didn't dare look her in the eye. Looking a white woman in the eye or even thinking about speaking to her was reckless."

Later, Raveling came to know the story of Emmett Till, the fourteen-year-old boy who had been lynched in Mississippi in 1955 after allegedly flirting with a white woman inside a grocery store. Could such a thing have happened in Washington, D.C., in the early 1950s? "I never took a chance on finding out," he said.

The men who lynched Till were acquitted on murder charges. Till became a symbol of how Black people were often treated in the Jim Crow South. "Emmett Till was George Floyd sixty-five years before George Floyd was murdered," Raveling said. "The difference all these years later was technology. There wasn't any video of what they did to Till. That's why his killers were acquitted."

That, and the notion that a Southern white jury would not acquit white men of *any* act committed against a Black person in those days was pretty much unthinkable.

Raveling went to St. Michael's as a high school freshman. By the time he got there, he had grown to six feet four and was recruited to play basketball by Gene Vellela, a former NFL lineman who coached all the school's teams.

"Going to St. Mike's was a turning point in my life," Raveling said. "It wasn't just because of the classroom education I got. It was the life education I got there. I'd spent my whole life in a segregated city, rarely dealing with or even seeing white people.

"At St. Mike's, it was just the opposite. Almost everyone there was white — students, teachers, staff. It was definitely an adjustment for me, but I learned a lot. Before I went there, I had never given any thought to going to college, and I had no idea what a scholarship was until my junior year."

By then, with his height and playing skills, a number of Division 1 schools were recruiting him. "My senior year, I was one of the three leading scorers in the state," he said. "We played a game on the road in Scranton, and I scored thirty-eight points. Afterwards a guy came up to me and said, 'My name is Jack Ramsay, I'm the basketball coach at St. Joseph's. Have you thought much about going to college?'

"I really hadn't. I had to ask my coach exactly what a scholarship was. He asked me who the guy was I'd been talking to. I handed him the card he'd given me."

This was in 1956. The coach at Villanova in those days was Al Severance. He called Raveling and, sight unseen, offered him a scholarship — if he could pass an entrance exam to get into school. When the nuns who ran St. Michael's found out about the offer — and the exam — they made him stay after school for two hours of tutoring every day once the basketball season was over.

By then, Raveling was being recruited by several big-time schools, notably Michigan State. "If I was going to college, I was going to a Catholic school," Raveling said. "That meant Villanova and St. Joseph's were the leaders."

Raveling and Vellela finally made the thirty-mile drive to Philadelphia's Main Line to visit Villanova on a Friday afternoon. After taking the entrance exam the next morning, Raveling and Vellela met with Severance. "We'll have the test results back tomorrow," Severance said. "I'd like to know if you'll accept a scholarship if you're admitted here."

He left Raveling and Vellela alone to think about the offer. "Coach said to me, 'George, this is a gift from heaven. If you get in, you need to say yes.'"

Raveling got in and said yes. He was one of eleven Black students at the school during his four years — ten on athletic scholarships, one on an academic scholarship. "Remarkable group of people," Raveling said. "All of us graduated in four years. Five have PhDs. One went on to be mayor of New Haven; another won the four hundred meters in the Olympics; another ran Hallmark Cards."

Most of Villanova's schedule was in the east, but during Raveling's junior year, the team played at Wake Forest — which was a power in those days and had stars like Billy Packer and Len Chappell, who would lead the school to its only Final Four appearance, in 1962. The Wildcats were staying at the Robert E. Lee Hotel in Winston-Salem, and after Severance checked everyone in and gave them room keys, they headed to the elevators.

Raveling remembers the next few moments vividly: "We got on, and the elevator guy looked at us [Raveling and teammate Hubie White] and said, 'Where do you niggers think you're going?' He took everyone's bags and threw them into the lobby. Coach demanded to meet with the manager. [The manager] said, 'If we had known you were bringing niggers, we'd have never have booked the reservation. If we let you stay here, no self-respecting white person will ever stay in this hotel again.'

"There was a loud shouting match. Finally, all the [white] guys said, 'Let's get out of here. Let's go home, let's not even play.' There was no way to get out of town until the next day, so we decided to stay and play. Fortunately, I knew a guy named Cleo Hill who played for Big House Gaines at Winston-Salem State. They came and got Hubie and me, and we stayed with them that night. Sadly, we lost the game."

That wasn't anywhere close to Raveling's scariest moment. It came at West Virginia, a team then led by Jerry West.

"Jerry was going in for a layup, and I came in to try to block the shot," Raveling said. "He made a fake on me, and I piled into him and knocked him down. He's lying on the ground, and I'm standing there thinking, 'Please, dear God, let this white boy get up so I don't get killed right here and right now.'

"I reached down for him, and he took my hand and let me help him up. He knew the last thing I'd wanted to do was knock him down that way—he'd just made a great fake. He probably also knew that if he didn't take my hand, there might be a riot. That was one of my biggest sighs of relief ever."

Villanova's teams were solid during Raveling's time there, going to the NIT his junior and senior years, when the NIT was still a big deal. Raveling was both captain of the team as a senior and the team's leading rebounder—setting school records in a game and in a season. Drafted in the eighth round of the NBA draft by the Philadelphia Warriors, he was the sixty-second player chosen, since the league only had eight teams at the time.

Three years later, Jack Kraft, who had replaced Severance as Villanova's coach in 1961, asked him to join his staff as an assistant coach. Raveling had graduated with a degree in economics and had gone to work for Sunoco as a marketing analyst. His job was to put together plans to open new Sunoco stations in the Philadelphia area. One of the new Sunoco lessees at the time was Roger Penske, the great race car driver and, later, race car owner.

Raveling wasn't certain if he wanted to coach but decided to give it a try. Soon, he became known as one of the best recruiters in the country, in part because he successfully recruited Black players from south of the Mason-Dixon Line to play on the Main Line.

"None of the schools in the northeast had really done that," Raveling said. "Most of the big-time schools in the South were still segregated, so the opportunity to recruit kids to come up north was very much there."

Raveling's most significant Southern recruit was Howard Porter, who was from Sarasota, Florida. Led by Porter and several others recruited by Raveling, Villanova reached the Elite Eight of the NCAA Tournament in 1970 and the national championship game in 1971, before losing to UCLA. That finish was vacated by the NCAA because Porter had signed with the ABA's Pittsburgh Condors (for whom he never played) during that season.

By then, Raveling was at Maryland, hired by Lefty Driesell soon after Driesell arrived at the school in 1969. Sandy Grady, the college basketball writer for the *Philadelphia Daily News,* had written a long story on Raveling's success recruiting in the South. The piece was headlined "The Underground Railroad."

Driesell had seen the story. He had turned tiny Davidson College into a perennial top ten team and had vowed to make Maryland "the UCLA of the East." He never quite got there, but he did make Maryland an important player on the national map—aided by Raveling, his first hire. Together, the two men recruited players like Len Elmore, Tom McMillen, and Howard White.

Maryland was then the northernmost school in the ACC, and the influx of Black players in the league had been slow. The Terrapins had recruited Billy Jones in 1964. A year later, they recruited Julius Johnson, and Duke brought in C. B. Claiborne. Dean Smith brought Charlie Scott to North Carolina in 1967—winning a recruiting battle with Driesell and Davidson. Soon after, more and more Black players came into the league, first in a trickle, then in a rush.

If Black players were scarce in the late 1960s, Black coaches were even less easy to find. In fact, Raveling was the ACC's first Black assistant coach. The conference had no Black head coach until Maryland hired Bob Wade in 1987. Two years later, Wade Houston became the SEC's first Black head coach when he was hired at Tennessee.

In 1972, after Maryland had gone 27–5 and won the NIT, Washington State offered Raveling the job as head coach. Any opposition to the notion of hiring a Black coach was pretty much wiped out by the fact that the school had known so little basketball success and desperately wanted to win.

Raveling was the Pacific-8's first Black head basketball coach. In fact, he was the first Black head coach at a school in what are now the power-five leagues: ACC, Big Ten, Big 12, Pac-12, and the SEC. Fred Snowden was hired at Arizona the same year Raveling was hired at Washington State, but Arizona was part of the Western Athletic Conference at the time. John Thompson was also hired in 1972—by Georgetown—but there was no Big East, and the Hoyas were a long way from being considered a power school in any way, shape, or form.

Raveling brought Washington State the success it had been hoping for when he arrived. After three losing seasons while Raveling was putting the program together, the Cougars had winning records in seven of his last eight seasons and made the NCAA Tournament in 1980 — for the first time in thirty-nine years — and then again in 1983.

That spring, Iowa offered him the job after Lute Olson left for Arizona, which by then was part of the Pac-10. At Iowa, Raveling reached the NCAAs twice, after a losing record in his first season. There was a good deal of grumbling during that first cold Iowa winter, but when Raveling and the Hawkeyes turned things around the next two seasons, Raveling became a hugely popular figure in the state.

The way he was embraced was proof of Olson's line about coaching at Iowa: "The best thing about coaching at Iowa is the fan support," he once said. "The worst thing about coaching at Iowa is the fan support."

Outgoing by nature, Raveling enjoyed his popularity but never felt completely comfortable living in Iowa City. He had gone through a divorce while at Washington State and often felt lonely living in a state where less than 1 percent of the population was Black.

"If I wanted soul food, I had to go to Chicago," he said, laughing. "I felt isolated. The people could not have been nicer, but Iowa City just wasn't the right place for me at that stage of my life."

Which is why Raveling jumped at the chance to return to the Pacific-10 (Arizona and Arizona State had joined the league in 1978) in 1986, when USC offered him the chance to move to Los Angeles. Even though the Trojans would always be the number two college team in a town dominated by UCLA, and even though they played in the run-down Los Angeles Memorial Sports Arena that wasn't even on campus, Raveling believed he could recruit enough good players to compete and make the NCAA Tournament.

It took four years — and a record during those years of 38–78 — for Raveling to turn the program around. During those first four miserable years, there was great pressure to fire Raveling. Los Angeles is not a patient town. But Athletic Director Mike McGee stood behind Raveling, and his faith paid off. In Raveling's next four seasons, USC was 77–40, a remarkable turnaround. The key recruit was Harold Miner, who had grown up in Inglewood, just a few miles from the USC campus. Miner was dubbed "Baby Jordan" in high school because he was a spectacular dunker of the basketball. He was a good-enough college player that he led USC to back-to-back NCAA Tournaments, including in 1992, when the Trojans were 23–5 in the regular season and were a number two seed in the NCAA Tournament. They were upset in the second round by Georgia Tech on a miraculous, falling-down, off-balance three-pointer at the buzzer by James Forrest.

Miner then turned pro — he was the twelfth pick in the NBA draft — and had an unspectacular NBA career, though he did win the slam-dunk contest once. "Worst thing that ever happened to him was the 'Baby Jordan' thing," Raveling said. "How do you possibly live up to that?"

Raveling was twice asked to be an assistant coach on Olympic teams: he worked under Bob Knight in 1984 and then under John Thompson in 1988. He was the only "outsider" — non-Georgetown person — on Thompson's staff. Those two opportunities under two very different men were proof of how respected Raveling was in the coaching community.

Still, the whispers—which sometimes weren't whispers—that he "just couldn't coach" during the down years at USC stung.

"What bothers me," he said, "is that I think some of it was truly racist. When Walt Hazzard was at UCLA, he had a good deal of success, but when the team struggled, all of a sudden, he couldn't coach. It wasn't that he had trouble communicating or that some of his recruiting didn't pan out—he couldn't coach. I heard the same things about me. Did I get to LA and forget how to coach? You almost never hear anyone say a white coach who isn't doing well can't coach. It's almost always something else. There's always been a double standard there."

After Miner's departure, the Trojans weren't as good the next two years but were still good enough to make the NIT. Then, on the morning of September 25, 1994, Raveling's car was blind-sided while he was driving to work. He spent several days in intensive care because of internal bleeding and was in the hospital for a total of fifty-nine days.

He was fifty-seven and knew he would need extensive rehab to even think about coaching again. He retired just as the season was about to start and handed the job off to his top assistant, Charlie Parker. At the urging of his friend Billy Packer, he did some television work and then was hired by Phil Knight as Nike's global sports marketing director. In that job, he worked with coaches who were on Nike's payroll at clinics around the world, at summer camps, and as a liaison between Nike and the media—something the company desperately needed.

"I still remember we did a clinic in China," he said. "We were touring Tiananmen Square, and a man came up to me and just started rubbing my hand. He'd never seen a Black person before. I think he thought my skin might come off."

Now eighty-four, Raveling is retired but still full of ideas and opinions.

"For me—or anyone—to say 'The problem is...' is ridiculous," he said. "We have so many issues right now. Think about this: in all the mass murders we've had in recent years, how often has the shooter been Black? The irony is that there are so many angry white people out there, and we're the ones who spent two hundred and fifty years as slaves. We're the ones who were subjected to Jim Crow. We're the ones who had to fight for the right to vote. And even today, Republicans are passing laws to still make it difficult for us to vote.

"And yet, all we hear is, 'You're making race an issue.' Well, yeah, damn right we are. You know why? Because it is still an issue, and there are far too many people who don't understand that or don't *want* to understand that."

Raveling was part of the first wave of Black coaches who made an impact nationally in college basketball along with John Thompson, John Chaney, and Nolan Richardson. Thompson and Chaney are now gone—revered at the end of their lives after often being under fire when they were at the peak of their coaching powers.

"I still remember Chaney giving a speech to a group of young Black coaches," Raveling said. "He talked and talked and talked, the way he always did. Finally, he turned to leave, then came back to the microphone and said, 'I got one more thing to tell all you motherfuckers. You're going to be Black forever and judged that way forever. Don't ever forget that.'

"He was right. That's just the way it is. When you speak up for change in anything, you are going to make a lot of people uncomfortable. Chaney did it; Thompson did it; Richardson did it. That's what's going on right now."

He paused. "I wish Dean Smith was still around. He was always a leader and spoke out on issues. He helped desegregate restaurants in Chapel Hill and never backed off on talking about issues. I guarantee you, if he was alive, he'd have been marching this past summer [2020]. We need more of that—in sports and in the world."

Leonard Hamilton is seventy-three years old, eleven years younger than George Raveling.

That means he is old enough to vividly remember growing up in North Carolina when Jim Crow was still the law in the South. Which is why when he is asked about progress in race relations, he laughs.

"For me not to acknowledge the progress that has been made would be ridiculous," he said. "I no longer have to drink from a colored water fountain or use a colored bathroom. I no longer walk into a hotel with my team and listen while the hotel manager says I can't stay there because I'm Black. I no longer have to get on a bus with my mother and know we have to sit in the back, and I don't have to sit in the balcony at the movies because downstairs is only for white people.

"That's the way it was in my childhood. It wasn't something you got upset about. It just *was*. I remember my father saying to me, 'Don't judge people because they are Black or they are white. Just always make sure whatever you do that you are paid fairly, that you make as much as the white guy who has a job like yours. And *never* let yourself get outworked. Because if you do that and the choice about who to promote is close, chances are your boss will pick the white guy. You have to leave him no choice.'"

Hamilton has done a good job of giving his bosses no choice for most of his adult life. In March 2021, he signed a five-year extension as the coach at Florida State, meaning he is likely to coach the Seminoles until at least 2026, the year he will turn seventy-seven. The contract was worth $2.25 million in guaranteed annual salary with bonuses that could add another $400,000 per year. Very good money, although it only made Hamilton the tenth-highest-paid coach among the fifteen ACC coaches.

Hamilton began the 2021–2022 season, his twentieth at Florida State, second only in seniority to Mike Krzyzewski, who had already announced his intention to retire at the end of his forty-second season at Duke in the spring of 2022. In 2021, after North Carolina hired Hubert Davis to replace the retiring Roy Williams in the spring, and after Boston College brought in Earl Grant to take the spot vacated when Jim Christian was fired, five of the ACC's fifteen coaches were Black. That may not sound impressive, but it is miles better than the Pac-12, which began the 2021–2022 season without a Black head coach for a third straight season.

Hamilton has now been a college head coach for thirty-four years: four at Oklahoma State, ten at Miami, and twenty at Florida State. After the Seminoles lost in the NCAA Tournament's round of sixteen in 2021 (to top-seeded Michigan), Hamilton stood one victory shy of six hundred career wins.

But getting the chance to be a head coach took a while. Hamilton grew up in Gastonia, North Carolina, and was recruited very little coming out of high school. He went to junior college for two years and then transferred to the University of Tennessee–Martin. He knew he wanted to coach when he graduated and got a job as an assistant coach at Austin Peay State University.

In 1974, Joe B. Hall hired him as an assistant coach at the University of Kentucky. This was only four years after Kentucky had first successfully recruited a Black player—Tom Payne—and nine seasons after the famous Texas Western upset of an all-white Adolph Rupp–coached team in the 1966 national championship game.

Hamilton knew Kentucky's history when he accepted Hall's offer, and he knew that Hall wanted him on his staff to help him recruit Black players. He was fine with all that.

"I knew what Kentucky had been in the past," he said. "I knew that anywhere I went — anywhere — there were going to be people who judged me because I was Black. That still goes on today; we all know that. My attitude was, if you don't like me — for any reason — that's fine. I'm just going to deal with people who don't have an issue with whether I'm Black or white. It worked out fine."

In fact, in 1975, Hamilton's first season, Kentucky went to the national championship game before losing to John Wooden's last UCLA team. The Wildcats then won the national title in 1978 and reached the Final Four in 1984, losing to John Thompson's Georgetown team — the one that made Thompson the first Black coach to win a national championship.

In 1986, at the age of thirty-seven, Hamilton got his first crack at a head coaching job when he was hired by Oklahoma State. The Cowboys had a great history, dating to their days as Oklahoma A&M when Henry Iba had coached them to back-to-back national titles in 1945 and 1946. But that record was part of a glorious, very distant past. In the twenty-one years before Hamilton's hiring, the Cowboys had enjoyed only five winning seasons. As would become a pattern in his career, Hamilton's first two teams had losing records. The Cowboys then won 17 games in each of the next two seasons to reach the NIT — their second and third postseason trips since an Iba-coached team had reached an NCAA regional final in 1965. Their first-round victories in those two years were the school's first postseason wins since Iba.

That success got the attention of the University of Miami, which was making the transition into the Big East. The school had shut down its basketball program entirely from 1971 to 1985 before slowly working its way back into the sport as an independent. Bill Foster, the former Clemson coach, had been able to piece together respectable records against benign independent schedules, but the Big East would be an entirely different story.

This time, Hamilton had to endure four losing seasons before the turnaround came. The Hurricanes didn't make the NCAA Tournament until 1998—for the first time since 1960. But that began a three-year string that also included a Big East regular-season title in 2000.

Then, Hamilton made arguably the worst mistake of his coaching career: he trusted Michael Jordan, the CEO of the Washington Wizards, to understand that Jordan was turning over to his next coach—Hamilton—a bad team that would need several years to become respectable again. After the Wizards went an unsurprising (but awful) 19–63, Jordan decided to blame Hamilton and fired him (it was announced as a "resignation") after one season. Two years later, Wizards owner Abe Pollin fired Jordan when, even with Jordan making yet another on-court comeback, the team twice failed to reach the sixteen-team NBA playoffs.

By then, after a year off, Hamilton was at Florida State. It wasn't as if Florida State hadn't had any success after joining the ACC in the early 1990s: a Pat Kennedy–coached team had reached the Elite Eight in 1993. But the Seminoles were coming off four straight losing seasons when Hamilton arrived. In keeping with Hamilton tradition, his first team was 14–15. The Seminoles have not had a losing season since then and have been to eight of the last twelve NCAA Tournaments. In 2020, Florida State was 26–5 and won the ACC regular-season title before the pandemic shut basketball down before the NCAA Tournament could begin.

Hamilton is now a respected elder in the game. He is one of those coaches who Shaka Smart refers to when he talks about the guilt he feels in describing the racial issues he has had to face. Smart says the issues he has dealt with are minor compared with what men like John McLendon, Big House Gaines, John Thompson, Nolan Richardson, John Chaney, and Hamilton have been through.

Hamilton doesn't worry about that. But he does believe that there is no way to make real progress on the issues of systemic racism until future generations have a better understanding of what's gone on in the last four hundred years in this country.

"I would like to see someone sit down with a group of white kids," he said, "actually with all white kids and say this: 'Picture your family walking down the street on a Sunday morning. Mom, dad, brother, and sister. Suddenly, a group of Black men swoop down, grab you, put you in chains, and take you to a ship, where you are thrown with hundreds of others into the ship's hold. You cross an ocean, barely fed, watching people die and finally land some-where—Ghana, Nigeria, Uganda—some place like that, and you are sold to a Black family that owns a plantation.

" 'There, you're put to work without being paid, working from morning until night. If you complain, you get beaten up. Years pass, and then you're set free. But you have no education, no job training beyond what you've been doing working in the fields. And if you complain, people say, "Why are you complaining? You're free." '

"That's the Black experience in this country, but it is *not* part of the history our children are taught. It's barely mentioned at all in most schools. We need to educate our kids—*all* our kids—about what has happened here over the last four hundred years. Has it gotten better? Yes, like I said, things have changed considerably since I was a kid.

"But does the next generation really understand it? How can they possibly understand it? We're taught about what happened at Jamestown and the first Thanksgiving, but we aren't taught about what it was really like to be a slave, what it was like to pick cotton in the heat for days on end, what it was like to be beaten, what it was like to be treated as *less than human.*

"How are kids going to understand what's going on now if they don't understand what was going on then? I think it's a good thing that people got to *see* what happened in the George Floyd murder. It was right there; no way you could say it didn't happen. It did happen, we all saw it happen, and that's why the jury really had no choice but to find the police officer [Derek Chauvin] guilty.

"But what's going on right now is like treating a symptom. You have to go back and find out the cause of the illness. *Then* you know how to treat it. It's like anything else: to understand where we are now, we need to have an understanding of how we got here.

"None of this is new. Lynchings were very much a part of Southern society through a lot of the twentieth century. The KKK flourished in the South for much of the twentieth century. Very few people objected to hearing the word *nigger* for much of the twentieth century.

"Kids growing up today need to understand that the history we're talking about isn't just about slavery. That was only the beginning—even though it lasted two hundred and fifty years. It set a tone that still exists today: that white people are *granting* rights to Black people. 'We're granting you the right to be free; we're granting you the right to vote; we're granting you the right to live among us.'

"But the attitude was—is, 'You aren't our equals. You should still look up to us and be thankful for anything we give you.'"

That was why John Thompson became angry when he was asked

in 1982 how he felt being the first Black coach to get a team to the Final Four. The implication was that forty-three years after the first NCAA Tournament was played, a Black man had finally been capable of coaching a team to reach that moment. Thompson's point was simple: if men like McLendon and Gaines had been given the chance to coach at the elite level, they would have done so years earlier than when Thompson finally did it in 1982. Thompson laughed years later when I asked him about "playing the race card."

"Of course I played the race card at times," he said. "Hell, white folks played the race card on me from the time I was a kid. You don't think there were white coaches who played the race card on *me*—especially with white players?" Thompson described what white coaches would tell white athletes who were considering playing for Thompson: " '[If] you go play for him, you'll never get a fair chance. He's gonna play the Black guys.' If there is one thing I can tell you about myself for certain, it's that I always played the best guys because my first goal was always to win.

"I liked the fact that people thought Georgetown was an HBCU. It was proof that the basketball team was the most important thing the school had going for it even though Georgetown is a great school academically.

"Do you think if we'd played exactly the same way we did in the eighties with a white coach and a lot of white players, we'd have been called the names we were called by the white media? We had three strikes against us every night: we had a loud Black coach, we had Black players, and—worst of all—we *won*. That combination made a lot of people crazy."

The opposite side of that argument is the label that was put on Duke when Mike Krzyzewski began to win a lot of games: "America's White Team." In 1986, the first time one of Krzyzewski's teams played in a national championship game, Louisville had four Black starters; Duke had three. But Duke continued to recruit great white players: Danny Ferry, Christian Laettner, Bobby Hurley, Mike Dunleavy, and JJ Redick among them.

Krzyzewski's first truly critical recruit was Johnny Dawkins. Later, he also recruited Tommy Amaker, Grant Hill, Brian Davis, Shane Battier, Nolan Smith, Chris Carrawell, Jason Williams, Carlos Boozer, and a slew of one-and-done players. All were Black.

And Duke—especially the talented white players—was *hated* for one of the same reasons Georgetown was hated: the Blue Devils won, a lot more often than Georgetown did, as it turned out. Duke won five national titles and went to twelve Final Fours under Krzyzewski.

"It was a different kind of racism," said Thompson, who was close to Krzyzewski. "In basketball, the Black player is supposed to be superior, the old white-men-can't-jump BS. They tried to make fun of my players, almost all of whom graduated, for not being able to read or write. But it was okay that they could play, because Black guys are supposed to be able to play. They made fun of Duke's players because they thought they *could* read and write but weren't supposed to be able to play. That made me almost as angry as the things directed at my players. All of it was just stupid."

In 1992, a group of coaches was sitting around late one night in the Nike suite at a hotel in Minneapolis. They were attending the annual coaches convention at the Final Four.

Thompson was there. So were Richardson, Raveling, and Chaney. Several younger Black coaches were there, too. The older guys were holding court, telling stories, reminding the younger guys about some of the things they had been through as they had climbed up the coaching ladder. The older coaches often had to deal with racism that had been far more blatant in the past than it was in the enlightened 1990s.

"At some point," Raveling said, "the thought occurred to me that we should formalize these sorts of meetings. Why not get all the Black coaches together to talk about the issues that were unique to being a Black coach—old or young?"

Four years earlier, Black coaches in football and basketball had banded together to form the Black Coaches Association, whose goal was to make Black coaches more visible and to help open doors for them to be taken more seriously in the job market. The BCA—led by Thompson, Chaney, Richardson, and Raveling—had made an impact in 1989 during the controversy over the NCAA's Proposition 42 rule, which imposed minimum academic standards for athletes to receive a scholarship.

It was Thompson who walked off his bench just before tip-off of a nationally televised game to bring attention to the issue. His support among coaches—white and Black—was almost unanimous.

This gathering was different, however. It was about educating people, not lobbying them. For years, the older coaches brought in the younger ones—and, eventually, members of the Black media who covered college hoops—to tell stories, to advise, and, occasionally, to scold.

"It was almost always on Sunday night, late," said Kevin Blackistone, one of the handful of Black writers invited to the meetings. "Everyone would start to gather at some point, but the meeting never really started until Big John [Thompson] got there. He was the king. Once it started, most of us stayed quiet or asked questions. We weren't there to express opinions. Those started with John and John Chaney and the other older guys. I think most of us learned a lot just listening for a lot of years."

Hamilton was a relatively new head coach in those days, having first been hired at Oklahoma State in 1986. Now, though, younger coaches and other people in basketball look to him much the same way others looked to Thompson, Chaney, Richardson, and Raveling years ago.

And while Hamilton insists that education about the Black experience — dating to 1619 — is absolutely paramount, he has one question that may sum up the issue that has plagued this country for more than four hundred years.

"We figured out a way to put men on the moon," he said. "Why can't we figure out a way for all of us to get along on earth? Why is that so hard?"

Sadly, no one has an answer to the question.

CHAPTER NINE

The Younger Generation

S HAKA SMART IS A BIT RELUCTANT to talk about his experiences growing up Black in the Midwest and what it has been like for him to be a Black basketball coach — a very successful one.

"I'm a little uncomfortable saying I had it tough, or I had difficult experiences," he said. "Because I know what I've gone through doesn't come close to what the real trailblazers dealt with, whether you go back to John McLendon and Big House Gaines or the guys who followed them, like John Thompson, John Chaney, Nolan Richardson, and Tubby Smith. The adversity I dealt with isn't close to what they experienced."

Smart is forty-four, part of the next generation of Black coaches who, in his words, "got opportunities because of what all those men had done."

He grew up in Madison, Wisconsin. His father was from Trinidad, his mother was white and grew up in Chicago. Smart never thought much about race or about being Black until his parents split and his mother moved to a different neighborhood in Madison. But he vividly remembers the first time he was made aware of the fact that he was Black.

"It was on the schoolyard," he said. "As I remember it, I was six. There was a skirmish during a game, and a kid called me a nigger. I didn't know what it meant, but when he started throwing punches right after using the word, it was pretty clear it wasn't meant as a compliment.

"I had to go home and ask my mom what it meant. After that, I knew exactly what someone was saying when I heard the word."

Smart's father, Winston Smart, was in and out of his life during his formative years. When Shaka was very young, Winston went home to Trinidad to visit family and didn't come back for two years. He had four children with women other than Shaka's mother and continued to drift into and out of Shaka's life right through high school. It was from his father, and his father's experiences, that Shaka became conscious of how different life is if you're Black.

"My father was very educated," Smart said. "He had four degrees, including a law degree from Wisconsin. He applied for a teaching position at the University of Illinois and thought he was going to get the job. At the last minute, the school hired someone else—someone who was white. My dad was stunned. When he checked into the other guy's background, he found out he wasn't close to being as qualified. He had Ds and Fs in core courses and a résumé not close to my father's.

"He sued Illinois for racial discrimination. He must have had a pretty good case because the school offered to settle for quite a bit of money. It would have changed his life and, presumably, our lives, financially. But he turned it down. It was about the principle to my father. He wanted to win in court and embarrass the school for what it had done.

"He was obsessed, not just with the case but with the discrimination he had faced. He's an example of how the negativity one can feel because of discrimination can take over your life. I think it drove him crazy. He fired his lawyer because he [the lawyer] had told him to take the settlement and went into court as his own attorney. Then he got mad at the judge for several rulings, turned around, and walked out of the courtroom. Never went back.

"It was right about then that I saw him for the last time. He came to our house and was angry and profane, dangerous. My mother told him to get out and not come back. That was on December 12, 1994 [Smart was seventeen]. I still remember the door slamming when he left. I never saw or heard from him again. I don't even know if he's alive right now. But his experiences were definitely an influence on me and on my feelings about race. I realized that if you obsessed about racism, it could drive you crazy. That's what it did to my father."

Smart's mother, Monica King, understood that Shaka would have to deal with a world different from what a white kid would face. She encouraged him to push for a Black education month at Oregon High School—which was largely white. Shaka got the school to do it, and a women's history month followed. He wrote a letter to Stu Jackson, then the basketball coach at Wisconsin, asking him to come and speak, and Jackson accepted the invitation.

"There was a lot of pushback," Smart said. "A lot of kids said, 'Why are we doing this? We don't need this.' What is almost impossible to understand if you are white is that race is always the elephant in the room if you're Black.

"What's going on now is similar to what I experienced then. A lot of white people don't want to hear from Black people on this topic. It gets back to white fragility: 'Don't tell me there's a problem or that *I* have a problem when it isn't affecting my life.' What happened after George Floyd was, a lot of white people started to understand that this *was* a problem, that it wasn't just about the one moment we all saw on video, that it went well beyond that.

"And yet, there are still millions who don't want to deal with it. Look how many people still voted for Trump the second time. That's pretty scary stuff."

Smart was a good high school player, but because he lacked size, wasn't recruited by any big-time Division 1 programs. His grades and board scores got him into several Ivy League schools, but he wanted to go to college someplace where he knew he could play. He ended up at Kenyon, which had a solid Division 3 program and was a very good school academically. As a senior, he was all-conference and graduated magna cum laude with a degree in history. He knew he wanted to try to coach, and when Bill Brown, the coach who had initially recruited him at Kenyon, offered him a job as a graduate assistant at another D-3 school, California University of Pennsylvania, he took it. He stayed long enough to earn a master's degree in social sciences and left for the University of Dayton to learn more about the craft of coaching. He started at Dayton as the director of basketball operations—known in basketball circles as a DOBO—and from there moved up the ladder at each stop: Akron, Clemson, and then Florida, under Billy Donovan.

"I decided to coach because it was the closest thing to playing I could find," he said. "I was like a lot of guys: basketball was my identity. I even went to a couple of tryout camps to play overseas. I thought I did pretty well, but not well enough, apparently. So I moved on to coaching."

When Anthony Grant left Virginia Commonwealth University in 2009, then VCU athletic director Norwood Teague continued the school's recent tradition of hiring young, up-and-coming assistant coaches: Jeff Capel had been twenty-seven when he got the job in 2002, and Grant had been thirty-nine when he was hired in 2006. Smart also had the advantage of being a Donovan assistant—just as Grant had been when he was hired.

Smart quickly became a star in Richmond. In 2010, his first team won 27 games and, after narrowly missing an NCAA bid and being shunned by the second-tier NIT, won the third-tier College Basketball Invitational. A year later, after barely making the NCAAs, the Rams won five games to reach the Final Four. It was the first season the NCAA added four more at-large bids, making it a sixty-eight-team field. VCU got one of those last four bids.

Once they were given the opportunity, the Rams beat Southern California in the so-called First Four in Dayton, and then crushed sixth-seeded Georgetown and third-seeded Purdue (both by 18 points). They squeezed past Florida State in the round of sixteen and, finally, stunned top-seeded Kansas in the regional final.

The joyride ended in the Final Four with a loss to Butler, but that was the point: it ended in the *Final Four*. All of a sudden, Smart was a young star in the coaching pantheon. VCU moved from the Colonial Athletic Association to the Atlantic-10 the next year, and although there were no more Final Four trips, the program continued to shine. The Rams never won fewer than 26 games in a season under Smart and made the NCAA Tournament every year from 2011 to 2015.

The Siegel Center, VCU's arena in downtown Richmond, became an impossible ticket. Since January 2011, the 7,637-seat building has been sold out 152 straight times. COVID-19 restrictions during the 2020–2021 season technically ended that streak, but when they are lifted for the 2021–2022 season, the building will probably again be full whenever VCU plays.

"The support we got in the entire community once we made the Final Four run was amazing," Smart said. "It was good before that, but once 2011 happened, it felt as if almost everyone in Richmond wanted to be part of it."

With his upbeat, outgoing personality, Smart became the symbol of that popularity. At his opening press conference, he had declared that his team would play a style of defense that would "wreak havoc" on opponents. *Havoc* became the Rams slogan and their brand—both in terms of the way they played and in marketing.

Smart and his wife, Maya, were the unofficial mayor and first lady of Richmond. If Smart had actually run for mayor, he might have been elected by acclamation.

In 2012, Shaka and Maya hosted a rally for Barack Obama during his reelection campaign. For Shaka, this was especially gratifying. "In 2008, when I was working at Florida, I tried to go to an Obama rally in Jacksonville and couldn't get in—it was too packed," he said. "Now, four years later, I'm introducing him at a campaign rally. It was a real thrill, one of the highlights of my life."

Not all of Smart's fans at VCU were quite as thrilled. "Virginia has leaned blue in recent years, but [Richmond is] still the city that was the capital of the confederacy," Smart said. "There are lots of people who vote Democratic, lots that vote Republican."

Many of those who voted Republican were not thrilled with the notion of their basketball coach introducing the country's first Black president. And they said so.

"If we hadn't been winning quite as much as we were, there might have been more backlash," Smart said. "As it was, there was some, but it wasn't really that bad. I was definitely glad that we did it."

Living in Richmond, Smart was reminded every day of the city's heritage. Because his drive to work took him down Monument Avenue, he had to pass the statues of Confederate war heroes — statues that became the subject of great controversy in 2020 in the wake of George Floyd's death.

"Actually, I could have driven to work without going past the statues," he said. "But I made a point of driving past them. My thinking was, I can drive past a statue of Jefferson Davis or of Robert E. Lee, know what they stood for, and still say to myself, 'That's okay, win the day anyway.'

"It was something I actually learned from Maya. When we'd get a bad call during a game, she'd always say, 'It's okay. Rams win the game anyway.' It's a very good way to approach things. You don't brood about what's happened in the past — whether it's the past thirty seconds or the past four hundred years. You accept that it happened and keep moving forward. Try to make things better by doing what you do as well as you possibly can. Driving past the statues actually got me pumped up for the day ahead."

Smart left VCU to coach at Texas after the 2015 season. His eventual departure was inevitable. He was too coveted a coach — a young coach — not to be coaxed at some point for the huge money that the power schools can afford to pay. He had turned down opportunities in the past, including jobs at UCLA and North Carolina State. Part of it was that he felt so comfortable at VCU; part of it was that he still vividly remembered how he had felt after his freshman year at Kenyon when Brown left.

"So much of my decision to go to Kenyon was tied into playing for Coach Brown," he said. "I realized then that most athletes pick a coach at least as much as they pick a college. I knew most of the guys who came to play at VCU picked *me* because they trusted me to help make them better players, but also to take care of them. The coach–player relationship in basketball is very close because there aren't that many players on the team. Football's different because there are so many players; you are usually much closer with your position coach than the head coach. Not so in basketball."

Ed McLaughlin, who had succeeded Norwood Teague as VCU's athletic director in 2012, understood that a time would come when Smart had to leave. "I've known since the first day I got the job that my toughest moment was going to come when Shaka decided it was time to leave," McLaughlin often said. "I know a lot of our fans won't understand it. I will."

The moment McLaughlin had been dreading came on the night of April 2, 2015. Smart was being courted by Texas, and the money on offer was more than two and a half times what he was making at VCU. He was being paid $1.2 million per year plus performance incentives to coach in the Atlantic-10. Texas, with all its Big 12 football money, offered him $3.2 million a year for five years.

VCU had been to the Final Four more recently than Texas had — 2011 as opposed to 2003. Basketball will never be the number one sport at Texas. Football is number one; spring football number two. But with the recruiting budget that Texas can afford, in addition to the TV exposure that a Big-12 team gets, the chances to make a Final Four and win a national championship are, realistically, better at Texas than at VCU.

Smart's first Texas team went 20–13 — his worst record as a head coach — but still made the NCAA Tournament. Five days after Donald Trump was elected president, after his team opened his second season with a victory, Smart was asked in a postgame press conference how he felt about Trump's election.

Always honest, Smart said, "When someone is elected who has a history of being hateful, of being racist, of being sexist, of saying certain things that are derogatory toward a certain group, it feels like a slap in the face. That's how some of [our players] felt. But you know what? We're going to have to move forward. There's not going to be another election. It is what it is, and we have to respond the right way...Our country's spoken. America's got some issues. But this is not surprising, based on the history of America."

As a history major in college, Smart is keenly aware of the country's shameful back story, dating back four hundred years to when the first Africans were kidnapped and brought here in chains. "It's worth remembering that we were slaves [245 years] for longer than we've been free [155 years]," he said early in 2021. "Some of it is about that legacy, but a lot of it is about the attitudes that all of us still face today."

If Smart needed any further evidence of how polarized things were in 2016, he got it quickly after his postelection comments. Texas is a blood-red state: Trump defeated Hillary Rodham Clinton by a margin of almost 10 percent in Texas. Joe Biden did better four years later but still lost Texas by almost 6 percent. Not surprisingly, then, Smart's comments did not play especially well with many Texas fans and boosters.

Among those not happy with him was the school's president, Gregory L. Fenves, who told Smart that he needed to stay away from politics in his public comments. It was a politer version of Laura Ingraham's infamous "Shut up and dribble" comment directed at LeBron James on *Fox News*.

There's no evidence that Fenves (now president of Emory University) was or is the kind of right-wing Trumpist that Ingraham is. But as the university's chief fundraiser, he knew that many of the school's wealthiest boosters were Trump supporters. No doubt he heard from many of them after Smart's comments.

As (bad) luck would have it, Texas had an awful season, going

11–22 that winter after losing players to the NBA draft, to transfer, and to injury. It was the first time in eight years as a head coach that Smart had failed to coach his team to 20 wins.

He rebuilt, reaching the NCAAs again in 2018 and, after just missing the tournament in 2019, winning the NIT that year. In 2021, the Longhorns won the Big-12 Tournament for the first time in school history, an achievement that quieted those calling for Smart to be fired. Texas is a place, it should be remembered, that fired Rick Barnes after he had taken the Longhorns to the NCAAs sixteen times in seventeen years, reaching the Final Four once and the Elite Eight on two other occasions.

Smart had reached the NCAAs three times out of five (there was no tournament in 2020), and, perhaps even worse, he is two things Barnes was not: Black and politically outspoken at times. These qualities can create shaky ground in a hurry. The ground became shakier, even after the victory in the Big 12 Tournament, when the Longhorns were victims of one of those first-round NCAA Tournament upsets that makes the event unique: losing to in-state rival Abilene Christian, 53–52. Texas was a number three seed, and Abilene Christian number fourteen. The Texas loss was *not* the biggest upset of the first round: the defeat of number two Ohio State by number fifteen Oral Roberts was the biggest—but the Longhorns loss set off another round of anti-Smart sentiment in Texas.

During the pandemic, Smart had let his hair grow. Previously, he had always kept it cropped close to his head, but with barbers no longer accessible, he allowed it to grow out, black and curly. He had decided to cut it himself when Maya and their ten-year-old daughter, Zora, stopped him.

"I literally had the razor in my hand and they said, 'No, don't cut it,'" he said. "So I left it alone."

After the season, Smart was talking to a friend who is a high school coach in North Carolina. "You realize, don't you," his friend said, "that letting your hair grow out was an act of defiance."

Smart hadn't thought about it that way, but when he did, he realized his friend was right. "It was about saying it was time to change the status quo," he said. "Wanting people to understand that change is a good thing and, right now, something we need in this country."

Even with the Abilene Christian loss, Smart clearly had the Texas program on solid ground after finishing 19–8 and winning the conference tournament. But there were always going to be Texas supporters who weren't going to forget his anti-Trump comments of 2016.

"If we won a national championship, some of them might forgive or forget," Smart said with a laugh. "But there were always going to be some who will never forgive or forget. That's just the way it is. I knew that."

That was not the reason Smart accepted an offer to move back to his home state to become the coach at Marquette. "It was just a better fit for me and for my family, I think," he said. "Texas can be a great job. It's a great school, but I don't think it was the right fit for me. Or, I wasn't the right fit for it—depending on your point of view.

"Marquette is much smaller, and it is a basketball-first school. Clearly, that was never going to be the case at Texas."

Smart will never say it, but there was very likely both a political and a racial element to his not being accepted by many at Texas. That was the message Fenves had been trying to send him in November 2016: most of those who support our program financially do *not* agree with your politics.

Being both liberal and Black meant he had two strikes against him in some minds before he won or lost a game. If you are going to start out with those two strikes, you have to win big to gain acceptance. Smart won—but he never won big.

Some in the college basketball world believed that Smart left Texas for Marquette because he thought he was going to be fired. Given that he had two years left on his contract and had just won the school's first Big 12 Tournament title ever, that seems unlikely.

Even if he had been fired, Smart probably would have landed in the same place: Marquette. And he would still be optimistic about the short-term future there while still worrying about what's ahead in the country in terms of race relations.

"You know, I tend to be optimistic about things," he said. "I don't look back and 'what-if' things; I move on to what's next. But when I look at where we are today when it comes to race, I wonder if my children's generation or my grandchildren's generation will get to see major progress. I'm honestly not sure they will unless there's some kind of revolution or a major upheaval of the status quo.

"I look at the NBA, which is probably our most progressive league, and I see Steve Nash, who has never coached, being handed a job with one of the league's best teams. Does that ever happen with a Black coach? Sure, Doc Rivers got hired by the 76ers this past season, but he's been an NBA coach for years and he won an NBA title. Completely different thing.

"But it isn't as simple as Blacks and whites getting along better or respecting one another more. As a Black coach, I have to do a better job with younger Black coaches and with my Black players. I might have an advantage going into a Black family's home because I'm Black, but that family is going to expect more from me if their son comes to play for me. I'm Black, so I should be able to understand what it is like for a Black kid dealing with college and all that comes with it.

"I try very hard to do that. But sometimes, your relationship with a kid comes down to one thing: playing time. That's one thing that's never going to change. I have to accept that I'm never going to get it exactly right, but I have to try to get as close to exactly right as I possibly can."

Like many other people, Smart wasn't overjoyed by Derek Chauvin's guilty verdict in the George Floyd murder case. "I was relieved," Smart said. "Relieved that the jury got it right but, more than that, relieved it was over. I felt like every time the media showed that video again, it was creating post-traumatic stress disorder for a lot of Black people — a lot of people, period.

"It bothered me that some people thought the verdict was worthy of celebration. It was the right verdict, but the fact that it was such a big deal that a jury came to the right conclusion when the evidence was overwhelming just means we've still got a long, long way to go."

Even so, Smart will continue to try to win the day. One day versus four hundred years can be difficult, but he's still going to keep fighting the good fight.

Once they are hired, Black coaches are often on a shorter leash than white coaches are. Shaka Smart might have become a victim of that short leash had he not left Texas for Marquette when he did.

Getting fired from a job that isn't right for you can also be the proverbial blessing in disguise. The best example of that cliché is Tommy Amaker. Now in his fourteenth season at Harvard — it would be his fifteenth except the Ivy League opted out of playing basketball in the winter of 2020–2021, during the pandemic — Amaker has become a respected figure on a campus where gaining respect as a coach can be difficult.

The funny thing is, Amaker never dreamed that Harvard would turn out to be his dream job. "I was too big-time for the Ivy League as a player," he said, laughing. "My goal as a player and then as a coach was to be at a so-called power school."

He was a basketball prodigy, albeit a very small one, even in high school. "I was about five seven and 108 pounds soaking wet as a freshman," he said. "But I could play."

He was from a middle-class family; his father, Harold (the younger Amaker's full name is Harold Tommy Amaker), was a colonel in the army, having gone through ROTC in college. His mother, Alma, was a junior high school and high school teacher for fifty years. When Tommy and his older sister, Tami, were in junior high school, their mother was their guidance counselor.

"Tami hated it," Amaker remembered. "She wanted to be independent. I loved it. It meant I got to see my mom during the school day."

His upbringing was relatively sheltered from racial issues. Some of the reason was growing up in a middle-class neighborhood. Some of it was knowing where to go and where not to go.

"There was a fence behind our house," he said. "Our side of the fence was where the Black neighborhood began. The other side of the fence was the white neighborhood. There were parks and basketball courts and rec centers. But we never went there. We went in the other direction. I played a lot of my basketball as a kid at the James Lee Rec Center. I saw very few white people there. The youth teams I played on were all Black. I didn't really play in the winter with white kids until I got to high school."

Amaker went to Lefty Driesell's basketball camp at the end of fifth grade. There, he met a kid who was a year older named Johnny Dawkins—who would become his backcourt mate at Duke years later. His idol was John Lucas, Maryland's great guard of the mid-1970s, who was the first pick in the 1976 NBA draft. When Tami, who was two years older than Tommy, went to Maryland, there was little doubt in her younger brother's mind that he would follow her—and Lucas—to College Park.

Because his mother was a schoolteacher, Amaker had his choice of high schools in Fairfax County. He chose W. T. Woodson—or, more specifically, he chose Red Jenkins, who probably ranked only behind DeMatha's Morgan Wootten on the list of star high school coaches in the Washington, D.C., area at the time.

During the summer between his sophomore and junior years, he first began to think about going to college someplace other than Maryland. The reason was Mike Krzyzewski.

In the summer of 1981, after Krzyzewski's first season at Duke, the coach was at the Jelleff Recreation Center in downtown Washington, scouting Dawkins, who was playing in the Jelleff Summer League. Jelleff was one of *the* summer basketball leagues in the country. At halftime of Dawkins's game, Krzyzewski was approached by Reginald Kitchen, who was Amaker's Amateur Athletic Union coach. In the Jelleff League, you played for your high school team, so Kitchen was just there to watch.

"Are you the Duke coach?" he asked Krzyzewski, who at that moment was identifiable to most people only because he was wearing a shirt that said DUKE BASKETBALL on it.

Krzyzewski confirmed that he was. "I know you're here to see Dawkins," Kitchen said. "But one of my players is in the next game. He's really small, but you might want to stick around and watch him. He's really good."

Krzyzewski decided to stick around. By then, Amaker had "grown" to five feet nine and 135 pounds. By halftime, Krzyzewski was in love.

Kitchen returned. "What'd you think?" he asked.

"I love him," Krzyzewski said.

"Well, his mom is sitting at the other end of the bleachers," Kitchen said. "I know you aren't allowed to talk to her, but you might just wave and let her know you're enjoying watching Tommy play."

At that moment, Krzyzewski didn't really care much about the NCAA's oft-violated "no-bump" rule. He walked over to Alma Amaker, introduced himself and said, "Mrs. Amaker, your son is going to look great in Duke blue."

From that night on, Krzyzewski ardently pursued both Dawkins and Amaker — eventually convincing both to come to Duke. "I've always thought a close relationship with your coach is very important when you choose a college," Amaker said. "I knew I'd have that with Coach K."

Amaker started every game he ever played at Duke and, as a junior, was the point guard on Krzyzewski's first great Duke team, one that went 37–3 and reached the national championship game before losing to Louisville. A year later, with the other four starters having graduated, Amaker led a very young team to the Sweet Sixteen.

"I'm probably as proud of what that team did as our Final Four team," Amaker said. "That was an important year for Coach K. It proved he wasn't going to be a one-hit wonder."

To put it mildly. Beginning in 1988, Duke went to five straight Final Fours and won two national titles.

Amaker was part of the two national championship teams as an assistant coach. His size — six feet and 165 pounds, still soaking wet — had kept him out of the NBA. He returned to Duke to pursue an MBA and worked initially as a graduate assistant. When Bob Bender left Krzyzewski's staff to become the coach at Illinois State, Krzyzewski offered Amaker a full-time job. Amaker decided to try it.

"I was actually surprised by how much I liked coaching," he said. "I'd always thought, when I couldn't play anymore, that would be it for me in basketball. But I enjoyed it, enjoyed working with the kids and feeling like I was still competing—which you were. You didn't work for Coach K without understanding how important winning was to him."

In 1997, Amaker was offered the job as the head coach at Seton Hall. A job in the Big East for any assistant coach was rare. He took it and, in his third season, took the Pirates to the Sweet Sixteen after they upset Temple, the number two seed in the eastern regional, in the second round. Two years later, in the midst of the Fab Five scandal, he was offered the Michigan job. (Michigan booster Ed Martin was charged with making large payments to key players, laundering money from an illegal gambling operation. The IRS, FBI, and US Department of Justice all investigated it and eventually punished several players, while the NCAA placed sanctions on the university's basketball program.)

Michigan was a mess. The two "Fab Five" Final Four banners had been ordered taken down by the NCAA. Many Michigan alumni still supported the Fab Five, but others did not. Recruiting took a huge hit. Amaker had to rebuild almost from scratch, going 11–18 in his first season. By his third season, Michigan won 23 games and just missed making the NCAA Tournament. It did win the NIT, but three more years of missing the NCAAs eventually cost Amaker his job. He was fired in 2007 after going 22–13. Good but not good enough.

That's when Harvard came into the picture. The school had just fired longtime coach Frank Sullivan, who had done remarkable work to keep Harvard consistently competitive in the Ivy League in spite of the fact that Harvard's admissions requirements for basketball players were far more stringent than for the other seven league schools.

Amaker knew about these high standards. He took the job only after the school agreed to give the basketball team the same flexibility the football and hockey teams had enjoyed for years: the admissions standards remained the same, but players would be evaluated on a case-by-case basis rather than just being eliminated by numbers. Amaker knew the only way to make that work was to ensure his players graduated.

There aren't any gut courses for athletes to slide by on at Harvard. Other Ivy League coaches went crazy when Harvard began taking players who would have had no chance to get in when Sullivan was the coach. Yet it wasn't as if Amaker was recruiting academic suspects — his recruits did graduate.

"If we took a bunch of kids who didn't make it academically, then the admissions people wouldn't trust me," he said. "It made no sense to take a kid unless I was convinced he was going to graduate."

What bothered the other Ivy coaches was that, given equal footing, Amaker was turning Harvard into an Ivy League power. The Crimson went 8–22 in his first season but won 21 games by his third.

There followed a run of six straight winters in which the Crimson won at least 20 games. In the first of those years (2010), Harvard went to the pay-to-play CollegeInsider.com Postseason Tournament (CIT) — the first time the school had played in any postseason tournament since 1946. A year later, after a tie for first place with Princeton in the Ivy League, Harvard lost a playoff game to the Tigers at the buzzer and went to the NIT. For the next four seasons, Harvard was the Ivy League champion and went to the NCAAs each year, twice upsetting high seeds in the first round.

By then, Lavietes Pavilion on game nights had become one of *the* places to be at Harvard. A mostly white student body had fallen in love with a mostly Black basketball team. It wasn't just that the team was winning; it's that the players were actually *part* of the student body. They weren't given special treatment or put on pedestals the way football and basketball players are at power schools.

"Of all the things we've accomplished, I think seeing the way our team has brought the campus together might be the most gratifying for me," Amaker said. "Harvard is a place that is both brilliant and isolated. There's the business school, law school, the college. Each exists on its own little island. The same is largely true of sports. There are fans of hockey and of tennis who come from those worlds. Even football, with all the success that Murph [football coach Tim Murphy] has had, is different. The players wear masks; the stadium is much bigger than the basketball arena. In basketball, you can sit close enough to feel the game and the sweat. Our crowds are diverse in ways that are unique. White kids, Black kids, Asian kids come. White faculty and Black faculty come.

"Our former president, Drew Faust, once said to me that basketball games had become the most diverse place on our campus. That made me feel very proud."

Amaker has taken that feeling a step further. Shortly after he arrived on campus, he teamed with longtime law professor Charles Ogletree to form the Harvard Breakfast Club. Amaker was well aware of Ogletree—who represented, among many others, Anita Hill—when he first arrived in Boston. The coach was thrilled when Ogletree and his wife invited him and his wife, Stephanie, to dinner and a jazz concert. Soon after, Amaker reciprocated, inviting Ogletree to breakfast at Henrietta's Table, the iconic restaurant located in Cambridge's Charles Hotel.

"I asked him if we could maybe get together for breakfast every once in a while," Amaker said. "I liked him, and I also knew I could learn from him. The next time, he brought a couple of friends. It grew from there."

After the group had grown to about ten people, management suggested they meet in a private room in the back of the restaurant. "I think it was because we were too loud," Amaker said, laughing.

Now, about thirty people show up for the meetings, which are monthly during the school year and took place on Zoom during the pandemic. Harvard has a large and distinguished Black faculty. Many members come to the meetings, as do white professors and Amaker's players. Speakers have included men like Harry Edwards, the former San José State professor who helped inspire the Tommie Smith–John Carlos victory podium salute in Mexico City; Satch Sanders, longtime Boston Celtics star and former Harvard basketball coach; Julius Erving; and James Brown, former Harvard basketball player and TV star.

Both men who have been Massachusetts governors during Amaker's time at Harvard—Democrat Deval Patrick and Republican Charlie Baker—have attended. Patrick, one of just a few Black governors in the country's history, first showed up while still serving as governor, although he had not been invited.

"I've heard all about this thing, but no one invited me," he said when he walked in.

"We told him we figured he came for the free breakfast," Amaker said, laughing.

All of this makes Amaker feel as if he's in a perfect place to coach. He has had numerous chances to return to the big-time. In 2014, after Harvard had beaten Boston College six years in a row, the ACC school handed him a contract and, in essence said, "You fill in the numbers." Amaker was flattered but said no thank you. UC–Berkeley made a similar offer several years ago. No thank you.

Three years later, Boston College came up with a different solution to its "Harvard problem": it stopped playing the Crimson except in closed preseason scrimmages.

As much as he enjoys all this, Amaker is still keenly aware of how far there is to go in terms of race relations in this country. Like most people, he watched in horror the eight-minute, forty-six-second video of Minneapolis police officer Derek Chauvin keeping his knee on the neck of George Floyd on May 25, 2020.

"One thing that made the protests after George Floyd's death different than in the past was the number of white people who were involved," he said. "Maybe it was because more people were at home and saw the video because of the pandemic, or maybe it was just a tipping point, not just for Black people but for white people too.

"I think that's important. It can't just be Black people protesting or being angered by the way we've been treated. It has to be white people, too, recognizing what's been going on in this country for far too many years. You have to feel *affected* by something, not just say, 'Oh yeah, too bad, but not my problem.' It's everyone's problem."

With his short-cropped hair and his elegant taste in fashion, Amaker could easily be mistaken for a lawyer — or, at fifty-six, a judge. But he's still sometimes mistaken for being a Black man who might be trouble or might be in a stereotypical job many white people view as belonging exclusively to Black people.

"I was in California a couple of years back on a recruiting trip," he said. "I was crossing a street after a game, talking to my mother on my cell phone. All of a sudden, a motorcycle roared up and a cop was shouting at me, 'What are you doing? What do you think you're doing?!'

"I told my mother I'd call back, and I said, 'Officer, I'm sorry. What is it I'm doing?'

"He pointed his finger at me and said, 'Do you know what the hell you just did?! You can't cross the street here! You're jaywalking!'

"He was right; I was jaywalking. There were no cars around, but

I *was* jaywalking. I told him I was sorry, I hadn't been paying enough attention. I kept my hands where he could see them the whole time. It was clear to me he was looking for a confrontation. I know when someone is trying to instigate. He wanted me to get angry and give him an excuse to start something. I wasn't going to give him anything. I just kept saying I'd made a mistake jaywalking. It was bizarre. He asked me what I was doing in California. I said I was the basketball coach at Harvard and I'd just been watching a game. He finally decided to let me go. I think he was disappointed."

A few years later, Amaker was on another recruiting trip, waiting outside his hotel for his car. He was dressed, as always, neatly, since he was going to visit a recruit and his family at their home. A woman walked up, handed him her valet parking ticket, and described her car to him.

Politely, Amaker explained that he wasn't a valet, that he was also a hotel guest. "She wasn't rude," Amaker said. "She just saw a Black person and assumed he was *not* a hotel guest."

Amaker is one of those people who almost always see the good in others. He also understands that many Americans—most of them white—are still uncomfortable with the changes that are slowly coming.

"I still agree that you often have to be twice as good as a Black person to get a job—especially a big-time job. Most of the time when a Black guy gets hired as a coach in college football or college basketball, he's taking over a program that's been losing or gotten into trouble. Look at where Michigan was when I got hired. Where was Florida State when Leonard Hamilton got hired? Or when he got hired at Miami? Boston College just hired a Black coach because after it fired a successful Black coach twelve years ago, the white coaches they hired failed.

"The exception to the rule was Tubby Smith at Kentucky. But the athletic director was C. M. Newton."

Newton was always a leader in breaking down racial walls. While coaching at Alabama in the early 1970s, he recruited the school's first Black basketball players. He later coached at Vanderbilt, which was the first SEC school to recruit a Black basketball player (Perry Wallace) in the 1960s.

"I guess the point really is that people *need* to see color and understand that being Black is a different experience than being white," Amaker said. "And we as Black people don't always have to be the same or agree on everything."

In the late 1980s, two of Amaker's boyhood heroes, John Thompson and Arthur Ashe, the first Black man to win Grand Slam tennis tournaments, clashed over the infamous NCAA Prop 42 rule that required athletes to meet minimum academic requirements to receive an athletic scholarship or be eligible to play as freshmen. The requirements were tied to grade point average and the SATs or ACTs.

Thompson saw the rule as a way of denying Black athletes a chance to receive a college education. He argued that numbers — especially the culturally biased numbers of the SATs and ACTs — should not be used to judge whether someone could thrive or survive in college.

Ashe, the last male American tennis player of any color to graduate from college and win a major title (UCLA, 1966), argued that Black people should require more of athletes. He believed that the athletes should be educated and be forced to focus on academics before being allowed to play a sport in college.

"They disagreed, and they were both right," Amaker said. "Arthur was right that we need to force people to educate athletes long before they get to college. John was right that athletes shouldn't pay a penalty for a flawed system. The more leaders like the two of them debate issues, the better off we'll all be."

Which may explain why Amaker has been pushing Harvard to establish a Black history major. "The history that's been taught for years is often white history," he said. "We need young people, Black and white, to be more aware of what's gone on in this country for four hundred years."

And yet, there are others who aren't enamored with the idea of separating Black history from history. "It makes me uncomfortable," said Dalen Cuff, who played for Columbia against Amaker's team for four years and now works for ESPN. "Black history is part of American history. I don't think it should be separated out. We should just make schools do a better job of teaching *all* history, not just white history."

Two smart Black men who want the same thing but see the road to getting there differently. Not unlike Ashe and Thompson thirty-plus years ago.

Dalen Cuff's father was Black; his mother white. He remembers as a young boy in Pittsburgh being called "Oreo" by other kids because his skin was light enough that many people thought he was white. When he went to high school in Florida, he was often asked by white kids why he had "nig-hair."

He still vividly remembers his first schoolyard fight. "I was five," he said. "A kid and I got into it, and he started screaming that I had 'Black blood.' I wasn't even sure what he meant, but I knew it wasn't a compliment. I went home and asked my mother what that meant. She explained to me that she was white and my dad was Black and that was why some people might want to label me as Black, because it mattered to them. I remember saying, 'But Mom, my blood is red. Isn't everybody's blood red?'"

Dalen was the third of Dennis and Patricia Cuff's five children. His father had played basketball at Duquesne and was good enough to be drafted by the New York Knicks. But it was 1966, the Vietnam War was raging, and the US Army also drafted him. When he got out of the army, he returned to Pittsburgh and became a pharmacist. In 1997, when Dalen was thirteen, Eckerd Drugs transferred Dennis to Palm Harbor, Florida. It was there, in high school, that Dalen began to flourish as a basketball player.

He was recruited by a number of mid-majors and several Division 2 schools. When Columbia became interested, his father, retired by then, told him if he got into Columbia, he was *going* to Columbia.

Which he did.

New York City was a culture shock for Cuff. He had never met anyone who was gay before—or who openly said he or she was gay. Columbia was a campus that had racial issues, the difference being that those issues were often discussed in class.

"I went there for an education and I certainly got one," he said. "The racial divides were clear. In class, the white kids would say that affirmative action was bad, that racism wasn't nearly as bad as some people claimed it was. They'd say to us, 'Look at you; you're here.' The biggest difference was that they thought they *belonged* at Columbia; we were *allowed* to be there.

"I actually loved the interaction. I learned from it. But there was still a tendency for the Black kids to hang out with the Black kids. It was just more comfortable. In many ways, it was a divided campus. But it was a great place to learn lessons about the real world."

Cuff is verbally quick on his feet. And because he wasn't a great player and had to study hard to understand the game to succeed, he is much better at explaining the game on air than are many analysts who were stars and tend to rely on talking about themselves when they have nothing else to say.

Cuff met his wife, Adrienne, while he was working at an ad agency in New York after graduating from Columbia. "She was completely unimpressed with me when we met," he said. "But I wore her down."

They now have a three-year-old daughter, Lyra. Like her father, Lyra is light-skinned to the point where people might mistake her for being white. Adrienne is darker-skinned. The Cuffs live in Fairfield, Connecticut, which is about forty miles from Bristol, where Dalen goes often to host studio shows for ESPN.

"Sometimes, when Adrienne takes Lyra for walks, people think she's her nanny," Cuff said. "They'll say things like, 'Oh, how long have you been with her?' She usually says, 'Since birth.' There's an assumption people make that if they see a child who appears to be white with someone who is Black, that the adult must be an employee."

One day, both Cuffs took Lyra for a walk in downtown Fairfield. They were stopped by a woman who asked about Lyra and clearly thought something wasn't right about the threesome.

"About a hundred yards down the street, we were stopped by a cop," Cuff said. "I guess the woman had called the police, thinking Lyra didn't belong with us."

Much the same way the woman at the hotel assumed Tommy Amaker was a valet. Or, as Ed Tapscott put it, "every Black man wakes up in the morning with two jobs—his job and being a Black man."

Even, as it turns out, if you are a biracial, light-skinned Black man. It's never easy.

CHAPTER TEN

Exceptions

T HERE ARE EXCEPTIONS TO EVERY RULE in sports and in life. Glenn "Doc" Rivers is an exception to this rule: if you are Black, getting a second or third chance to coach a professional team is, at best, unlikely.

Rivers is currently the coach of the Philadelphia 76ers — his fourth job as an NBA head coach. Previously, he has coached the Orlando Magic, the Boston Celtics, and the Los Angeles Clippers. When the Clippers fired him in September 2020, it took the 76ers five days to name him as their new coach.

A closer look at Rivers's résumé might help explain why people continue to hire him: In 1999, he took over an Orlando team that had lost Shaquille O'Neal a couple of years earlier and kept the team afloat for four years, never finishing below .500 and making the play-offs three times. A 1–10 start in the fall of 2003 got him fired, but a year later, he was hired by the Boston Celtics. In 2008, the Celtics became NBA champions for the first time in twenty-two years and, two years later, lost to the Lakers in the finals in seven games. Three years after that, the Celtics agreed to accept a first-round pick from the Clippers in return for giving them Rivers to coach the team.

"That was a mistake on my part," Rivers said of his decision to accept the move to Los Angeles. "I knew how bad an owner Donald Sterling was, but I had enough ego to think I could get the organization turned around even with him as the owner. I didn't think I could change Sterling, but I did think I could change the Clippers. I honestly thought if I could turn the Clippers around, I'd be remembered more for that than for winning a championship with the Celtics. We did get it turned around, but it never would have happened if Sterling had still been there."

Sterling wasn't there, because of racist remarks that his girlfriend had recorded and released to TMZ in April 2014. The story broke right in the middle of a playoff series between the Golden State Warriors and the Clippers—led by first-year coach Doc Rivers.

On the tape, Sterling can be heard talking to a woman named V. Stiviano (she used other names at other times) about an Instagram photo Stiviano had posted of herself with Magic Johnson.

"It bothers me that you want to broadcast that you're associating with Black people," he is heard saying. "Do you have to?"

Stiviano responds that she was simply posting a photo taken with someone she admired.

"I think the fact that you admire him—I've known him well, and he should be admired," Sterling then says. "And I'm just saying that it's too bad you can't admire him privately. And during your entire fucking life you can admire him, bring him here, feed him, fuck him, I don't care. You can do anything. But don't put him on an Instagram for the world to see so they have to call me. And don't bring him to my games, okay?"

The release of the tape—not surprisingly—caused an instant

uproar. When Commissioner Adam Silver first heard about it, it was suggested to him that perhaps the voice on the tape wasn't Sterling.

"I needed to hear the tape right away," Silver said. "When I heard it, there was no doubt it was Donald. I'd known him for years. It was definitely him."

Fortunately for Rivers, Silver acted quickly. Even though he definitely didn't have the authority to do so, he banned Sterling from the NBA for life and made certain that the owner didn't show up in Los Angeles for game 5 of the Clippers–Warriors playoff series, which was played four nights after the tape had been released.

"I had never had a course in crisis management that taught you how to deal with a racist owner in the middle of a playoff series," Rivers said, able to laugh about what had taken place seven years later. "It was more unfair to the players than to anybody else. They'd done nothing wrong, and now they're caught in the middle of this. I walked into the locker room and said, 'Fellas, my name is Glenn Rivers, and I'm from Maywood, Illinois. I'm a Black man, and I know how you feel about all this because I know how I feel about it. Right now, we have to speak with one voice coming out of this locker room. It doesn't have to be mine. If you want it to be someone else, just say so — as long as we all agree that we're all on the same page with all of this. We do that, we'll be okay.'"

It wasn't quite that simple. The players decided to obscure the Clippers logo on their warmups before game 4 in Oakland. They were blown out by the Warriors in that game, leaving the series tied at 2–2. Game 5 was scheduled for two nights later in Los Angeles. During the team's game-day shootaround, Rivers got a call from the head of the team's human resources office saying the team's entire office staff was threatening to walk out. Everyone had worried about a player boycott; no one had considered the possibility that the staff might walk.

"I'd already been fighting with [team president] Andy Roeser that day over the issue of Donald coming to the game that night," he said. "I told him it just couldn't happen; he had to keep him away. When I got the call from our HR person, I got in my car and drove to our team offices. I talked to everyone possible and said I would get something done. Remember, this is a few hours before we're playing game five of a two-two playoff series.

"I got in my car and called Adam [Silver]. He had told me if I needed any help at all to call him. I said, 'I need help here, right now. I'm losing it. I'm a basketball coach—that's all.' He said to me, 'Doc, worry about coaching your team. This is going to be taken care of today. After today, you won't ever have to deal with Donald Sterling again.'"

Silver was as good as his word. Even though only the league's Board of Directors had the authority to do so, he banned Sterling from the NBA for life on the spot and forced him to sell the team with remarkable speed. On May 29, Steve Ballmer, who had just retired as CEO of Microsoft, agreed to buy the Clippers for a record $2 billion.

"I never could have come back if Sterling had still been there," Rivers said. "But once Donald was gone, it was okay. I could just be a basketball coach again."

The Clippers—who won that series with Golden State in seven games before losing to the Oklahoma City Thunder in six games— were consistent winners during the next six seasons but never reached a conference final. That led to Rivers's departure in September 2020, followed by his hiring in Philadelphia five days later.

In 2021, at the age of sixty, Rivers stands on the doorstep of becoming the tenth coach in NBA history to win 1,000 regular-season games, having finished the 2021 season with 992 victories.

"I guess it's fair to say I've come a long way from Maywood," he said, laughing. "But it hasn't exactly been nothing but smooth sailing, even going back to when I was a kid."

Maywood was a largely Black suburb of Chicago surrounded by mostly white suburbs. "It was a little bit like East Germany and West Germany years ago," Rivers said. "In our case, if we crossed First Avenue into Oak Park or Merrills Park, it got dangerous in a hurry. I'm not just talking about the police. I'm talking about everyone."

Rivers's father, a police officer in Maywood, counseled his children to be careful about leaving Maywood. He told them how to deal with a police officer should they encounter one outside the safety of their hometown. "We got The Talk from him early," Rivers said. "Look, I've always said that I support good police work and I understand firsthand how important it is. But, unfortunately, I have to put the word *good* in there as a qualifier because, as we've seen, not all police work is good."

Rivers vividly remembers the first time he encountered what was clearly racism. "It was in the sixth grade," he said. "My dad had gotten me into a basketball camp in Lombard, which was a wealthy, mostly white suburb. He thought it was worth the money for me to compete with some good players and to deal with a white environment because I was going to have to do that sooner or later.

"I'd shown some potential by then. I was a good player. One afternoon, I made a steal and went in for a layup. Kid I stole the ball from yells, 'You fucking nigger!' I'd already heard the term when I was in third grade. Back then, I'd had to ask my parents what it meant and they'd told me.

"So, I turned around and went after the kid, wanted to fight him.

Counselors intervened and told *me* to get out because I had started the fight. My dad sat me down that night and said, 'You can't start a fight every time someone calls you a name. Someone lays a hand on you, that's different. But the way you react to name-calling is you beat the guy—on the court. Let him know you're as good or better than him, and you won't lower yourself to his level.'

"The next day, he made me go back to the camp. Woke me up and said, 'You're going back. You aren't running away from this.' The team I was on ended up winning the tournament at the end of the camp, and I went home with pretty much every trophy. *That* was my answer, as it turned out. I think when the incident happened, the other white kids weren't thinking they needed to back me up. By the end of the camp, I think I'd earned the respect of most of them."

Rivers was highly recruited coming out of Proviso East High School and ended up at Marquette, where he played for Hank Raymonds, who had succeeded Al McGuire when McGuire retired after winning the national championship in 1977.

Rivers picked up his nickname in college. When he showed up at a summer camp wearing a Julius Erving T-shirt, Rick Majerus, then a Marquette assistant, said, "Hey, look, it's Doc"—invoking Erving's "Dr. J" nickname. The name stuck.

And so it was that the Atlanta Hawks drafted "Doc" Rivers in the second round of the 1983 NBA draft. He played thirteen seasons in the NBA, making the all-star team in 1988. After eight years in Atlanta, he was traded to Los Angeles—to the Clippers. It was during his one season in Los Angeles that he had firsthand experience with being pulled over for DWB—on multiple occasions.

"We played in the old Sports Center," he said. "It was in a rough neighborhood, and you had to drive through south-central LA to get there. It happened to almost everyone on the team—Black guys driving nice cars through south-central LA; I'm not exaggerating when I say it happened to me once every two weeks.

"One day, a cop pulled me over and asked to see my license. I'd been through it before, but that day, I lost my temper for a minute. I said, 'For what? The only thing I've done wrong is being Black.' He said, 'I don't have to tell you why.' I thought about it for a moment, and I remembered my father giving me The Talk. Thank goodness I remembered it because I was about to lose my composure. The cop had a gun. I didn't. I gave him the license. He went back to his car and took his sweet time before he finally came back and said, 'You're free to go.' No apology, of course. Fortunately, I kept my composure and didn't say anything else.

"Ken Norman [a teammate] had it worse than I did. He stopped to get gas one day; cops pulled up, assumed he'd stolen the car, and threw him across the hood and handcuffed him. He wasn't even Driving While Black; he was Getting Gas While Black.

"Cops are supposed to be there to make sure we get home safely, not to make us worry that they might be the reason we *don't* get home safely."

Rivers went on to play for the Knicks and Spurs before retiring in 1996. Coaching was a natural next step for him, since he defied many of the racial stereotypes scouts often use to describe players. Rivers was the rare Black player whom scouts labeled "cerebral."

"Most of the time, even today, I can read a scouting report and, if I've never heard of the player, know if he's Black or white," he said. "Black guys are described as 'athletic, a leaper, physical.' White guys are 'cerebral, coaches on the court, hustlers.' It's the same with coaches. I've always been described as a 'players' coach' or 'a great motivator.' That's fine. But there was a stretch of seven years where my teams ranked either number one or number two in efficiency coming out of a time-out. That's Xs and Os coaching. But you never hear that about me or, generally speaking, about Black coaches."

Rivers was happy to see how many young people—both Black and white—were involved in the Black Lives Matter protests in the summer of 2020. He thinks it is important for today's athletes to speak out on issues.

"I like the fact that these young people are very serious about all this," he said. "They're on it now. Once, it was old people talking about what was wrong and what needed to be changed. Now, it's younger guys, a lot of whom are in the spotlight, who are speaking up and doing things. That's a very good thing.

"But it needs to go beyond that. We still aren't educating kids the way they need to be educated about what's been done to Black people in the last four hundred years. A lot of times, kids in high school are given a 500-page history book. One day, the teacher says, 'Okay, turn to pages 221 and 222. Today, we're going to study Black history.'

"It's almost as if we don't *want* to look back at what happened in the past. When they wrote the Constitution, slaves weren't even considered people: they were three-fifths of a person. When that finally changed, a lot of white people thought they were doing us a favor *allowing* us to be considered equal in the eyes of the law.

"I hate to bring up Nazi Germany in any context but think about this. There are millions of people who think it's wrong to take down Confederate flags, to ban them at racetracks, because—they say— that flag is part of their history and heritage. The swastika flag is a part of Germany's history and heritage, but it is completely banned in Germany because it is a shameful part of their history and heritage. Here, though, there are millions who don't see that Confederate flag as being a shameful part of our history and heritage. But that's exactly what it is."

Like most people, Rivers was stunned by the video he saw of police officer Derek Chauvin killing George Floyd. He was just as stunned two months later, when a police officer in Kenosha, Wisconsin, pumped seven bullets into the back of Jacob Blake as he was trying to get into his car. If you believe the police version of the incident, Blake was a dangerous criminal intent on harming the police.

If you believe the video, it's clear that Blake is simply attempting to leave the scene. His three young sons were in the back seat of the car. As Blake leaned into his car, officer Rusten Sheskey, with another officer right behind him, fired seven shots at his back. Blake ended up paralyzed from the waist down. Sheskey was never charged with any crime and was returned to regular duty in the spring of 2021.

"The guy was trying to break up a fight," Rivers said. "If they wanted to arrest him, okay, fine, arrest him. But seven shots in the back? My dad always told me you pull your firearm if you think someone is in danger—another person or you. What danger was the guy to anybody at that moment? He had three little children in the car. Who was he going to harm?"

The Blake shooting, in the wake of the Floyd shooting—not to mention the killings of Ahmaud Arbery and Breonna Taylor—set off another round of protests and brought professional sports to a halt for two days. Players boycotted playoff games in the NBA and the NHL, and several Major League Baseball teams refused to play. Many NFL players walked out of their training camps.

The shooting took place the week of the Republican National Convention. Rivers had seen one speaker after another talking about the "fear" Americans needed to feel if Joe Biden were to be elected president.

When the playoffs resumed, Rivers was asked in a postgame press conference to talk about the Blake shooting. "It was just too much for me," Rivers said. "Kenosha is fifty miles from where I grew up. I'd seen the video, and there it was again, a white cop shooting a Black man in the back. It all got to me. Plus, I'd been listening to the Republicans and Trump talking about fear. Seriously?"

Rivers talked about Trump and the Republicans: "We're the ones who should feel fear. We're the ones getting shot, getting killed. We're the ones who in the past have been hung and killed. It's ridiculous that we have to deal with this sort of thing every day. What white father has to give his son a talk about being careful if you get pulled over? It's ridiculous."

He then said, "You don't need to be Black to be outraged watching that video. You need to be American watching that video to be outraged."

Rivers talked about his father being a cop. "I'm not saying we should defund the police, not at all," he said. "But police unions have to be taken down. We need to demand more. We need to train the police better. All we're asking is that they protect us, just like they protect everybody else. Do what the Constitution says they should do. I'm a coach. I should just be able to be a coach."

And then Rivers, choked up, delivered a line that resonated with millions: "It's amazing that we keep loving this country and this country doesn't love us back."

Months later, Rivers still gets emotional when the subject comes up.

"What I get sick and tired of hearing is that this is somehow a new phenomenon," he said. "That's laughable. I remember watching *Sanford and Son* back in the seventies, and there's a scene where Lamont [the son] is trying to get Fred [the father] to change his diet. He says to him that eating bad food is the number one killer of

Black men. Fred looks at him and says, 'Oh really? I always thought it was the police.'

"That's almost fifty years ago. I think I understand the way a lot of people with money in this country think. Imagine, you drive from a rich white suburb in Chicago to get to Comiskey Park [the White Sox home when Rivers was growing up], and you have to drive through some tough neighborhoods. You see people sitting outside, you figure there's drugs being sold, and you say to yourself, 'Why should I have to give money to help make these people have better lives?' You get angry about it; you think it's all terribly unfair.

"Well, here's the answer: Imagine a basketball game. One team gets to play the first three quarters without the other team on the court. They score and score. Then, at the start of the fourth quarter, the other team gets to play. When they say, 'Hey, we're so far behind, it's not fair,' the other team says, 'What are you complaining about? We're letting you play.'

"That's this country financially and educationally. We were slaves for two hundred and fifty years; we didn't get to play for three quarters. And now people say, 'What are you complaining about? You're free.' For the record, if 'freedom' is what existed in the fifties and sixties, thanks, I'll pass."

He paused. "I try to stay optimistic. But right now, I'd say I'm optimistic, realistically. I'm not exactly sure what that means, but that's the way I feel."

Steve Kerr wasn't coaching in the NBA in 2014 when Doc Rivers was dealing with "Sterling-gate" and it became a front-page story. He had spent several years successfully working for Turner Sports as a commentator on NBA games and on college basketball games during the NCAA tournament. Kerr was so good at the job that when CBS agreed to allow someone from Turner to join its Final Four announcing team, Kerr was their choice.

During that winter, Kerr started to think about getting back into the game in a more direct way—as a coach. He and his wife, Margot, were about to become empty nesters. The travel schedule of a coach didn't seem as daunting as it had in the past.

Kerr's story is a remarkable one. As a boy, he had spent time in Los Angeles and in Beirut and Cairo because his father, Malcolm Kerr, a college professor, had taught in all three places. When Steve was a senior in high school, Malcolm was named president of the American University in Beirut, which had been his dream job.

"We had a family meeting to discuss dad taking the job," Kerr, one of four children, remembered. "We all knew the Middle East was dangerous; we'd lived there. I remember my brother Mark saying, 'Dad, I don't want you to make Mom into a widow.' I wasn't thinking in those terms. We'd lived there in the past and knew the dangers, but the kind of thing Mark was talking about was something that happened to other people."

By then, Kerr was hooked on basketball and had become a very good player at Pacific Palisades High School. He and his family spent part of the year in Los Angeles and part of it in Beirut. As a high school senior, he was only lightly recruited by college teams. It was then that Jay Hillock, the coach at Gonzaga, came up with the line Kerr often used to describe himself as a player.

Kerr had gone to Gonzaga on a recruiting visit that had become a two-day tryout. When it was over, Hillock said to him, "Steve, you can really shoot. The problem is you're not a step slow, you're two steps slow."

Kerr amended the line as he got older: "You know I have deceptive speed," he would say. "Most people think I'm a step slow. I'm actually two steps slow."

That line is typical of Kerr's self-deprecating humor. At the last possible minute, he was offered a scholarship by new Arizona coach Lute Olson, who was taking over a team that had gone 4–24 the previous season and had lost a number of its best players — the definition of *best* being a loose one.

Olson had seen Kerr playing in a Los Angeles summer league while watching players who were about to be high school seniors. He noticed the kid making one jump shot after another and turned to his wife, Bobbi, who often accompanied him on scouting trips and said, "That kid can shoot."

"She laughed at me," Olson said years later. "When she realized I wasn't joking, she said, 'Lute, you can't be serious.'"

He was serious enough to offer Kerr a scholarship — but only after Malcolm Kerr had intervened when Olson didn't follow up on his initial contact with his son. He called Olson and said, "Are you interested in Steve or not?"

Olson had heard that Kerr was going to Cal State Fullerton. When Malcolm Kerr told him that Steve wanted to go to Arizona, Olson offered him his last scholarship. It proved to be one of the smarter coaching decisions he ever made.

As a freshman, Kerr was the third guard on a bad team — the Wildcats were 11–17, the only season during Olson's twenty-four-year tenure in Tucson that they failed to make the NCAA Tournament. On January 18, 1984, Kerr got a phone call in his dorm room. His "other people" theory had been proven tragically wrong.

His father had been murdered by members of the Palestinian

Liberation Organization, shot in the head twice as he walked down a hallway on his way to his office in Beirut.

What happened next has been written about (often by me) and talked about for years. Two nights later, Arizona, which was 3–11 at that point in the season, played archrival Arizona State, which had won nine straight games against the Wildcats. After talking to his mother, Kerr decided to play. "She said to me, 'There was nothing your dad enjoyed more than watching you play basketball,'" he remembered, years later. "I knew he would want me to play."

Before the game, Arizona planned a moment of silence in honor of Malcolm Kerr. Assistant coach Scott Thompson asked Kerr if he wanted to be in the locker room during the moment of silence or on the court.

"I want to be out there," Kerr said. The entire team went with him.

Not surprisingly, he broke down during the moment of silence, as did the Arizona coaches and his teammates—and many others inside the McKale Center. Eight minutes into the game, Kerr came into the game in his normal rotation. The first time he touched the ball, he drilled an eighteen-foot jump shot. Then he made another one. The game became a rout: Arizona, fueled by the emotion in the building, winning 71–49. Kerr, who averaged 3.7 points per game, scored 12 that evening.

A year later, Kerr was the starting point guard and Arizona made the NCAA Tournament for the first time since 1977. The following year, he was first team All-Pacific-10 and was chosen to play for the US team in the World Championships in Spain. During a semifinal victory over Brazil, Kerr tore the ACL in his knee. The ACL is still a very serious injury, but back then, it was potentially career-ending.

After returning home to Los Angeles, Kerr sent an open letter to Arizona fans thanking them for their support, adding, "I will be back for the 1987–88 season to help our team win a third straight Pac-10 title." He was as good as his word, coming back to lead the Wildcats to their first Final Four ever. What had been a 35–2 joyride ended with a national semifinal loss to Oklahoma. Kerr shot 3 of 12 in that game and, to this day, broods about that loss.

When I said something to him one day about how disappointed I knew he had been to shoot 3 of 11 in that game, he instantly said, "Three of twelve. Trust me, I remember."

No one, Kerr included, thought he would have much of an NBA career. "Just getting drafted [second round by Phoenix] and making a team was a big deal for me," he said. "But playing for fifteen years? Thought never occurred to me."

In those fifteen years, he played on five NBA championship teams—three in Chicago, two in San Antonio. He famously fought with Michael Jordan during Jordan's first practice with the Bulls after the superstar's first retirement before becoming close friends with him. In game 6 of the 1997 finals, he hit the shot that clinched the title for the Bulls.

"Michael turned to me during the last time-out and said, 'When they double me, I'm reversing the ball to you,'" Kerr said. "Then he pointed his finger and said, 'You better make it.' *That* was pressure."

Kerr made the shot; the Bulls won the title. Three years later, Kerr landed in San Antonio, where his coach was Gregg Popovich. There, he was a part of championship teams in 2000 and 2003.

"I'm not sure we win in '03 without Steve," Popovich said. "We were in a very tough series [the Western Conference finals] with Dallas, and [point guard] Tony Parker got hurt. Steve stepped in the last couple of games and played a key role in our winning. He made a bunch of threes in game six that, without them, we don't win the game."

Kerr made four three-pointers in the second half of that game, and the Spurs closed out a contentious series that night. They went on to beat the (then) New Jersey Nets, 4–1, in the finals.

Kerr was thirty-eight and figured that being part of another championship team was pretty close to the perfect way to retire. "By then my body was pretty beaten up," he said. "I'd worked really hard to be able to take the pounding you take playing in the NBA. I figured it was time."

He was able to jump right into TV work because of his outgoing personality and ease in front of the camera. Popovich remained both a friend and an important influence in his life. Kerr had played for, among others, Phil Jackson, but it was Popovich who became his role model—as a coach but even more so as a person.

Popovich has never been afraid to express an opinion—on anything, especially politics—and Kerr is much the same way. Kerr has always been an outspoken advocate for gun control—dating to his father's death—and has become more and more involved in political issues through the years.

In May 2010, as president and general manager of the Phoenix Suns, Kerr, along with managing partner Robert Sarver, decided to print the name "Los Suns" on the team uniforms for a playoff game against the Spurs. This move was in response to Arizona's controversial immigration law that required all immigrants to carry identification papers at all times. Kerr publicly compared the law to the politics of Nazi Germany. Popovich wanted to outfit his team in "Los Spurs" jerseys that same night but couldn't get them made in time for the game. Instead, Popovich endorsed what the Suns were doing and criticized the law.

In 2014–2015, Kerr's first season as the coach at Golden State, the Warriors won the NBA title. Like most professional sports teams who win a championship, they were invited to the White House by then president Barack Obama and happily accepted the invitation.

Two years later, after Donald Trump had been elected president and the Warriors won another NBA title, Kerr's star player, Stephen Curry, said he had no interest in visiting the White House as NBA champions. Trump promptly withdrew the Warriors invitation.

"It's not very likely that anyone on our team would have gone anyway," Kerr said, sitting at breakfast in Washington, D.C., on the very day the Warriors would have gone to the White House if they had accepted the invitation and hadn't been uninvited. "I think what we're going to do today will be a lot more fun and have a lot more meaning for everyone."

The Warriors spent the day with kids from the Boys and Girls Club in Prince George's County, Maryland, where Kevin Durant had grown up. They accompanied the kids to the Black History Museum in downtown Washington.

"One of the best days I can remember having," Kerr said later.

A year later, the Warriors won a third NBA title, and going to the White House wasn't even on the table. Kerr has often said that Trump won the election by playing on the biases of white men toward women and minorities. He also compared the behavior of Trump's supporters at campaign rallies to *The Jerry Springer Show*.

But the Kerr who publicly endorsed Joe Biden in October 2020 was a very different person from the Kerr who had been critical of Trump in the past. "George Floyd's death really changed me, really made me think," Kerr said. "I know I'm not the only one who had that sort of reaction. Watching that video was horrifying in a vacuum, but it also made me think about my attitude toward Black people and what they go through every single day of their lives. I played with Black kids growing up and, obviously, in college and in the NBA. But I never stopped to think about what their lives were like and how different they were from my life. The Floyd murder was like getting hit over the head. I realized how incredibly ignorant I had been."

Kerr's first memory of understanding the difference between being white and being Black came in 1974 when he watched Henry Aaron hit his 714th and 715th home runs. "I was eight and I remember how exciting it was to watch that," he said. "It was only later that I heard about all the death threats and racist letters he'd gotten. I always knew it was there, but never took the time to learn more about it.

"Even before the Floyd murder, I'd talked about what was going on with my staff. One of my assistants, Aaron Miles, told me a story about the aftermath of the Ahmaud Arbery murder in Georgia. He said his eight-year-old son walked in while he was watching the news, and before [Aaron] could change the channel or turn it off, [his son] heard the people on television saying that Arbery had been shot while out for a run. He said to his dad, 'Does this mean that we can't run in our neighborhood because we're Black?' Imagine having to explain that to your eight-year-old."

Arbery had been jogging through the Brunswick, Georgia, neighborhood where he lived on February 23, 2020, when three white men pursued him and shot him three times. The white men claimed that Arbery fit the description of someone who had been burglarizing homes in the neighborhood—without explaining why they hadn't called 911. Prosecutors initially failed to bring charges against the men. Only after a video of the shooting went viral in May did the Georgia Bureau of Investigation get involved, and the men were charged and arrested.

It turned out that one of the men had been heard saying "fucking nigger" while standing over Arbery's body. Several racial slurs were found on one of the men's phones, and there was a Confederate flag on the toolbox of one of the two trucks that had pursued Arbery.

"When Aaron told the story about his son, it really hit me over the head," Kerr said. "I never had to worry about anything like that. I never had to talk to my kids about being afraid in the neighborhood where we lived.

"One of my other assistants, Khalid Robinson, who grew up in Harlem, told me whenever he went for a run in Oakland, he made sure to make plenty of noise if he came up behind a white woman so as not to startle her when he went past her. In my entire life, when I've been out for a run, regardless of where it is, I've never worried about that. Khalid and I are about the same size, but I've never given any thought to the idea that my presence might frighten someone. He *has* to think about it.

"My hope is that what happened to Floyd turns out to be an aha moment, one of those things where we look back years from now and say *that* was when we started to have real dialogue on the issue; that was when we all had to stop and think. Lately, we've seen a lot more commercials with biracial couples. Twenty years ago, ten years ago, you would never have seen that. The same is true for gay couples. It's slow progress, very slow progress, but still, it's going in the right direction.

"If you think about the history of mankind, it's a fact that the world changes very slowly. We all know that. Muhammad Ali was hated in the sixties. So were Tommie Smith and John Carlos. I had Carlos come in and talk to our team because I wanted the players to understand that what he and Smith did in 1968 had helped to make their lives what they are today—they had taken a stand, and even though it took years, most reasonable people understand that now.

"I think the same will happen down the road with Colin Kaepernick. People will understand that what he did took courage and it brought about a dialogue — even if it was often an angry one — that was needed. He was sitting next to our bench last year in Portland, and I walked over to say hello and tell him how much I admired what he had done."

Stuck at home during the pandemic, Kerr went on a reading binge with books on race and racism, as did so many white, well-meaning allies. He read *White Fragility,* by Robin DiAngelo, and Isabel Wilkerson's *Caste,* among others.

"What I learned," he said, "was how much more I needed to learn.

"What's sad is that there are still lots and lots of people who don't get it — don't *want* to get it. I got an email from a woman the other day saying, 'Who are you to speak out on these issues?' I made a mistake and tried to engage with her. She insisted that Floyd was a criminal who had held a pregnant woman at gunpoint. Patently false, of course. Her angry racism was truly frightening. She was like the people who stormed the Capitol who think of themselves as patriots.

"Wow. You talk about a divide in our country. As far as we've come, we've still got miles and miles left to go. I think I understand that a lot more clearly now than I did a year ago. I'm embarrassed that I was as ignorant as I was. And I know I've still got a lot to learn."

Duke basketball coach Mike Krzyzewski, a Republican for most of his life, is also someone for whom Black men — as friends, players, and coaches — have been extremely important. Before the pandemic and the Floyd killing, he was much like Kerr, thinking he understood what it was like to be Black.

"I was wrong," he said, shortly before announcing that he would retire from coaching in the spring of 2022. "Really wrong. I wasn't just living in an ivory tower when it came to having a sense of what it was like to be Black; I was living *above* the ivory tower. If the building was twenty stories high, I lived my life on the twentieth floor."

For Krzyzewski, the realization began to hit when the pandemic began. He had long sessions with his assistant coaches, deciding how to handle the disappointment of their pandemic-shortened season and figuring out what needed to come next.

"All my assistants played for me, so I've known them a long time," he said. "Three of them were Black [Chris Carrawell, Nolan Smith, and Nate James, who has since left to become the head coach at Austin Peay]. They opened my eyes to a lot of things. Remember, I've coached kids for forty years who had the chance to go to Duke and, in most cases, graduate from Duke. The other group I coached were guys on the US National team who are all zillionaires. My thinking, which was naive, was, 'These guys have all had it pretty good' in terms of dealing with race.

"I should have been more aware. My dad used the name 'Cross' at work because so many people assumed things about someone who was Polish. And yet, I had missed the fact that racial abuse is a fact of life for almost anyone who is Black and is something they carry with them their entire lives."

After talking at length with his assistants, Krzyzewski decided to organize two Zoom sessions with his players—past and present. In all, about a hundred players took part.

"It was eye-opening, to say the least," he said. "I asked the guys to be very honest, and I think they were. Some were very emotional talking about their experiences. Some cried. They all talked about systemic racism they'd faced. All of them. It was intense. I'm not going to say there was an aha moment. It was just an education for me.

"That's why after the Floyd murder and after we did those Zoom sessions, I decided to do the Black Lives Matter video. I wanted people to know that I now had a better understanding of the issues and that I completely supported what the protesters were doing and why they were doing it and that it was important for more white people to figure out why BLM was so important."

Krzyzewski's video was posted on June 26, a month after the Floyd murder. There was no script. Instead, he asked Nolan Smith to stand next to the camera so he could speak to him and not speak to the camera.

The video was two minutes and forty-seven seconds long and both emotional and emphatic.

"Black Lives Matter," he began. "Say it. Can't you say it?" That line was directed at those refusing to say the words or insisting on saying "All Lives Matter."

He went on: "This isn't a political statement. This is a human rights statement, a fairness statement. I've had opportunities to learn in the last couple of months and so have you... This is a problem, a disease, a plague that has been with our country for four centuries."

There was more—about systemic racism, about the denial of opportunities to Black people, and the importance of acknowledging the problem. Krzyzewski then added a quote from the Cadet prayer he had learned at West Point more than fifty years earlier: "Help me choose the harder right instead of the easier wrong."

He concluded: "It is time to choose the harder right.... It's time. Black Lives Matter."

It was a powerful message—done in one take. More than 1.3 million people viewed the video, although not all agreed with it.

"There was backlash, certainly," Krzyzewski said. "I knew there would be. I got notes from some of my West Point classmates saying, 'How could you say those things?' I wrote back and said, 'If you knew what I now know, you'd feel exactly the same way.'

"It's important that more white guys come to understand this. One of the best things about the BLM protests was that a lot of white people were involved in them. There was some violence, but in the context of the whole summer, not that much.

"We *all* have to realize a simple truth: it's harder to be Black. A white person doesn't wake up and wonder how he's going to be judged that day and by whom—people he's never met. Their lives *are* different. I go crazy when I hear white people say that Blacks who succeed should be grateful for their success. Are you kidding me? That's BS. They were the ones who achieved, most of the time *in spite* of the way they were treated, certainly not *because* of it. You think players get opportunities because someone is trying to help them out? No. It is because someone thinks their team will be better if they're on that team. Period.

"I feel now like these are things I should have felt and understood years ago, but I didn't. Now, I do, and I'm going to work the rest of my life to try to make it better. I wish we could put an answer on speed dial, but we can't. We can't just say, 'Let's start anew,' because so many people have been abused for so many years. So, let's just dig in and work.

"We need to make a real effort to get more people into positions of authority in athletic departments and on professional teams. I'm not just talking coaches and athletic directors. I'm talking other positions that aren't as visible but are still very important. I thought for a long time we were making progress—and we were and are. But not nearly enough. We've got miles and miles to travel before we can even think about resting."

The Floyd murder wasn't an aha moment for Gregg Popovich. His had come a long time ago. He had lived in East Chicago until the sixth grade before moving a couple of towns over to Merrillville, Indiana—a few miles outside Chicago. His parents both worked in steel mills.

"I would go over to Gary and East Chicago to play basketball, usually by myself," he said. "I never thought twice about going alone. It was just what I did."

Popovich was recruited mostly by Division 3 schools in high school but had friends who were recruited by Army and by Air Force to play football. His mother came home one day with an Air Force Academy recruiting brochure. "It had an eagle on the cover and a picture of someone skiing on the inside cover," Popovich said. "I thought, 'Wow, this looks cool.'"

He decided to go to Air Force for the chance to play Division 1 basketball. "It had nothing to do with wanting to fly or be in the military," he said. "I wanted to see if I could play D-1 ball."

Like most plebes at any of the academies, he was miserable his first year. "It was like taking a fire hose, putting it in your mouth, and turning it on full blast," he said. "I hated it. I felt as if I repeated the phrase 'No excuse, sir,' about a hundred times a day."

He stuck it out and became a solid player, leading the Falcons in scoring as a senior. His life-changing moment, one he still remembers vividly, came during his junior year.

"We were playing out east, somewhere in North Carolina," he said. "I don't even remember who we were playing. We had a night off, and four of us went to a club. We were lined up to go in. I was last in line, and Jimmy Love, who was Black, was right in front of me. We got to the door, and the guy points at Jimmy and says, 'You can't come in.' We were stunned—which, looking back was probably pretty naive. This was 1968. The three of us got angry and started to argue. I mean, we were pissed, beside ourselves. Jimmy just said, 'It's fine, guys.' He even tried to convince us that we should go in without him. No way that was happening. We all left.

"That was the first time I realized how white I was. It just hit me over the head. I tell my players that if I was Black, I'd have probably been sent to jail on a number of occasions.

"It's disgusting the way some white people—far too many white people—look at Black people. The racism level in this country ratcheted up when President Obama was elected, and it peaked on January sixth at the Capitol.

"What's going on now is much more insidious than what went on in the fifties and sixties during the Civil Rights Movement. Back then, racists got right in your face and tried to tell Black people that they were somehow inferior. That dates to the Civil War. White people felt it was their right to grant any sort of equality to Black people. Jim Crow was still legal until the midsixties. There's this constant perpetuation of whites as being somehow superior. It's gone on for hundreds of years, and it's still going on.

"Now, you've got Republicans out there passing voter suppression laws and trying to claim it's about fairness. Are you kidding? Nothing they do is about fairness. That's the problem: Democrats are always trying to be fair. Republicans will cut your heart out to get their way. A lot of times, it works.

"Sometimes, I get very down about what's going on and what's coming next. But then I have moments where I think there's hope, some hope at least. I think we're doing a better job in the NBA than we've ever done. Do I wish that [Spurs assistant coach] Becky Hammon would get hired as a head coach because she's more than qualified? Yes. Now, unfortunately, when she gets interviewed, it's just so someone can say, 'Hey, look, we interviewed a woman.'

"But we *do* have progressive leadership in the league. I was in New York a few years ago after our season ended, and I was walking around on a Sunday afternoon. I look up, and here comes a parade. I stop to watch. It's the Gay Pride parade. I stood there and watched the floats go by me. And here comes one, and who is on top of it? Adam Silver. I was so proud of him. I stood there and thought, 'That's the commissioner of my league, a league that's not perfect, but is at least progressive.'

"Adam is smart and he's progressive and he's empathetic. He gives me hope—at least within the context of the NBA. But looking at where we are as a country right now, I wonder about the future. The recent past certainly hasn't been encouraging."

There are those who will point out that the NBA embarrassed itself when Houston Rockets general manager Daryl Morey posted a tweet in October 2019 supporting protesters in Hong Kong: "Fight for Freedom. Stand with Hong Kong."

The NBA's first reaction to the tweet was to grovel at the feet of the Chinese government. An official NBA statement called Morey's tweet "regrettable." There was instant backlash—especially from the right wing—to those comments. How could the NBA call itself progressive and talk about how proud it was that players were frequently outspoken on political issues, but the minute someone said something that might have a negative economic impact on the league, Silver and others appeared to be rushing to apologize to an authoritarian government?

It was a legitimate question. The NBA does a great deal of business in China, which is a basketball-mad country. Silver clarified the league's comments a few days later, saying the NBA would never tell anyone what to say—or not say. But he also said the Chinese government had the right to react negatively to what Morey had said.

"I made the point that we [the NBA] supported Daryl's right and [the right of] anyone connected to the league...to speak out on any issue," Silver said. "Remember, it was Daryl who took the tweet down. We never told him to do that. He wasn't fired.

"I'm a little baffled by the right attacking us for doing business with China. A lot of American companies do business with China, and China isn't exactly the only country in the world with authoritarian issues. We probably should not have used the word *regret* in our initial statement. Beyond that, I'm okay with how we handled it."

Regardless of Silver's intent, the Chinese went ballistic. They canceled all business with the Rockets—the team that Chinese hero Yao Ming had played for—and stopped televising NBA games in China for a year. They even went so far as to demand that Silver have Morey fired, which he didn't have the authority to do and would not have done, regardless.

One year after the tweet, Morey stepped down as Rockets GM after twelve mostly successful seasons. No doubt the tweet, not any playoff failures, was the primary reason for the separation. Three weeks later, the Philadelphia 76ers gave Morey a five-year contract for $10 million a year to become president of basketball operations.

Not surprisingly, Kerr was asked for his reaction to Morey's tweet soon after it happened. Like almost everyone in the league, he dodged the question, saying he didn't feel he knew enough about the China–Hong Kong situation to comment. The right wing couldn't line up fast enough to pillory him — and LeBron James, among others — for not speaking up when money was involved.

"They were right," Kerr said in April 2021. "I fucked up. I should have supported Daryl right from the start. Even if I disagreed with him — which I didn't — I should have supported him. The funny thing is, for all the groveling we did as a league, the Chinese didn't forgive anyone at all. It was, 'How dare you criticize us in any way.' We all should have spoken up because it was the right thing to do. Plus, as it turned out, staying quiet didn't do any good anyway in a business sense. So we blew that one."

The China incident was a bit like LeBron James's tweet right after Derek Chauvin was found guilty on three counts of murder for killing George Floyd. His tweet showed an officer at the scene of the shooting of sixteen-year-old Ma'Kia Bryant with the caption "you're next" — which was clearly directed at the police officer. The tweet included the hashtag #accountability, the point being that in the future, cops who killed Black people would be held accountable. Naturally, some chose to take the tweet as James saying that the next person to be shot for no reason would be a police officer.

James took the tweet down quickly and then tweeted: "I'm so damn tired of seeing Black people killed by the police. I took the tweet down because it's being used to create more hate — this isn't about one officer. It's about the entire system and they always use our words to create more racism. I am so desperate for more ACCOUNTABILITY."

James's prediction that the original tweet would be used to create more hate and racism was accurate. The right-wing media ran amok with the tweet, making James the story rather than the continued shootings of Black people. One famous golfer texted a copy of the tweet to friends and added, "James is an ignorant, racist, goon."

James is none of those things. He was, as he said, frustrated that Black people continue to be shot by police. But right-wingers weren't concerned about that. They wanted to make James's tweet — not people dying at the hands of the police — the issue.

"It's called misdirection," Doc Rivers said. "They don't want you to look at the real problem, so they jump up and down and say *this* is the issue. LeBron was right. The tweet gave the right an excuse to change the subject. They're very good at that."

PART THREE

BASEBALL AND OTHER PASTIMES

CHAPTER ELEVEN

Baseball

E VERY YEAR, ON APRIL 15, Major League Baseball honors Jackie Robinson. It was on April 15, 1947, that Robinson made his debut for the Brooklyn Dodgers and broke the color line that had existed in baseball since 1889, when baseball unofficially banned Black players because of Jim Crow laws. Before then, Moses Fleetwood Walker had played for the Toledo Blue Stockings, who were part of the American Association — the league that later became the American League.

It wasn't until Dodgers general manager Branch Rickey famously signed Robinson and brought him to Brooklyn, after a year with Triple-A Montreal, that Black players — Negroes in those days — were allowed back into baseball. Integrating the game was a slow process: only in 1959 — three years after Robinson had *retired* — did Elijah Jerry "Pumpsie" Green make the Boston Red Sox the last of baseball's sixteen teams to put a Black player into uniform. The Detroit Tigers had integrated a few months earlier, when they traded for Larry Doby, who had been the first Black player in the American League when he played for the Cleveland Indians — three months after Robinson's debut in Brooklyn. The fabled New York Yankees first signed a Black player—catcher Elston Howard—in 1955.

The racism that Robinson dealt with—including from some of his Brooklyn teammates—has been well documented in books and movies. In 1997, baseball decided to honor him once a year by having all players wear his number—42—on April 15. It was also decided that the number would be retired throughout baseball once those who were wearing it at the time retired. The last MLB player to wear 42 on a regular basis was Mariano Rivera, who retired after the 2013 season. In a twist that seems to fit, Rivera was the first player ever elected unanimously to the Hall of Fame.

Even though baseball honors Robinson's legacy, the number of Black players in the sport has dropped sharply in the last thirty-five years. In 1986, almost 20 percent of MLB's players were Black—lower than the NFL or the NBA, but still a healthy number. Since then, the ratio of Black players has dropped to as low as 6 percent. In 2020, MLB proudly announced that the number had climbed back to almost 8 percent. The largest number of minority players in the game—by far—are from Latin America. For the past several years, the percentage of players from Latin America has hovered at about 27 percent.

Some of these numbers have to do with logistics: while it is easy to find a basketball court to play on almost anywhere, baseball diamonds—especially decent ones—can be harder to find in city settings. Football is different because, even though there aren't a lot of football fields not directly connected to a school anywhere, finding a handful of kids to play football is easy. It can be done anytime with four kids, two on two. You need at least a dozen kids to get any kind of baseball game started.

There is—always—the issue of money. More and more white

parents are spending money to pay for their kids to be on travel teams, forking over thousands of dollars and often starting when they are nine or ten years old. Parents are frequently told that this is the starting point for their kids to play in high school, college, or—perhaps someday—the big leagues.

Baseball has made efforts to get more Black kids involved in the game through clinics and city leagues, but the results, so far, have been minimal.

"When I was young, growing up in Brooklyn, I played with a lot of Black and Latino kids," said Willie Randolph, who played in the major leagues for seventeen full seasons and later managed the New York Mets. "But when I got older and started playing American Legion ball, there were a lot more white kids than Black kids. Our team was, for the most part, Black and Puerto Rican kids. When we played teams from other neighborhoods, mostly white teams, there was always a simmering animosity. But it never really got out of hand. We all wanted to play ball, not fight with one another.

"I stuck with baseball because I was really too small to play football or basketball at a high level. For me, baseball was a chance to get out of the ghetto when I got older."

As a high school senior in 1972, Randolph was picked in the seventh round of the MLB draft by the Pittsburgh Pirates and was sent to Pirate City in Bradenton, Florida, where the Pirates had a rookie league team.

"They gave me five thousand dollars to sign," Randolph said with a laugh. "I was seventeen. I thought I was a millionaire."

It was in Bradenton that, for the first time, he occasionally encountered white people who clearly didn't want to be anywhere near Black people. It helped that one of his coaches was Gene Baker, who had played in the Negro Leagues and was willing to spend extra time with a willing pupil. By the time he was nineteen, Randolph had reached Triple-A ball. In 1975, he was a late-season call-up on a Pittsburgh team that won the National League East before losing to the Cincinnati Reds, the Big Red Machine, in the National League Championship Series.

That winter, he was traded—along with pitchers Ken Brett and Doc Ellis—to the Yankees for Doc Medich, in one of baseball's more one-sided trades. Randolph was the Yankees starting second baseman for thirteen seasons, making six all-star teams and playing on two World Series champion teams and four American League champion teams.

His final big-league season was in 1992—with the Mets—and he finished his career with 2,211 hits. The question for him after he turned down an invitation to go to camp with the Yankees in 1993 was what to do next.

Randolph was one of those players for whom Steinbrenner always had a soft spot. It was Steinbrenner who had invited him to come to the Yankees camp in 1993. When Steinbrenner offered him a chance to coach, Randolph decided to see if he would like it.

Randolph worked with a lot of young players early on, notably a rising young shortstop named Derek Jeter. He ended up being Joe Torre's bench coach during the Yankees renaissance, when they won four World Series titles in five seasons and reached the postseason thirteen times in a row. Randolph was there for ten of those seasons, and after a few years with Torre, he was convinced he had what it took to be a manager.

"I can't even remember how many jobs I interviewed for," he said. "I'm pretty sure it was at least ten—maybe more. Some of them, I knew when I walked out the door that I had just been there so the team could say 'We interviewed a minority' before they hired whoever it was they wanted to hire. It got frustrating after a while — very frustrating. I got to the point when I would get a call and I would say, 'If you're just interviewing me to say you interviewed a minority, find someone else.' I didn't want to prepare for the interview, get on a plane, and fly someplace and then find out I never really had a chance for the job.

"After we won the '99 World Series, I got a call from Dan O'Dowd in Colorado to interview for their manager's job. I was ready to fly out there when he called again and said, 'Look, Willie, I'm going to be honest with you, we're going to hire Buddy Bell. Can we just do a phone interview so I can honestly say I interviewed you?' I told him, 'Dan, let's not and say we did.'

"I remember before I went to interview with the Phillies [before the 2001 season], Claire Smith [who covered the Yankees for the *New York Times*] told me I was wasting my time, that they were going to hire Larry Bowa. I went anyway. I thought I had knocked their socks off. Maybe I did. Didn't matter. They hired Bowa."

Major League Baseball had informally created the so-called Selig Rule — named for then commissioner Bud Selig — in 1999. It was a forerunner of the NFL's Rooney Rule, but for a long time, its major impact seemed to be to give men like Randolph token interviews for jobs.

The number of Black managers was still minimal. Frank Robinson had been hired as a player-manager in Cleveland in 1974 and had gone on to manage the San Francisco Giants; the Baltimore Orioles; and the Montreal Expos, who became the Washington Nationals. Dusty Baker, still managing today in Houston, was first hired in San Francisco in 1993.

Since then, most who have managed major league teams have

gotten one shot and one shot only — Lloyd McClendon did manage the Pirates and then the Mariners. Remarkably, in 2014, McClendon was the only Black MLB manager. Now, there are two: Baker and Dave Roberts, who won a World Series for the Dodgers in 2020.

Randolph remembers interviews in the early 2000s that went on at great length. During these encounters, he became convinced the interviewers were just trying to milk him for information on the Yankees success — specifically Joe Torre's formula that had brought the team so many championships.

"After a while I wanted to say, 'Look, if you want to pay me a consulting fee, fine, but that's not what I'm here for,'" Randolph said.

Not surprisingly, when Randolph's chance finally came, it was another nonwhite official who gave him the opportunity. Omar Minaya had been named general manager of the Mets at the end of the 2004 season. Previously, he had been baseball's first Latino GM, running the Montreal Expos while they were still owned by Major League Baseball.

Minaya's three biggest moves of his first off-season with the Mets were to sign Carlos Beltran and Pedro Martinez as free agents and to hire Randolph as his manager.

"I could tell during the interview that this was different than my other interviews," Randolph said. "The team that Omar was shaping had a lot of Latinos and Blacks on it. He wanted someone who could relate to those guys, and it was clear he thought I was the right fit."

Randolph was the right fit. Under Art Howe in 2004, the Mets had gone 71–91. In Randolph's first season, they were 83–79. A year later, in 2006, they were 97–65 and ran away with the National League East, breaking the Atlanta Braves' eleven-year stranglehold on the division. The Mets then swept the Dodgers in the National

League Division Series before losing in seven games to the St. Louis Cardinals in the league championship series.

Game 7 ended with the Mets trailing 3–1 in the bottom of the ninth with the bases loaded and Beltran, their best hitter, at the plate. On an 0–2 pitch from Adam Wainwright, Beltran never took the bat off his shoulder as strike three sailed past him.

A year later, the Mets led the division by 7 games with 17 games to play, only to end the season 5–12, allowing the second-place Phillies, who went 13–4, to finish 1 game ahead of them. Randolph became the fall guy for the collapse. When the team started 34–35 a year later, he was fired.

"The way they did it was messed up," Randolph said, anger still in his voice thirteen years later. "We'd had a tough start, and we had some injuries. But we were starting to get it together. You know how New York is; there are always rumblings and rumors. I'd heard them. Before we left for the West Coast trip, I went to Omar and said, 'Look, if you're going to make a change, do it now before I get on the plane and fly coast to coast.' He said, 'No, you're all right, you're fine.' So, I went west, and we won three of four, and we *won* the night I got fired.

"Omar called me in after that game [in Los Angeles]. I thought, 'Uh-oh, I'm going to have to fight for [pitching coach Rick] Peterson and [first base coach Tom] Nieto.' Omar was all over the place, and it suddenly occurred to me that he wasn't talking about Peterson and Nieto. I said, 'Omar, are you firing me?'

"He hemmed and hawed and finally said, 'Yeah, yeah, we're making a change.' I couldn't believe it."

To this day, Randolph and most others believe that Minaya was carrying out orders from Jeff Wilpon, the trust-fund son of Mets owner Fred Wilpon, who had been handed the keys to the Mets castle by his father in 2002. Jeff Wilpon was infamous in baseball circles for meddling with the team, and Randolph's firing appeared to be another example.

"Look," Randolph said, "the Mets were the ones who gave me an opportunity. I really believe we were going to continue to get better. [David] Wright and [José] Reyes were young players who were only going to keep improving. Having grown up in New York, I was proud of the fact that Omar and I were the first minority combination leading a team in the city and having success. Maybe we had too much success too quickly. They had won seventy-one games the year before I got there. In my second year, we won ninety-seven and just missed the World Series. That certainly turned up expectations.

"When it ended, I was surprised and hurt. But I thought I'd learned a lot as a first-time manager and it would benefit me in my next job."

It never occurred to Randolph that there would be no next job. Baseball managers are recycled more than coaches in any other sport. Jeff Torborg, one of Randolph's predecessors with the Mets, managed five major league teams and had a winning record with only one of them (the White Sox, where he went 250–235). He never won a division title but kept getting rehired because he was an extremely nice guy. Similarly, the Yankees job was Torre's fourth of five. Among the thirty men managing MLB teams at the start of 2021, *ten* were on at least their second jobs. Only one of those, Houston Astros Dusty Baker, was nonwhite.

Baker, though, has won everywhere he has managed, making the postseason ten times in twenty full seasons in San Francisco, Chicago (with the Cubs), Cincinnati, and Washington before being hired in Houston in the spring of 2020 in the wake of the Astros sign-stealing scandal. The Astros were desperate for a manager with a sterling reputation after the scandal sullied their 2017 World Series title. The manager of that 2017 team, A. J. Hinch, was hired by the Detroit Tigers about fifteen minutes after his one-year suspension from baseball ended. Those who win — Black or white — get hired and rehired, regardless of how they win. (See Pitino, Rick, in college basketball.)

Unlike many of baseball's recycled managers, Randolph had a winning record (302–253) and, as a person, was liked by everyone who ever worked with him. There is also the fact that the Mets had losing records every year from 2009 to 2014 after his departure.

And yet, Randolph has only been seriously considered for another managerial job once — in 2009, when he and Ken Macha were the two finalists for the Milwaukee Brewers job. General manager Doug Melvin hired Macha — who had been drafted by the Pirates one round earlier than Randolph in 1972 — and asked Randolph to be Macha's bench coach. Two years later, Macha was fired and, instead of hiring Randolph to replace him, Melvin hired Ron Roenicke without interviewing Randolph. Melvin's Selig Rule interview was with Joey Cora, then a White Sox coach.

Alex Cora (Joey's younger brother), who was Hinch's bench coach in Houston in 2017, led the Red Sox to a World Series title the next season and, like Hinch, was suspended for the 2020 season. He was rehired by the Red Sox as soon as his suspension was lifted. He replaced Ron Roenicke, who, in his second chance as a manager, had steered the Sox to last place during the pandemic-shortened season.

Randolph worked for Buck Showalter in Baltimore for one season but hasn't been a manager or a coach in the majors since the 2011 season.

"Honestly, I don't understand it," he said. "We [he and Minaya] turned the Mets around. I'll take the hit for what happened at the end of 2007, but do you judge someone's entire career on seventeen bad games? I don't think I've been an asshole; that's not it. So what is it?"

Randolph has never thought or claimed that his firing in New York had anything to do with race. In fact, Jerry Manuel, his successor, is also Black. The Mets have hired four nonwhite managers—Randolph, Manuel, Carlos Beltran (who resigned without ever having managed a game after his role in the Astros sign-stealing scandal was revealed), and current manager Luis Rojas. Their New York counterparts, the Yankees, on the other hand, have never had a Black manager.

In 1972, in what turned out to be his final public appearance, Jackie Robinson spoke to the crowd in Cincinnati before game 2 of the World Series.

"I am extremely proud and pleased to be here this afternoon," Robinson said. "But I must admit I am going to be tremendously more pleased and more proud when I look at the third base coaching line one day and see a Black face managing in baseball."

Robinson went on to name three men who he thought would make good managers: Frank Robinson, who had managed in winter league ball in Puerto Rico, and Jim Gilliam and Elston Howard, who were among the ten Black men who had been MLB coaches.

Jackie Robinson didn't live to see a Black manager in the majors. Nine days after speaking in Cincinnati, he died from a heart attack brought on by a long battle with diabetes. In 1974, Frank Robinson, still a player, was named to manage the Cleveland Indians.

In 2021—seventy-four years after Jackie Robinson's debut as a player and forty-seven years after Frank Robinson's debut as a manager, there were two Black men managing in the major leagues on

Jackie Robinson Day: Dave Roberts of the world champion Los Angeles Dodgers and Baker, in Houston. There were four Hispanic managers: Rojas with the Mets, Davey Martinez with the Nationals, Charlie Montoyo with the Blue Jays, and Cora, back with the Red Sox.

Progress? Sort of...maybe

Becoming a nonwhite general manager is even more challenging in baseball these days. As the 2021 season began, three nonwhite people held positions of authority in major league front offices: Kenny Williams became the White Sox general manager in 2001 and is now the team's executive vice president. Kim Ng became the first woman to be named a general manager when the Miami Marlins hired her during the off-season. And Al Avila has been the Detroit Tigers general manager since 2015.

Ng (pronounced "Na") was hired by Derek Jeter, the CEO of the Marlins. The former shortstop turned part owner is the only non-white person in an ownership or CEO role in the sport.

The first Black general manager in baseball was Bill Lucas, who was hired as the GM of the Atlanta Braves in 1976 and held the job until he died of a cerebral hemorrhage in 1979 at the age of forty-three. It wasn't until 1994 that Bob Watson became the second Black GM, when he was hired by the Houston Astros. Two years later, Watson was hired by the Yankees, and when the Yankees won the World Series in 1996, he became the first Black general manager to win a championship. A year later, he left the Yankees to work for Major League Baseball.

When Dave Stewart retired from baseball in 1996, he knew he wanted to be a general manager. It took him eighteen years to get the chance.

"But then I never did anything quickly or easily," he joked.

Stewart's nickname was "Smoke," which he earned in high school, not because he threw smoke on the pitcher's mound but because he threw it from his position as a catcher.

He grew up in Oakland, the son of David, a longshoreman, and Nathalie, who worked in a cannery and was a three-sport athlete in high school.

"My first love was football," he said. "But baseball was second. I liked basketball too, and to be honest, I was pretty good at all three of them. For a long time, my plan was to go to college and play football."

Stewart's father was a baseball fan, and Dave vividly remembers the first time his dad took him to a baseball game in San Francisco. "It was 1963, so I was six," he said. "The Pirates were in town. It was Bat Day. I got to see Willie Mays and Roberto Clemente. And, after the game, we waited around until Willie came out, and he signed my bat."

David Stewart was a baseball fan, but the thought that his son might grow up to be a baseball player was, as far as he was concerned, out of the question. Dave remembered his father's attitude: "Someone asked me at some point what I wanted to do when I grew up. I said I wanted to be a baseball player. My dad was there, and he looked at me and said, 'You're an idiot. You aren't going to make a living hitting a ball with a stick.'"

As it turned out, the father was right: the son ended up making a living throwing a ball that men holding a stick only rarely hit.

Dave Stewart's plan to play college football changed when he was recruited by a number of big-time schools—USC, Cal-Berkeley, and Oklahoma among them—and had a chance to get a close-up look at some of the players. "I was a linebacker and a tight end," he said. "I was six two and weighed maybe one eighty. No way could I compete with the size those guys had. I decided I needed to focus on baseball."

The Dodgers selected him in the sixteenth round of the 1975 draft. "I didn't even know I'd been drafted until my sister Carolyn noticed it in the *Oakland Tribune* the next day," he said, laughing. "It was a couple more days before I heard from them."

The team offered him $3,000 to sign. Stewart pointed out he could still go play football and baseball in college. The offer eventually grew to $22,000, and Stewart signed. It was when he arrived for rookie ball in Bellingham, Washington, that he found out the Dodgers wanted him to be a pitcher.

"At first I refused," he said. "I honestly thought it was a joke. Bill Berrier was the manager. He told me I had two choices: pitch or go home. Actually, I should have seen it coming. They'd sent me to a workout camp before I signed, and I caught for three innings and pitched for one. So I should have realized they were at least thinking about converting me."

Stewart's first two years were miserable. He couldn't throw strikes, and he didn't win a single game. After the 1976 season, the Dodgers sent him to Vero Beach, Florida, where he was assigned to work with Sandy Koufax.

"I honestly didn't realize when I first got there that I was working with a Hall of Famer," he said. "He acted like he'd just been another pitcher with control problems early in his career. He broke my mechanics down completely. I mean, we went to square one."

It was Koufax who first told Stewart to pull his cap as low as he could. That look became his signature: cap pulled low, glaring in at the batter, a picture of intimidation.

"That was never the intent," Stewart said. "He told me to pull my cap low to cut down on my field of vision. He wanted me to see the batter only from the shoulders down because that's where I needed to throw the ball. Everything he told me worked. He turned my career around."

In 1977, Stewart went 17–4 pitching in the Midwest League— with a 2.15 ERA—and then won his only start in Double-A. Late in 1978, after a solid season with Double-A San Antonio, he threw two shutout innings in September for the Dodgers.

And then, things got murky again. He spent the next two seasons at Triple-A Albuquerque and finally made the Dodgers out of spring training in 1981, beating out Don Stanhouse for the final spot on the pitching staff. He pitched mostly in relief during that strike-interrupted season and was part of the Dodgers World Series winning team.

The next five seasons he was both a starter and a reliever. He was traded to Texas in 1983 and then to the Phillies in 1985. Two important things happened to him while he was in Texas. First, pitching coach Tom House taught him to throw a forkball, the pitch that would make him a star a few years later. And second, he was involved in an ugly racial incident that he never forgot.

Stewart had been exposed to little racism as a kid in Oakland. He had played on all-Black teams until high school and then played on integrated teams in high school. "Never once heard anyone direct the word *nigger* at me," he said. "I was aware of what was going on from watching TV. I remember when Martin Luther King was shot vividly."

One night, however, as his father stood near a picture window in the Stewarts' house, a rock crashed through the window. Remarkably, no one was hurt. The Stewarts learned later that the rock had been thrown by a police officer. "I have no idea why we were targeted," he said. "I asked my dad why he didn't follow up and file a report and he shrugged and said, 'Do you really think anything would have happened?'"

It was while playing minor league ball in the South that Stewart first heard the N-word directed at him. "I was with San Antonio and we were coming out of a restaurant in Jackson [Mississippi] late one night, and a car tried to run us down. As it went by, one of the guys rolled down his window and shouted, 'Niggers don't need to eat on this side of town.'"

The ugly incident in Texas happened years later, in 1985. Stewart had given up a late home run to lose a game, and as he walked to the dugout, he heard a fan in the front row screaming, "Get out of town, nigger. Go live with the other spear-chuckers!"

"I snapped," Stewart said. "I was ready to go after him, but Buddy Bell and Toby Harrah grabbed me and got me into the dugout and the clubhouse. Buddy said to me, 'Go sit in the training room for a while. Cool off. Do *not* talk to the media right now. You'll say something you'll regret.'

"I didn't listen. Guys came to my locker, and after a few questions about the game, someone said it looked like I was ready to go into the stands after the guy who was yelling at me. I said, 'These god-dang fans: this is what happens when you put a little alcohol in them. They're a bunch of cowboys and rednecks. They go home and screw their cows and beat their wives.'

"Probably went too far with that last sentence, but I really didn't care at that moment."

Eddie Chiles, the owner of the Rangers, cared. He told Stewart to apologize. Stewart said no. Then Bobby Valentine, the manager (who had the same agent as Stewart), told the pitcher he needed to apologize, or "There would be trouble."

Stewart wasn't backing down. Valentine hadn't been kidding. In early September, Stewart was traded to Philadelphia. Pitching strictly out of the bullpen, he floundered and was released by the Phillies in May 1986. That turned out to be the best break of his career.

The Orioles asked him to come to Baltimore for a workout. "They told me they were looking for someone to pitch in Double-A," Stewart said. "But they decided not to sign me."

As luck would have it, the Athletics were in Baltimore during Stewart's workout, and general manager Sandy Alderson was intrigued. Jackie Moore, the manager, and Wes Stock, the pitching coach, were not as intrigued. But Alderson had heard that Bill Lajoie, the general manager of the Tigers, was interested in signing Stewart.

"Sandy told me later that when he heard Lajoie might sign me, he said, 'Heck with it. Let's sign him,'" Stewart said. "After he signed me, he told me that Moore and Stock weren't wild about the idea. I'm glad he told me that, because I didn't understand why I wasn't being used at all."

Stewart was signed on May 23 and got one start in the next month. On June 19, the White Sox fired Tony La Russa as their manager. Roland Hemond, who had hired La Russa in 1979, had been fired and was replaced by Ken "Hawk" Harrelson, who decided to fire La Russa and pitching coach Dave Duncan on the same day. That decision proved to be a disaster for the White Sox and a boon for the Athletics — and for Stewart.

Nine days after the La Russa sacking, Alderson fired Moore and Stock and, on July 7, replaced them with La Russa and Duncan. La Russa's choice to start his first game as manager? Dave Stewart.

"He remembered that I'd pitched a shutout against the White

Sox when I was in Texas," Stewart said. "And since I'd only pitched once since they signed me, I was the freshest arm on the staff."

The Red Sox were the opponent. Roger Clemens, who was 14–1, was Boston's starting pitcher. The A's and Stewart won 6–4.

With Duncan encouraging him to use the forkball he had learned from House more often, and with La Russa giving him the ball every fifth day, Stewart became Oakland's best pitcher. He was 9–5 the second half of 1986 and then won at least 20 games for the next four seasons. He was the pitcher the A's always gave the ball to for game 1 of any postseason series. The Athletics made postseason four years out of five from 1988 through 1992, going to the World Series three times, winning it once.

During that stretch, Stewart was 8–3 in the postseason with a 2.65 ERA, and was the MVP of the 1989 World Series. The Athletics swept the Giants 4–0 in that series, Stewart going 2–0 with a 1.69 ERA. That series was most remembered because of the devastating earthquake in the Bay Area that occurred just prior to the start of game 3 in San Francisco and caused a weeklong postponement. Stewart spent much of that time bringing food to people left homeless in Oakland. He continued that work after the series was over.

"It was devastating," he said. "I was working at a site right near where I grew up. People died; people lost their homes, everything. [If] you live in the Bay Area, earthquakes aren't that unusual, but this one was on another level. There was only so much any of us could do to help. I didn't sleep very much during that stretch."

Stewart left the A's after the 1992 season. The team was cutting payroll, and the Toronto Blue Jays, who had just won the World Series, offered him $8.5 million for two years — far more than the A's were willing to pay. He was part of another World Series champion team in 1993 and retired after the 1995 season, with an overall record of 168–129.

To this day, many people think his nickname — "Smoke" — came from how hard he threw as a pitcher, but in fact, it came from his high school days as a catcher. Actually, he didn't throw especially hard. His best weapon was his forkball, which he could throw in about four different ways at all different speeds. That is what kept batters off-balance.

There is also the image: Stewart peering out from under his cap, glaring in at the batter, a picture of intimidation. The off-field Stewart could not be more different from that image. He is outgoing, friendly, and thoughtful with a high-pitched voice and laugh.

While he was playing in Oakland, Stewart had become friends with team owner Walter "Wally" Haas Jr. They had lunch together about once a month and talked about life and family and baseball and what Stewart thought he wanted to do after baseball. Stewart told Haas he'd like to be an executive, to work in a front office. When Stewart retired, Haas passed that information on to Alderson, who quickly hired Stewart as an assistant general manager.

"He told me I had to spend time in the office, learn about budgets and administration and how to hire a staff," Stewart said. "I already knew baseball. I had to learn the rest."

He learned it well enough that Kevin Towers offered him a job in San Diego as his number two man. By then, Stewart and family were living in San Diego — "I like warm weather," he said — and he had young kids. Reluctantly, he left Oakland because he felt that San Diego was a step up and a chance to work in a city he wanted to live in. Two years later, Stewart was hired by Gord Ash in Toronto. In 2001, when Ash was fired, Stewart thought it was his time to become a general manager.

It wasn't.

Blue Jays CEO Paul Godfrey hired J. P. Ricciardi, who was Billy Beane's chief scout — director of player personnel — in Oakland.

"That was the first time in my post-baseball career that I ran smack into racism," Stewart said. "There was no comparison in our résumés. J.P. was a glorified scout, nothing more. He had no real front-office experience. I had worked for three very good general managers, I had established the Padres Dominican Academy, the list went on. I had run the minor league system for teams. I was angry.

"So I quit. I wasn't going to work for a guy who wasn't as qualified as I was. What really pissed me off was when Godfrey came in as I was cleaning my office out and said, 'Ricciardi was the best guy for the job.' I told him that was BS and he knew it."

Stewart worked in Milwaukee as the Brewers pitching coach for a year but resigned after Davey Lopes, who hired him, was fired. He then became an agent, a job he enjoyed. "Allowed me to be around the game and around players," he said. "I think I was pretty good at it too."

The agent stint lasted until December 2014, when La Russa, who had become the chief baseball officer (English translation: team president) for the Diamondbacks, offered him the general manager's job. Stewart couldn't resist the chance to finally prove what he could do running a team.

But he only lasted two seasons. "The problem was, they gave me the title but not the responsibility," Stewart said. "I did *not* want to sign Zach Greinke, but they insisted he was a franchise changer. He certainly changed the salary structure: his contract was one-third of our payroll. I still thought we'd done some good things and were on the right track when we [he and manager Chip Hale] got fired after 2016. The team made the playoffs the next season, so we must have done something right."

Stewart now works for Wally Haas on a youth program Haas started twenty-five years ago. He also does pre- and postgame shows for the A's. He's sixty-four and he's happy, but he still wonders if things might have been different if he'd gotten a chance in Toronto (the Blue Jays never made postseason in Ricciardi's eight years as GM) or if he'd been given more time in Arizona.

"I'll never know what might have happened in either situation," he said. "Look, I've been lucky through most of my life, but being Black definitely makes things different. I was stopped in Los Angeles once for running a red light I didn't run. I'd done two things wrong: I was driving a nice car and I was Black. It's part of the deal. I've talked to other guys about it. The first question is always the same: where'd you get this car?

"Look at the number of Black guys working in positions of authority in baseball. As far as I know, Derek Jeter is the only Black guy who has final say with any of the thirty organizations. Kenny Williams has a lot of authority with the White Sox—which he earned. That's about it. I agree with people who say it's not only harder to get a chance at that level if you're Black; it's harder to keep the job once you get it. And getting a second chance? Not likely."

Williams was named general manager of the White Sox in October 2000. He came from a remarkable family. His biological mother was a Black Panther. His father had been the first Black firefighter in San José but had to sue the city to get the job.

"Imagine having to sue someone for the right to put your life at risk," Williams says with a laugh.

His dad had graduated from San José State, where he was a teammate on the track team with John Carlos. The two became close friends: Carlos is Kenny's godfather.

"I learned a lot, to say the least, just sitting around my house as a kid," Williams said. "John would come over, and sometimes he'd bring Tommie Smith with him. They would talk about what it was like in Mexico City, but also what it was like *after* Mexico City. For a long time, they were treated like pariahs.

"The message I got was to never let being Black be an excuse for not achieving or for not going after what you wanted. I think I've always remembered that."

Williams was selected in the third round of the 1982 draft by the White Sox when he graduated from high school. He reached the majors in 1986 and played in Chicago until he was traded to Detroit in 1989. He moved on — briefly — to Toronto and Montreal and retired in 1991. A year later, White Sox owner and CEO Jerry Reinsdorf hired him as a scout. Three years later, Williams became the team's director of minor league operations — at the age of thirty-one — and was promoted to vice president of player development. In that role, he not only oversaw the team's minor league operations but was also involved in decision making at every level of the organization.

On October 26, 2000, Reinsdorf named Williams to replace Ron Schueler as the White Sox general manager. As Williams drove home after his introductory press conference, he tuned in to a Chicago sports station, curious to hear what people were saying about his hiring.

"Mistake," he said, years later.

A drive-time host named Mike North, long known for his conservative views on *everything*, was ranting about Williams's hiring. "He kept saying that the only reason I'd gotten the job was because I was Black," Williams said. "He said there was nothing in my résumé to indicate I was ready to be a general manager. We had just been voted the minor league organization of the year, and I was the one in charge of the minor leagues. So I thought there was *some* reason to hire me.

"I remember thinking, 'Okay, I'm going to have to deal with some of this stuff.' Then, I got home and it got worse."

When Williams reached his house, he saw that it had been spray-painted on the side. The words were impossible to miss: "No nigger should run the Chicago *White* Sox."

Williams called his father, who had dealt with a good deal of blatant racism as a firefighter in San José working for what had been an all-white fire department. "You have to talk to your boys about this right away," his father told him. "They're going to have to deal with this going forward, and you have to prepare them for that."

That night, Williams sat down his two oldest sons—then fourteen and eleven. "I felt as if I was taking some of their innocence away," he said. "But it had to be done." He paused. "That was twenty-one years ago. I'm not sure they even remember it at this point."

Like almost every Black person who has had enough success to drive a nice car, Williams has dealt with being pulled over for DWB. "Almost without fail, the first question is, 'How'd you get this car?'" he said. "I've had it happen ten or twelve times over the years."

I asked how he managed to not lose his temper in those situations, especially since it had happened so often.

"It's easy," he said. "You remind yourself that you don't want to die."

Williams did lose his temper once. "I was driving through a construction zone," he said. "Cars were lined up to get through, and no one was going more than fifteen miles per hour. I looked in my rearview mirror, and I saw a cop pull into the closed-down construction lane, go around a couple cars and pull in right behind me. A minute later, he pulls me over. I said to him, 'I saw what you did. How, with all these cars lined up, did you pick *me* out?'

"He said I had been speeding. He wrote me a ticket for going forty miles an hour in a construction zone. I said to him, 'I'll see you in court. I don't care if I have to pay the fine, I'm going to get what you just did on the record.'"

Williams went to court and told the judge exactly that. "I don't care if you find me guilty. I want what happened on the record."

Williams walked through what had taken place. "The judge looked at the cop and said, 'I've driven through that construction zone to get to the courthouse. There's *no way* anyone could drive forty miles per hour there.' He dismissed the case on the spot. *That* was a bonus. I made my point and didn't have to pay a fine."

Williams had success as the White Sox GM, building a team that in 2005 won the team's first World Series since 1917. A year later, the team won 90 games but missed the playoffs. In 2012, Williams was promoted to executive vice president, a title he still holds today.

"The funny thing is, you can't look at me right now as evidence of progress," he said. "I've been here twenty-one years. The progress was when I got the job. Now, I'm just someone who's been here a long time. We need to see more progress around baseball. I'm not just talking about jobs like mine; I'm talking about front-office jobs like scouting director, legal counsel, marketing director. There are certainly plenty of qualified minorities for those jobs. We need more of them to get some of those jobs."

One qualified—and proven candidate—who hasn't gotten a second crack at a managing job is Willie Randolph. When I started to ask Williams about Randolph, he blurted, "How the——has he not gotten another shot at managing? I mean, that's impossible, isn't it? Except it isn't impossible."

He paused for a moment and then continued: "In 2012, when I hired Robin Ventura, I should have talked to Willie. I was just so locked in on Robin because of his connection to the team [Ventura played for the White Sox for ten years] that I never got past that to other candidates. I still regret that I didn't at least talk to Willie."

Williams's—and the White Sox's—record on diversity may be baseball's best. When Williams took over as GM, Jerry Manuel— who is Black—was the manager. Williams hired Ozzie Guillen, who is Latino, to succeed Manuel in 2004, and Guillen led the team to its World Series victory in 2005. Ventura succeeded Guillen for five years before Williams hired Rick Renteria, also Hispanic. In 2021, Reinsdorf decided to bring Tony La Russa back (at the age of seventy-six) to correct the "mistake" he believed he had made when he fired La Russa in 1986.

Williams has served on MLB's diversity committee for many years. Since the pandemic and the George Floyd murder, he thinks the discussions on the committee have become more intense.

"Before the pandemic, we might meet two times a year," he said. "But when the pandemic started, we started meeting by Zoom once a month or so. That gave us more chance to explore issues in depth. And then, when the Floyd murder happened, I think it made everyone think again about how far we still had to go in baseball, in sports, in the world, toward the kind of progress we all want to see."

Williams finds the lack of diversity in front offices and in major league dugouts disappointing, but he insists he remains optimistic about the future. "Optimism is a choice," he said. "There was a time a few years ago I was ready to give up. There just didn't seem to be any progress. But now I look and I see some things that make me think there's hope for the future. I have to think that way — I want to think that way.

"The Chauvin verdict was a step in the right direction, as long as we all understand that's all it was — a step. We need a lot more of them."

The old saying goes that a journey of a thousand miles begins with a single step. In the context of what has happened to Black people in this country in the last four hundred years, the journey might be longer than a thousand miles.

Even so, every step in the right direction matters.

CHAPTER TWELVE

Outliers

I F THE NUMBER OF BLACK BASEBALL PLAYERS has gone down a good deal in the last thirty-five years, swimming, golf, tennis, and hockey have never had that issue. That's because none of those sports have ever had more than a handful of elite Black athletes.

Even though the numbers have always been remarkably low in those sports, some of the greatest players in their history have been Black. Golf has Tiger Woods, who, depending on how you judge someone to be the greatest of all time, is either the best player in the sport's history or, at worst, the second-best player, behind Jack Nicklaus. Woods has won fifteen major championships, three shy of Nicklaus's all-time record of eighteen. He is also tied with Sam Snead for most tournaments won (eighty-two) and once won four major titles in a row—something no player has done in the modern era.

If he hadn't blown up his personal life and hadn't been injured so often, there's no telling what kind of numbers Woods might have put up. But as the great football coach Bill Parcells liked to say, you are what your record says you are.

Tennis has produced a number of important Black players,

starting with Althea Gibson, who won Wimbledon (twice), the US Championship (twice), and the French Open, between 1956 and 1958. Arthur Ashe won the first US Open in 1968 and won Wimbledon and the Australian Open.

Additionally, Serena Williams is arguably the greatest female tennis player in history. She has won twenty-three major titles, and while that number might be one short of Margaret Court's all-time record of twenty-four, Court won eleven of those championships in Australia during a time when international players rarely made the trip Down Under. It was almost like winning an intramural championship. Court *was* great; Williams is greater. Additionally, her older sister, Venus, won seven majors, including five Wimbledon victories.

Nowadays, besides the Williams sisters, there are a number of Black American women who are important players in the world. Sloane Stephens won the US Open in 2017 and has been ranked as high as number three in the world. She defeated Madison Keys in that final. Keys has been ranked as high as number seven in the world. The latest American phenom is seventeen-year-old Coco Gauff, who has already reached a ranking of twenty-third in the world prior to Wimbledon in 2021.

Most of the current crop of Black American women were inspired by the Williams sisters. Sadly, the same thing has not happened in golf with Woods.

The Williams sisters first burst onto the scene in 1997, when unseeded seventeen-year-old Venus Williams made it to the US Open final. Two years later, younger sister Serena won the US Open a few weeks shy of turning eighteen. A family dynasty was born.

Tiger Woods also became a star—a megastar—in 1997, when he won the Masters by twelve shots at the age of twenty-one. But Woods's victory—and his subsequent dominance of the sport—has yet to inspire a younger generation of Black golfers. Even though millions of dollars have been raised to support First Tee, which was launched soon after Woods's victory and aims to bring more minority kids into the sport, it has yet to produce a Black PGA Tour player, much less a star.

Twenty-four years after Woods's breakthrough victory, there are a total of four Black players (other than Woods) who have had any success in professional golf. Cameron Champ, whose father is Black, is one of the better young players on tour, having won three PGA Tour events. Joseph Bramlett and Wyatt Worthington have been up and down between the PGA Tour and the Triple-A Korn Ferry Tour.

And Harold Varner III has been on tour now for six years. He hasn't won, but he finished tied for second at the RBC Heritage Classic in April 2021 and has been in position to win on a number of occasions. Shortly after Varner came on tour, he was, for a time, the only Black player out there, because Woods was injured and not playing.

"People would come up to me and say, 'Hey, do you know you're the only Black player out here?'" Varner said with a laugh. "I'd look at them and say, 'No shit.' I've been a minority all my life, so this wasn't any different."

Exactly why golf remains so lily white is difficult to say. There's no doubt that finding places to play golf is more difficult than finding a tennis court, but it goes beyond that. Arthur Ashe was the first great Black player of the Open era—which began in 1968—and he was a true role model on and off the court. He was outspoken on issues and ran clinics in the inner city to try to get more minority kids involved in his sport.

Tragically, Ashe died in 1993, struck down by HIV-AIDS, which he had contracted from a blood transfusion he received while being treated for heart problems. Before he died, Ashe said he believed the person best equipped to pick up the mantle from him was John McEnroe.

Ashe's assertion might have sounded strange to those who only knew McEnroe for his on-court hot temper, but Ashe was right. McEnroe was always sensitive to issues involving race and believed it was important to bring more Black athletes into tennis.

"If we don't go out and actively do something about it, the greatest player in history might never pick up a racquet," he said once, while still an active player. He and his brother Patrick McEnroe now run a tennis academy in New York — on Randalls Island — which is a stone's throw from the Triborough Bridge.

"We haven't produced any major stars yet," Patrick McEnroe said recently. "But we've got some kids in the program with a lot of potential, and we're working at it."

At a time when the United States hasn't produced a true male star since Andy Roddick — and hasn't had a major championship winner since Roddick's 2003 US Open victory — one of the most promising young Americans in recent years is Francis Tiafoe. Tiafoe, who is Black, is twenty-three and has been ranked as high as twenty-ninth in the world. For an American man nowadays, that's like climbing Mount Everest. In 2019, he reached the quarterfinals of the Australian Open but has struggled since then and had dropped to seventy-third in the world in the spring of 2021 before reaching the third round at Wimbledon, which moved him back up to number fifty-two.

Golf got lucky because arguably the greatest player ever — Woods — did pick up a golf club. But, unlike Ashe, Woods has made a point of never taking political positions of any kind in order not to offend his sponsors or golf's white, mostly right-wing fan base. He was forgiven long ago by a majority of golf fans for the numerous transgressions that ended his marriage, but—unfortunately—his role model has been Michael Jordan, not Ashe.

Jordan once refused to campaign in the state of North Carolina for Harvey Gantt, who was running for the Senate against Jesse Helms, an outspoken segregationist. "Republicans buy shoes too," Jordan told Dean Smith, his college coach, when Smith urged him to help Gantt's campaign.

Woods has always been keenly aware of the fact that Republicans buy golf shoes, golf equipment, and expensive watches. He is as much a role model to young white kids—who have access to golf courses and, in most cases, plenty of money—as to Black kids.

Varner is not the product of a First Tee program, but he participated in a summer program at what was then Gaston Municipal Golf Course. His father paid $100 a summer for a junior membership, which entitled Harold to play Monday through Friday in the afternoons. By the time he was a teenager, he was so good that members invited him to play with them on weekends.

"That's the kind of program we need more of," he said. "First Tee is a good idea, and I'm working with the programs in North Carolina now, but my view of it has been it's sort of like golf day care. The kids don't get enough access to golf courses in most places to get bitten by the game. I got bitten by the game because I got to *play* all the time. For a hundred dollars, I got to play four months of golf.

"Those are the kinds of programs we need. Kids need access to golf courses. They need to learn from good players and play with good players. My foundation has started a program where kids can play at clubs for five dollars a round. We're sponsoring some of it, but we need more and we need programs like that in more places."

Varner admits he was lucky as a kid. Never once did another

player or a parent at a junior tournament question his presence. Never once was he told he couldn't have the same access at any golf club during a tournament as the white kids who were playing there.

A little more than a year ago, Varner and his wife, Amanda—who is white—pulled up to the front door of the Greenbrier, a West Virginia resort that annually hosts a PGA Tour event, and were greeted by a valet who said, "Caddies park outside."

"Amanda said, 'We're guests at the hotel,'" Varner remembered. "The guy was embarrassed; said he was sorry. I don't think he was a racist. I just think he'd probably never seen a Black golfer not named Tiger Woods. In fact, he probably hadn't seen too many guests at the hotel who were Black."

Varner has the kind of outgoing personality that the PGA Tour needs more of, regardless of skin color. Many players enjoyed playing with no fans when the tour returned in June 2020 in the midst of the pandemic. They didn't have to deal with people screaming "Get in the hole!" when they were five hundred yards from the green. Nor did they have to deal with autograph seekers or, for that matter, the media. Varner missed all of it.

"When they let fans back in for Houston [in October], I was like a dog with a bone," he said. "I love having people to show off for because I'm good at golf. Fans make playing golf more fun; so does the media."

In 2018, Varner shot 79 in the first round of the US Open at Shinnecock. It was a windy day, conditions on the golf course very difficult. Players came into the clubhouse shaking their heads about how tough the golf course had been. Someone asked Varner if it had been a tough day for him.

"Tough day for me?" he said with a laugh. "It was a tough day for all those people out there trying to find my golf balls when I hit them into the rough. I was just playing golf. What they were doing was tough."

Varner's approach probably has a lot to do with his upbringing. Most talented young golfers are treated like newly discovered diamonds. They get lessons from expensive teaching pros, travel in style to posh country clubs where junior tournaments are being held, and are told again and again about the lucrative future that awaits them if they continue grinding at their game all year round.

"I was never that good until my junior year in high school," Varner said. "I mean, I was good enough that the guys at the club would let me play with them, but I wasn't any kind of junior star. When I was a senior, I was recruited by colleges, but it wasn't overwhelming by any means. I could have gone to Michigan State, but it was too cold up there. So, I went to East Carolina."

He had a solid college career but—again—was hardly a star. He didn't even think about turning pro until he was a junior and then had to figure out how to find some money to bankroll himself when he graduated. His personality helped him again.

"I've never had trouble asking people for money," he said. "Hey, if they say no, they say no. I'd made friends with a lot of older people playing golf, and several of them—all white—were willing to back me. When I made enough to start paying guys back, I went to pay one of them and he said, 'All I want is two tickets to the Masters when you play there.'"

Varner hasn't made the Masters yet, but he has qualified for the other three majors (he was in the last group on Sunday at the 2019 PGA) and has been a solid tour player for six years. He won the prestigious Australian PGA in December 2016, and in April 2021, he finished tied for second at Hilton Head behind winner Stewart Cink. He was thrilled when eighty-six-year-old Lee Elder was invited by the green jackets at Augusta National to join Jack Nicklaus and Gary Player in hitting the ceremonial opening tee shots to begin the 2021 Masters. Varner disagreed with those who said Elder should have turned it down since it took so long for the Augusta membership to get around to inviting him to take part. In fact, Elder's health was such that he couldn't actually hit a shot. Instead, he was introduced to a warm ovation as he waved to the crowd.

In 1975, Elder was the first Black golfer to play in the Masters. Several other Black players had won tournaments on the PGA Tour but had not been invited to play at Augusta. It was only after an invitation to the Masters became automatic if you won on tour, that Elder—after winning the 1974 Monsanto Open—was "invited" to play. The Masters likes to emphasize that it "invites" players to take part, as if the club were doing them a huge favor by allowing them to come play after they have qualified.

That was the way most golf people looked at Augusta's invitation to Elder to take part in the opening ceremony forty-six *years* after he broke the color line. What a wonderful thing they were doing recognizing him and allowing him to share the tee with Nicklaus and Player.

"I'm glad they did it, and I'm glad Lee did it," Varner said. "Could it have happened sooner? Sure. A lot of things should have happened sooner. But you have to look at progress and say it's a good thing, regardless of when or how it comes about. My kids will grow up in a world different than the one I grew up in, and that will be a good thing.

"I hope there will be a lot more Black role models for them to look at in golf by the time they're teenagers. Heck, I hope I'll have won the Masters four times and they'll be inviting *me* to hit a ceremonial tee shot.

"My parents taught me long ago that you don't judge people as Black and white; you judge them as good or bad. A good person is a good person — period. A bad one is a bad one — period. That's the way I look at people all the time. It's the way I want them to look at me.

"And if someone looks at me and judges me because I'm Black, that's their problem, not mine."

Cullen Jones feels the same way as Varner does when it comes to judging people. But his experiences as a Black athlete in an overwhelmingly white sport haven't always been as gentle as Varner's.

Jones made two US Olympic teams as a swimmer. He was part of arguably the most famous relay in history, the US 4 × 100 freestyle relay team at the 2008 Olympics in Beijing. The team came from way behind to catch France and win the gold medal — preserving Michael Phelps's quest for eight gold medals.

"I like to kid Michael that he couldn't have gotten the eight golds without us," Jones said, referring to the other members of the relay: Garrett Weber-Gale and Jason Lezak. It was Lezak who heroically caught French world record holder Alain Bernard from behind on the anchor leg. But all four Americans had to swim their best times to touch out the French at the wall.

Jones grew up in Newark, New Jersey. When he was five, he and his parents went to a water park in Pennsylvania. Cullen didn't know how to swim, but he felt fine wearing a tube until the tube flipped on him and trapped him underwater for close to thirty seconds. Lifeguards had to give him CPR. After that, his parents decided he *had* to learn to swim.

Which he did — although it took him a while to feel comfortable in the water. But once he got comfortable, he didn't want to leave.

He loved the water. Early on, he swam on youth teams that were diverse—he grew up in a neighborhood with Black, Latino, and white kids. But as he advanced to more elite teams, he began to notice that fewer and fewer of the kids he was swimming with and against were minorities. "I'd look around the deck at meets," he said. "And there weren't very many guys who looked like me. Sometimes, there were none at all."

The lack of diversity didn't deter Jones. By the time he was in high school, he was six feet five and weighed a lean 210 pounds. On first glance, he might have been mistaken for a linebacker or a small forward, in light of his size, but he was a swimmer—always a swimmer.

"It bothers me when I hear people put down the idea of being obsessed," he said. "I was obsessed. I wanted to be the best swimmer I could possibly be. I loved the competition and the challenge of trying to get better. And I loved the fact that there were people who didn't want to accept the idea that a Black kid could be as good as I was.

"I still remember a meet when I was a teenager where I beat a kid, who was also very good, in the hundred free. I was standing with my parents afterwards, and the kid's mother came up to me and said, 'Shouldn't you be playing basketball somewhere?' People have said that to me through the years, but at least some of the time, it's just a reference to my height. This was *not* a reference to my height."

At a dual meet in high school, Jones came from behind on the anchor leg of the final relay to win the race and the meet. Even before he climbed out of the pool, he heard profanities and racial taunts coming at him from all directions. "It got ugly quickly," he said. "They were screaming at me and at my teammates. We sprinted to the bus—no way we were going into the locker room. It was frightening. A couple of guys surrounded me for protection, but, honestly, I didn't feel safe at that moment."

Jones became a world-class sprinter in high school and was heavily recruited by swimming power schools around the country. One coach at a Southern school that had never had a Black swimmer told him he would love to have him on the team, but he was concerned about the reactions he'd get if Jones came to his school. "He wasn't worried about my teammates," Jones said. "He was worried about their parents."

He eventually settled on North Carolina State, an ACC school with a lot of swimming tradition. As a senior in 2006, he won the 50-meter freestyle at the NCAA nationals. That performance convinced him it was worth continuing to swim full-time to try to make the Olympic team that was going to Beijing.

Jones ended up making two Olympic teams—the 2008 team and the 2012 team that went to London. He had become the first African American to hold a world record in 2007, when he was part of the Americans' record-breaking 4 × 100 relay team at the World Championships. In Beijing, the 4 × 100 relay team was the first US team to win an Olympic gold medal in that event since 1996. Not only did it break the previous world record by an astonishing four seconds, but the first *five* finishers in the race also broke the previous world record.

Jones made the Olympic team again in 2012, qualifying for both the 50-meter freestyle and the 100-meter freestyle. He won three more medals in London, finishing second in the 50-meter freestyle, second in the 4 × 100 freestyle, and first in the 4 × 100 medley, swimming the anchor leg in the prelims since he was the second-fastest American in the 100 meters individually.

He took a crack at making the 2016 team but finished third in the

50 freestyle—two-tenths of a second shy of the second-place finish he needed to make the team. He felt lost. He was thirty-two, and he was certain his last chance to swim in an Olympics had just ended. Chuck Wielgus, then the CEO of USA Swimming, reminded him that he had always promised his mother that he would get his college degree. After four years, Jones had come up several credits short.

Deciding that Wielgus was right, Jones reenrolled at N.C. State that fall. "I was in a rhetorical writing class," he said. "This was right after Colin Kaepernick had started his protest against the way white police officers were treating Black men. I got put into a three-person pod with two guys who were both in ROTC. Both white, both from the South. I thought, 'This is going to be a disaster.'

"They schooled me," he said. "They pointed out to me that Kaepernick had started out sitting for the anthem, but that a Green Beret had convinced him to kneel because that's what guys do when they are at the gravesite of a fallen comrade. It's a way of honoring them. It was a great learning experience for me. It made me glad I went back to school and reminded me that we're all still learning."

Being back at State also inspired him to take one more crack at swimming. He asked Coach Braden Holloway if he could train with his team. Holloway, who had not been at the university when Jones had been there ten years earlier, loved the idea of having an Olympic gold medalist train with his younger swimmers. But he wondered if Jones could handle the workouts.

"I was at least twenty pounds overweight," Jones said, laughing. "I looked more like a whale than an Olympic swimmer."

Getting back into shape one more time proved cathartic for Jones and made retiring easier to accept after he just missed making the World Championship team in 2019. A year earlier, he had married longtime girlfriend Rupi DeSai and had gone to work for Speedo as their philanthropic sales manager—a position the company created specifically for Jones.

"It's allowed me to help kids—some of them are like I was as a kid. We work at getting them into the water to learn how to swim when they're young," he said. "I'm working on things that will make the sport more diverse for kids today and, someday, I hope, for my son."

Jones's son, Avyn, was born in 2019 and, according to his father, has already shown an affinity for the water. "Every time he goes near the water, my wife says, 'Oh no, another swimmer,'" he said, laughing. "My goal for him, if he does become a swimmer, is to do so in a world where people won't call him the N-word when he has success or tell him to go play basketball. We've got a long way to go to get there, though. The last year-plus has certainly reminded us of that."

The night after George Floyd's murder, Jones took his dog out for an evening walk. He was staying at his brother's house in Charlotte, North Carolina, because he and his wife were building their own home nearby.

"I'd gone about a block when a police car went past me," he said. "All of a sudden, the car screeched to a stop. The cop made a U-turn and came back to where I was walking. He said, 'Where'd you get the dog?' I told him it was my dog. He said, 'Really? What kind of dog is it?' I told him it was a French bulldog and it was seven years old. He lingered a little while longer and then finally said, 'Well, just wanted to make sure everything's okay,' and drove away.

"I was really angry. Do you think if I'm white there's any way he screeches to a halt and turns around to come back and question me that way? No way. He saw a six five Black dude walking in a nice neighborhood, and he decided something was up. Did he think I was stealing someone's dog?"

Jones had become a victim of a new phenomenon: WDWB—Walking Dog While Black.

"It turned out to be a good thing in the end," he said. "I have *always* been aware of the fact that I have to think every single day about my actions because I'm a Black man—a six-foot five-inch Black man. Every morning when I wake up, just like every person of color, I have to think about what I'm going to wear that day: Where am I going? Who am I going to be dealing with? Is it okay for me to wear a hoodie if I go out for a walk and it's cold? Maybe not. I'm very conscious of my diction because I don't want people to get the wrong idea about me, think maybe I'm not educated. These are things my white counterparts never have to think about. I have to think about them all the time. We all do.

"It can be exhausting, but it's a fact of life. Because of Floyd's murder and what happened twenty-four hours later, I've become more outspoken on these issues. I think it's very important for me and for others to speak up. Do I see progress? Of course I do. What happened this past summer, even though some people went too far, was progress. The more times Black and white people unite for a cause, the better for everyone. And that's what happened after the Floyd murder and with Black Lives Matter.

"But looking at my sport, we still have a long way to go. It is still almost all white. Black kids need to be encouraged to swim—and not just by guys who look like me. It's going to take more than me and Simone Manuel [the women's 100-meter freestyle gold medalist in Rio, who is Black] to change the way people view minorities in this sport. There is lots left to do.

"My goal now is to be part of the solution, bring more Black faces to my sport. It's going to take a while, but I think I can be a role model. That's a start."

*   *   *

Joel Ward is also a role model. Like Varner and Jones, his sport is almost all white. In 2021, 3 percent of those playing in the National Hockey League were minorities. It was a news story late in the season, when the Stanley Cup champion Tampa Bay Lightning — which defended its title successfully in July — put a line on the ice with three Black skaters.

"I hope there will come a time when this isn't a story," Lightning coach John Cooper said afterward.

For the moment, it is still a story.

Ward's parents were from Barbados but met in Canada after each had moved there.

Growing up, Ward saw few Black role models in the NHL. Willie O'Ree became the first Black player in the league in 1958, playing for the Boston Bruins, but scored a total of four goals and had ten assists — all in 1961 — before continuing to play (and star) at the minor league level for another eighteen years. The NHL didn't have another Black player until 1974, when Mike Marson became a member of the expansion Washington Capitals.

Ward grew up in Scarborough, a suburb of Toronto, playing both soccer and hockey when he was young. He had two older brothers who often took him with them to play soccer. Hockey, though, was his first love, and he pretty much gave up soccer by the time he was ten. Around then, he began to notice that he was often the only Black member of his team — regardless of level. Also around then, he first encountered the N-word during an on-ice skirmish in a hockey game. "Kid and I were jostling one another, and he said, 'Let go of me, nigger,' " Ward remembered.

"I kind of had to grow up fast on the subject of race after that," he said. "My mom explained to me that the word was bad — very bad—and, not surprisingly, I didn't react especially well after that when I heard it. She said people who used the word did so because they were jealous of me because I was a better player than they were. That was usually the case."

Ward's parents, Randal and Cecilia, frequently came to see him play. When he was thirteen, his team played a game at St. Michael's Arena in Toronto on a Sunday afternoon. At one point, late in the game, Joel noticed a lot of people gathered in the area where he knew his parents were sitting. He didn't think much of it at the time. But at game's end, he found out that his father had suffered a stroke and had been taken to the hospital.

"At first they thought he was going to be okay," Ward said. "But then he developed a blood clot and he died. It was a horrible shock, to say the least."

Cecilia Ward was a nurse, and she took on a second job and worked even longer hours than she had worked previously to make sure Joel could continue to play youth hockey. There were nights his mom worked an overnight shift in a hospital and Joel slept in an empty room so his mother could take him to school when her shift was over.

"It really wasn't too bad," he said. "At home, I shared a room with my brother. At the hospital, most nights, I had my own room. Mom always made sure I had what I needed—especially when it came to hockey because she knew how much I loved it."

There were plenty of racial incidents. During a junior league game in Lake Erie, Ward heard the N-word constantly throughout the game, and as he was leaving the ice, he heard repeated shouts of "Go back to basketball!"

After a while, he became almost immune to the comments—especially from fans. The problem, he decided, was theirs, not his.

But there were also moments on the ice, including one with a referee.

It happened when he was playing in the Ontario Hockey League for the Owen Sound Platers. One of his teammates, Brian Kazerian, skated over to him during a game and said that the referee, Kevin Pollock, had just referred to him as "a monkey." Kazerian was very upset and angry. So was Ward.

"The thing is, my teammates always had my back, and this was an example," he said. "We reported the incident to the league office, and there was a hearing. Pollock vehemently denied saying it or anything like it. My question was, why would Brian just make something like that up? I was willing to be told that Brian had misunderstood, that maybe the guy had said, 'Tell your buddy to quit monkeying around,' something like that. But he denied the whole thing."

Years later, both Pollock and Ward made it to the NHL, and Pollock worked games in which Ward played. "We would just nod at each other; that was it," he said. "Part of me wanted to say to him, 'What really happened? Why would my teammate make something like that up if it didn't happen?' I never did it, though. Maybe I should have."

Ward paused and laughed. "I'll say this: if you go back and look at the games he worked when we were both in the NHL, my team didn't do very well in those games."

Ward was a good player but wasn't a coveted star in juniors. Never drafted by an NHL team, he finally decided to go to college at the University of Prince Edward Island after coming to believe he was never going to get a fair shot with an NHL team.

"I was always one of the last guys to get a chance when junior teams had tryouts," he said. "I really do believe a lot of coaches saw a Black hockey player, not just a hockey player. I believed in myself. I thought if I got a fair shot, I could prove to people that I was a good player."

He finally got a shot after he was selected for a college conference all-star team that played in a Christmas event against the World Junior all-stars. A number of NHL teams scouted those games, and the Minnesota Wild liked enough of what they saw to invite Ward to a tryout camp. Ward stayed in college long enough to graduate and then spent most of three years playing for the Houston Aeros, the Wild's top affiliate, in the American Hockey League. In the fall of 2006, he got into eleven games for the Wild and had one assist.

He began to come into his own as a scorer in his third season in Houston, scoring twenty-one goals. That earned him a one-year two-way (major league/minor league) contract with the Nashville Predators. He made the opening night roster and scored his first NHL goal on October 10, 2008 — two months shy of turning twenty-eight. By then, he was a solid two-way forward, a defensive specialist who could also score.

After three seasons in Nashville, he signed a four-year $12 million deal in the summer of 2011 to play in Washington.

The Capitals were one of those teams that almost always made the playoffs and, just as often, flamed out in the spring. They drew the defending Stanley Cup champion Boston Bruins in the first round of the 2012 playoffs and, after taking a 3–2 lead in the series, lost game 6 at home (in overtime) and had to go to Boston to play game 7. It looked like another failed spring for the Caps.

Game 7 also went into overtime, tied 1–1. Ward was getting ready to come off for a line change almost three minutes into the extra period, when line mate Mike Knuble knocked a shot down at the Caps blue line and took off toward the net.

"I was going to come off, but when I saw Mike take off, I just went with him," Ward said. "I knew he wasn't going to just dump the puck in and head for the bench. It was one of those quick-change moments that happen, especially in overtime, when everyone's pressing to try to win the game."

Knuble flew down the left side and flipped a backhand shot at goalie Tim Thomas, who made the save, but couldn't control the puck. Flying in from the right side, Ward pounced on the puck before anyone could stop him and flicked it past Thomas to win the game, 2–1, and the series, 4–3.

"Greatest moment of my career," Ward said. "I was skating on the fourth line. We were out there to defend well and give our scorers a chance to catch their breath. And then, just like that, I get the chance to win the game. It was an amazing feeling."

The feeling didn't last very long. On the plane home that night, teammate Jeff Halpern told Ward he was seeing some "really ugly stuff" on social media.

Much of it — though not all — was coming out of Boston. There were the usual "stick to basketball" gems, and the N-word was all over the place. "We don't need a nigger like you polluting our sport" was a familiar refrain. Ward shrugged most of it off — until the threats started.

"At first, I didn't think much about it," he said. "I'd gotten used to systemic racism being part of my life. I still remember driving home for the off-season one year from Houston, and I got pulled over just as I crossed into Oklahoma. I wasn't speeding, wasn't doing anything wrong. The cop was one of those guys with a big hat and sunglasses. First thing he said was, 'What are you doing here?' as in, 'What's a Black guy doing driving into Oklahoma from Texas?' I explained to him that I was a hockey player heading home for the off-season.

"Needless to say, he had me out of the car in an instant after that. Fortunately, I had my ID and hockey equipment in the car.

"When we'd go through airport security as a team, one of us would get pulled out of line—almost always it was me. Again, my teammates were always there for me. They'd say 'What the hell was that about?' They knew the answer, and so did I.

"After the Boston goal, it went to a different level. People weren't just calling me names. They were saying, 'You should be dead.' I couldn't believe it. This was a hockey game. I tried to shrug it off, but there was a point when I couldn't do that, because it was too serious.

"I can tell you exactly when it got really serious: when the FBI called and said they felt I needed protection. That was serious."

Ward was given extra protection going in and out of arenas for the rest of that season and into the next season. "I felt like I had to be *on* every day for my entire career," he said. "I couldn't let up. The goal gave me a chance to take a deep breath—except, in the end, it didn't."

The Caps lost in the next round to the New York Rangers, a key moment coming when Ward was called for a double-high-sticking penalty in the final minute in game 5 with the Caps up a goal. The Rangers tied the game in the last ten seconds and then won it in overtime—all on the same penalty. Ward got racist tweets from Ranger fans this time, but no death threats. Just the "Stick to basketball, nigger," refrain.

After four years with the Caps, Ward signed with the San José Sharks and was part of a team that reached the Stanley Cup finals in 2016. He retired after ten seasons in the NHL—not bad for someone who no one bothered to draft when he came out of junior hockey.

"My mom told me when I was a kid that I better be prepared to be ten times as good as the next guy if I wanted to make it as a hockey player," he said. "As it turned out, she was right. It took me a long time just to get a chance to play professionally.

"Was some of that racial? Probably. But I did finally get a chance, and I think I proved myself to the teams that gave me a chance. But there's more to be done—a lot more. I want to see more minority kids playing hockey. And I want to see them get a real chance if they love the sport."

In June 2020, two weeks after George Floyd's murder, Ward was one of seven players named to the executive board of the newly formed Hockey Diversity Alliance. The goals of the HDA were direct: to work to get more minorities involved in hockey at the grassroots level, to encourage NHL teams to hire more Black executives, and to encourage more people involved with the NHL at the top levels to make minority involvement a priority.

In late August, after Jacob Blake was shot in the back seven times by a white police officer in Kenosha, Wisconsin, and left paralyzed, the HDA encouraged NHL players to shut down the Stanley Cup playoffs for two days to protest the Blake shooting. They were successful. The league is 97 percent white, but the players willingly went along with the NBA, which also shuttered its playoffs for two days. Soon after, the NHL also announced a new grassroots program for the Toronto area, designed to get more minority kids on the ice.

All good. But in October 2020, the HDA announced it would no longer be working with the NHL, because it believed the NHL's involvement was more about public relations and *talking* about the issue rather than actually doing anything.

Progress is never easy—regardless of the sport.

CHAPTER THIRTEEN

The Watchdog

O NE PERSON WHO HAS WIELDED a good deal of influence on the subjects of both race and gender in sports is known very little—if at all—to most sports fans. But sports commissioners, team owners, the media, and even college presidents are very aware of Richard Lapchick and what he does. For most of thirty-five years, Lapchick has been the watchdog, keeping an eye on the progress— or lack of it—being made when it comes to minorities, whether they be Black or Hispanic or women.

Lapchick is the keeper of the numbers. And as Gary Williams likes to say, numbers are very difficult to argue with—whether on a scoreboard or a scorecard.

Lapchick is seventy-six now but has been keenly aware of the issues that face minorities for almost his entire life. He is the son of Joe Lapchick, the Hall of Fame basketball coach who, in 1950 as the coach of the New York Knicks, signed Sweetwater Clifton as one of the first two Black players (the other being Chuck Cooper of the Boston Celtics) to play in the NBA.

"I was five years old," Lapchick said. "I can still remember looking out our window and seeing an effigy of my father that had been hung across the street. I wasn't quite sure what it was but found out why it was there soon enough. A lot of Knicks fans did *not* want a Black player on their team."

Lapchick was also deeply affected by a visit he, his mother, and his sister made to Dachau, the infamous Nazi death camp, when he was fourteen. Before he was even out of high school, he knew he wanted to do something that related to human rights.

His other passion as a kid was basketball. He went to a camp run by Jack Donohue, who was then the coach at Power Memorial High School. One of the other kids in the camp was a rising young star named Lew Alcindor—who later became Kareem Abdul-Jabbar. A lifelong friendship was born. Almost fifty years later, when Lapchick was presented with the Rainbow/PUSH Coalition's lifetime award for civil rights, his presenter was Abdul-Jabbar.

Lapchick received his undergraduate degree from St. John's, where his father coached for twenty-one years in two different stints. The younger Lapchick went on to earn a PhD in international race relations at the University of Denver, then the only school that had a PhD program in the discipline.

In his PhD dissertation, Lapchick compared apartheid in South Africa to the Nazi movement in Germany. After finishing at Denver, he became a professor at Virginia Wesleyan University in Norfolk, Virginia, and became very active in the anti-apartheid movement. He was heavily involved in trying to convince the US Tennis Association to refuse to play against South Africa in the 1978 North/Central Davis Cup zone final, and he led a group of seventy-five protesters during the US Open at Forest Hills in 1977.

"We were protesting against the US Tennis Association allowing South African players to take part in the Open," he said. "Back then, given the relative lack of interest in apartheid in this country, getting seventy-five people out there was a big deal."

During the protest, Arthur Ashe came outside the gates of the West Side Tennis Club to speak to Lapchick and his group. Ashe had won three of the four major tennis championships by then: the US Open, the Australian Open, and Wimbledon. He had traveled to South Africa in 1973 after being granted a visa to play by the South African government, which was trying to convince the International Olympic Committee to allow its athletes to compete again in the Olympics. The country had been banned in 1964 and was not allowed to return until 1992, when apartheid finally ended. Ashe had gone to South Africa to play, hoping his presence would help bring a halt to the segregation that ruled the country.

"It didn't happen," Lapchick said. "Arthur said when he got over there, they gave him tickets to give away in the Black community to see him play—but the Black fans were segregated from the white ones. He regretted the whole thing."

Ashe told the protesters that day that he had made a mistake going to South Africa. He became a leading voice in the athletic community against apartheid. Lapchick and others tried to convince the USTA to refuse to take part in the 1978 Davis Cup unless South Africa was expelled. The protests against the US participation in the Davis Cup drew more attention than the Forest Hills protest because they involved a team representing the United States.

Lapchick was teaching at Virginia Wesleyan at the time, and the proposed boycott drew considerable attention. One of the countries that *did* boycott was the Soviet Union. The Soviet stance says something about the attitudes Americans had toward race at the time.

"It certainly does say something, doesn't it?" Lapchick said when I brought that up.

*   *   *

Shortly before the matches were scheduled to be held in Nashville, two men broke into Lapchick's office, pinned him to the ground, and carved the N-word into his stomach. Except they misspelled it, and it came out "niger." Although Lapchick says now that the word was "more scratched than carved" into his stomach, he spent four days in the hospital with liver and kidney damage, a hernia, and a concussion. Hardly minor injuries.

And yet, the Norfolk police seemed more interested in investigating Lapchick than his attackers. "They told the local news media that they believed my injuries were self-inflicted," Lapchick said. "When I accused them of leaking a lie, they suggested that *they* give me a lie-detector test. I know how those things work. No way was I letting them give me the test."

He eventually went to an independent company for the test, which confirmed he was telling the truth. And still, no one was ever arrested for the attack.

Lapchick left the school soon after he recovered from his injuries, going to work for the United Nations as a senior liaison officer. A book publisher convinced him to write a book about the attack and the work he had been doing that led to the attack. "I was really on the verge of giving the [advance] check back," he said. "I just couldn't bring myself to sit down and write. But when I told the publisher how I felt, he convinced me to give it one more try. I did. It turned out to be therapeutic.

"He suggested I make half the book autobiographical and half of it on race relations. At first, I was hesitant because it all felt so personal. But then when I did it, I also included a chapter that was a study, a report card, really, on how three sports — football, basketball, baseball — were doing in terms of hiring people. That was really how the whole thing began."

When the book, titled *Broken Promises: Racism in American Sports,* was published, it was reviewed in *Sports Illustrated* by Jeremiah Tax, a semiretired longtime writer at the magazine. Tax trashed the book largely on the premise that Lapchick was creating an issue — racism — where none really existed anymore.

"Lapchick concedes almost nothing," he wrote. "He believes racism is more virulent than ever. It may also be risky for an ideologue to concede that any progress has been made because readers may assume that all problems have been solved. In any case, Lapchick's text is a message without hope."

Tax went on to cite those in sports who had worked to stem the tide of racism. According to him, everything was all good now, and Lapchick, by pointing out that racism was still very much an ongoing crime, was somehow an "ideologue." If anyone was an ideologue, it was Tax, who sounded then much like those today who scream that racism is no longer an issue in this country.

Forty-two years after Lapchick was attacked, seventy-four million people voted for Donald Trump in the 2020 election. Like Jeremiah Tax almost forty years ago, they no doubt believe that racism is no longer an issue. Why? Because it doesn't affect *them.*

In 1984, Lapchick moved to Northeastern University and founded the school's center for the study of sports in society. He stayed for seventeen years and, during that time, launched the National Consortium for Academics and Sports and began to study sports hiring practices as they related to race and gender. When his first full-fledged report card came out in 1988, he began to get attention nationally because the numbers couldn't be refuted.

"When I first started doing it, I think the people who ran sports leagues were pretty pissed about it because most of the numbers were not good," Lapchick said. "Now, they might still prefer the numbers not be out there, but I think they also see them as a way to insist that changes need to be made—that diversity still remains an issue for all of them."

In 1994, six years after he started doing his "report cards" (by then he had added gender to his studies), Nelson Mandela invited Lapchick to his inaugural as president of South Africa as a gesture of thanks for all his anti-apartheid work.

In 2001, Lapchick was asked by the University of Central Florida to run the newly endowed sports business school chair funded by the DeVos Foundation. He is still a professor emeritus at Northeastern in addition to his work at UCF.

"I'm seventy-five, and I'm still working," he said in the spring of 2021. "I guess that's a good thing."

His work has certainly become more important now than ever. He has expanded it greatly through the years, recently adding report cards on ownership, CEOs, college athletic directors, and umpires and referees to his work. What was once a one-man project is now backed by ten UCF business students who put all the numbers together for Lapchick to examine before he hands out grades.

"I knew when we started looking at owners and CEOs the grades wouldn't be good," Lapchick said. "That's why we didn't include them in the overall grades because it was almost unfair to do so. But that's where the changes really need to come—in the people who have hiring power. Kim Ng should have been a Major League Baseball general manager years ago, but it took a Black CEO [Derek Jeter in Miami] to give her a chance."

Almost forty years after Tax declared that racism in the United States and in sports really wasn't that big a deal, Lapchick—like so many others—finds himself shaking his head at how slow the progress has been, even now, in 2021.

"Why doesn't Eric Bieniemy have a head coaching job yet?" he asked in response to a question. "I have absolutely no idea. Every hiring cycle, there's at least one guy who appears to clearly be the 'next guy,' ready to be a head coach who doesn't get hired. The last couple of years, he's been it.

"It can get discouraging, especially when you look at some numbers. There are places where we do see improvement. There are more minorities and women getting jobs in front offices, and Ng's hiring was a breakthrough. But the positions of real authority, the ones at the very top, are still controlled almost entirely by white men.

"On the other hand, I stay optimistic about the future. I have to stay optimistic because if I don't, then all the work I've done for almost forty years now would feel as if it had no value. Last summer [2020] definitely brought about a sea change. It's only been five years now since Kaepernick and the anger directed at him. But a lot has changed.

"I still think the key to getting things to happen more quickly is going to be athlete activism. That will ultimately be the change-maker. We saw the power that athletes can wield through activism in the summer of 2020.

"Most people, especially white people, were very much against Kaepernick when he kneeled in 2016. The protests that followed probably would have died out if not for Trump's rant the next year. But last fall, after what happened in the summer, there was a Nielsen poll that showed that 70 percent of the people contacted approved of what athletes were doing, of having them speak out. That's a huge change from the past, and it's important that it continue."

There is no doubt that George Floyd's murder and the athlete activism that followed represented a transformation in the way many Americans view athletes' propensity to speak out on political issues. During the anthem protests of 2017, white football fans loudly booed players who knelt during the anthem. The fans complained that the peaceful protests were somehow ruining their enjoyment of football.

Right-wing pundits insisted that Black athletes had no right to protest, because they were making millions of dollars. In the fall of 2020, when Nielsen did its survey, far more people seemed to understand that there was good reason for athletes to make their voices heard.

Lapchick thinks the answer to the question about the lack of Black hires in positions of authority is simple: most of the decision makers are still white. "Most athletic directors at big-time college programs are white," he said. "Most owners in major sports are white. It's worth looking at the financial contributions to campaigns from owners in 2020: About five million dollars in contributions went to Republicans; about nine hundred thousand went to Democrats. That's a pretty big difference.

"It kind of tells you how many of them think. It goes beyond support for a candidate. It goes straight to 'We're okay with the way things are. We don't *want* change.'"

The NFL has thirty white owners. The Green Bay Packers are publicly owned, but their CEO, Mark Murphy, is also white. There are no Black owners. The only minority owner right now is Jacksonville Jaguars owner Shahid Khan, who was born in Pakistan, came to the United States at the age of sixteen, and graduated from the University of Illinois. Khan was one of seven NFL owners who contributed $1 million to Donald Trump's inaugural fund in 2017.

Coincidence or not, Khan has hired four coaches and two general managers since buying the team in 2011 — all white. The Jags did have a Black general manager pre-Khan in James Harris, although he never had the title. Like Ozzie Newsome before him in Baltimore, he was the "vice president for player personnel." He held the job for six years before leaving in 2009.

Lapchick is like Tony Dungy, Mike Tomlin, and others, in that he finds the lack of progress in Black people getting coaching jobs discouraging. "I honestly think that the Texans hired [David] Culley because they thought that might be a way to appease Deshaun [Watson]," he said mentioning the Texans star quarterback who had publicly attacked management but then become embroiled in a series of sexual assault charges soon after Culley's hiring. "I think Culley deserved a chance, just as Bieniemy and some others did — and do.

"But you can't force billionaires to do something they don't want to do. There are plenty of things I disagree with Roger Goodell on, but I think he's genuinely embarrassed about this and wants to see it change. That's why the Rooney Rule was bulked up last year. I think he hopes that what we've seen — or not seen — in hiring the last three years will change in the not-too-distant future."

Lapchick was encouraged by the number of Black coaches who were hired in Division 1 college basketball this spring. He had gone back to study past report cards earlier in the year and found that the number of Black head coaches in the college game had gone *down* since 2006.

"That certainly wasn't a good number," he said. "But there was a noticeable uptick this spring, and perhaps just as important, a lot of the hires were young coaches, assistants being given a chance to move up. The more of that we get, the better."

The same can be said of the NBA. Seven coaching jobs opened up at the end of the 2021 season, and six of those jobs were filled by Black men. Additionally, Nate McMillan, who had been named the interim coach in Atlanta during the season, had the interim tag removed. Becky Hammon and other female coaches are still awaiting a chance.

There's little doubt that the spate of minority hirings in college basketball was largely a result of what has happened since the Floyd murder. According to Lapchick's end-of-2020 report card, almost 81 percent of presidents and chancellors at the 130 schools that are part of the Football Bowl Subdivision —and also have major basketball programs—are white. Almost 77 percent of athletic directors at those schools are white men. Eight of the eleven FBS commissioners are white men, the Big Ten's Kevin Warren and the Sun Belt's Keith Gill becoming the first Black men to lead FBS conferences in the last two years. Judy MacLeod became the first woman named commissioner of an FBS league—Conference-USA—a year ago.

Lapchick likes to point out that most of the numbers he and his group have tracked have slowly improved but are still a long way from being close to where they need to be. Almost 50 percent of those who play football at FBS schools are Black; the number in power-five programs is closer to 60 percent. Thirteen of the 130 head coaches are Black. That's 10 percent. As with the NFL, that's not a good number.

Lapchick is still working at seventy-six because he enjoys what he does. Beyond that, his work is still very much needed.

One person Lapchick seldom calls out is NBA commissioner Adam Silver. "I think the NBA is in a different category than the other leagues when it comes to diversity and to being progressive," he said. "They're way ahead of everyone else."

It is highly unlikely that any other commissioner will be seen riding a float in a Gay Pride parade anytime soon. Goodell, who refused to be interviewed for this book, is the son of a former (moderate) Republican senator and is married to a former Fox on-air correspondent. He publicly steers away from talking about his politics, but one can take an educated guess about where he stands.

PGA Tour commissioner Jay Monahan grew up in a Boston suburb and attended the prestigious Lawrenceville School for a year after graduating from high school. He played Division 3 college golf and has been involved in the sport—largely in different jobs that involved sales—for most of his adult life.

Like any good salesman, Monahan knows his clientele. Most of those who play on the PGA Tour are either traditional Republicans or Trumplicans. The politics of the majority of "the 28,000 PGA professionals"—as the PGA of America likes to put it (the teaching pros at golf courses)—around the country are similarly to the right. The number of Black PGA professionals in the summer of 2021? 167.

Perhaps more important, Monahan is keenly aware that a majority of golf fans and those who run the corporations that keep the tour afloat from week to week also lean right or far right.

Which is why it wasn't surprising when athletes in every other professional sport except golf—basketball and hockey in the midst of playoffs, baseball during the regular season, and the NFL during preseason—boycotted in some form for two days in the wake of the Jacob Blake shooting in August 2020.

Golf did nothing other than putting out a statement saying it supported the actions taken by athletes in other sports. That was it. All sixty-nine players scheduled to play in the BMW Championship that week in Chicago showed up ready to go on the first tee on Thursday. Tiger Woods, famous throughout his career for never taking any kind of political position, put out a statement of his own, which said he supported the tour's statement.

Gutsy stuff.

"What happened [in Kenosha] was heartbreaking," Monahan said almost a year later. "We were in Chicago getting ready to play [the BMW Championship, one of the tour's three playoff events], and we were confronted with this in real time.

"I talked to players and to people on staff. I was up all night pacing, trying to decide what to do. Ultimately, I felt that our players have a platform to do good things in the cities where we play and to not play would take that platform away.

"Looking back, maybe in the short term that wasn't the best decision, but I was focusing on the long term. I'm aware that our sport's history when it comes to race has been questionable at times in the past. We had already been working on doing some things connected to issues of diversity and race and social injustice. I thought it was important that we keep pushing forward with those things."

One player Monahan said he spoke to repeatedly during that tense twenty-four hours was Cameron Champ, the only Black player in the sixty-nine-player field (Champ is biracial) other than Woods. Champ ended up playing on Thursday wearing one black golf shoe and one white golf shoe with Blake's name on his shoes. He talked about his frustration with the fact that white cops were still shooting Black men.

I interviewed Champ for a piece I wrote on the *Golf Digest* website. Among other things he said, "When I saw the [Blake] video, my jaw dropped. I thought, 'Not *again.*' But there it was. All I could think was, 'Wow.'"

Champ also posted a video explaining the thinking behind his shoes. It concluded with the words "This has to stop."

Champ received considerable blowback from golf fans for the video, many defending the actions of the police in Kenosha. So did I, and so did *Golf Digest.*

The tour publicly supported Champ for wearing the shoes and for the video. Did Monahan hear from fans angry with the tour for supporting Champ?

"I get blowback from people every single day," he said, semi-ducking the question. Then, laughing, he added, "Yes, I heard quite a few opinions that day."

A week later, during his pre-tour championship press conference, Monahan announced some of the tour's long-term plans. Most notable was a commitment to spend $100 million over the next ten years on programs that support minorities in the cities where the tour goes every year.

"We started talking about this right after George Floyd," Monahan said. "We knew that we needed to be involved in some way, and we had numerous meetings to discuss ways to do it. This was kind of both a start and a culmination."

The money will come from the tour's events, and each tournament will choose what it considers worthy projects to give money to once the programs begin in 2022.

"I think we understand that we, like everyone else, are just at the starting line," Monahan said. "But to make progress, you have to start. We won't be finished in a year or perhaps in ten years, but we can make progress during that time."

Fast-forward to March 25, 2021, when the Georgia state legislature passed a "voting rights" bill clearly designed to make it more difficult for Black citizens in the state to vote. This move came after Black voter turnout had played a key role in Joe Biden's winning Georgia in the presidential election and Democrats' winning both Senate seats in very close races.

The new law was quickly attacked by many in Georgia, including Coca-Cola and Delta, both Georgia-based corporations, and Viacom, the parent company of CBS. The big surprise was Major League Base-ball's decision to pull the 2021 All-Star Game out of Atlanta. Baseball commissioner Rob Manfred has given money in the past to Republi-can candidates for office; he's a member of Augusta National Golf Club, whose membership is, if anything, more to the right than are most—even in golf. He is also the leader of a sport where, according to a *Newsweek* report in October 2020, 75 percent of the money con-tributed by owners to political campaigns went to Republicans.

And yet, Manfred moved quickly to announce the All-Star Game would be moved (it landed, eventually, in Denver) and then withstood the many brickbats that came his way after the decision.

"I didn't mind the attacks coming from the right wing about it," he said. "I expected that, and I have a pretty thick skin. But when my wife and children began getting messages that were pretty ugly, that bothered me. I signed up for this. They didn't."

Manfred says that after Governor Brian P. Kemp signed the "vot-ing rights" bill that was clearly a response to the three critical Demo-cratic victories. He knew that MLB needed to look into moving the game.

Kemp signed the bill into law on March 25. Two days later, Tony Clark, the president of the Major League Baseball Players Associa-tion, was quoted in the *Boston Globe* as saying that a player boycott of the All-Star Game—scheduled to be played in Atlanta—was a possibility. Additionally, Los Angeles Dodgers manager Dave Rob-erts, who as manager of the world champions would be the National League manager, said he might turn down the honor if the game was held in Atlanta. Roberts was one of two Black managers in MLB at the start of the 2021 season.

"We had already dealt with a number of games being called off in August," Manfred said, referring to the Blake shooting in

Wisconsin. "So we had something very real right in front of us. This was going to be a live issue for the players right up until July 13 [the date of the All-Star Game]. I didn't want to put them through that.

"Second, we're a business. If we had to deal with pickets or players not wanting to cross a picket line, we were talking about potentially losing hundreds of millions of dollars."

Manfred, a lawyer himself, consulted with MLB's lawyers and brought in outside counsel. He asked them to compare the Georgia laws with voting laws in other states. MLB also consulted with the Brennan Center for Justice in Washington in order to understand exactly what the law did and why it might be objectionable to many people—Black and white.

"If there's one thing I think we can all agree on, hope we can agree on, it's that everybody should be able to vote," Manfred said. "That should be an absolute, right? It really should *not* be a political issue. From the day Tony [Clark] made his comments until the day we made the announcement that we were moving the game, that was all I did. Regardless of the decision, we had to move fast."

Manfred talked to MLB's eleven-owner executive council; he talked to members of the Player Alliance—a group made up of current and former Black players. He talked to on-field personnel and front-office personnel. He talked repeatedly to Clark. In essence, he talked to just about anyone who had any connection at all to the sport.

"I talked to guys who talked to guys who talked to guys," he said. "I wanted to get input from as many different people as possible."

On April 2, six days after Clark's comments, MLB announced it would move the All-Star Game out of Atlanta. There was—not surprisingly—great anger, especially in Georgia, directed at the decision. The Braves, for whom having the All-Star Game in their sparkling five-year-old stadium was a very big deal, were unhappy.

Because Manfred had kept board chairman Terry McGurk looped in on what MLB was thinking, the announcement didn't come as a shock to the Braves. Even so, many local officials complained that moving the game would hurt the local economy—which it did—and some of the local charities that would have benefited from the game. Manfred was angrily attacked by the right, including a piece in the ultraconservative *American Spectator,* with a headline that declared, "Baseball Is for Democrats Only."

Manfred understood. He also believed—and believes—he made the right decision.

"In an ideal world, sports and politics stay separate," he said. "We try in baseball to be as apolitical as possible. Sports is an escape from the real world that people look for, and we get that. But we don't live in an ideal world. Regardless of what we decided, this was going to be a political statement. If we stay, we're making a political decision. If we go, we're making a political statement. I think we made the right decision."

For Manfred personally, the timing could not possibly have been worse. Ten days after MLB announced it was moving the game out of Georgia was the first Monday of the Masters. Traditionally, the club's three hundred members break out their green jackets for the week—they can only be worn on club grounds—and take part in running the tournament.

Manfred opted not to go to the tournament. He won't discuss the decision, because no Augusta National member other than the club chair is allowed to discuss club matters publicly. Clearly, the absence of the commissioner of baseball from the Masters ten days after a controversial decision involving a voting rights law in Georgia (where the club is located)—a law that most members probably supported—would be a subject off-limits.

"It's a fact that I decided not to go," Manfred said. "Let's leave it at that."

PGA Tour commissioner Jay Monahan was at Augusta during Masters week, and he too had made a statement. The day after MLB's announcement to pull the All-Star Game from Georgia, Monahan announced that the tour would *not* be moving the annual tour championship from Georgia.

On that same day, the PGA of America announced it would not move its annual LPGA (Ladies Professional Golf Association) championship from Atlanta Athletic Club in June. The PGA of America had needed four full days to finally announce it was moving its 2022 PGA championship from a Donald Trump–owned golf course after the January 6 invasion of the Capitol. In its statement, the association insisted that leaving the LPGA in Atlanta was okay because the event is run by "three organizations that believe in diversity, equity and inclusion"—the three being the PGA of America, the LPGA, and the title sponsor.

This belief in equity is apparently true because the PGA of America says it's true. As noted earlier in this chapter, among the "28,000 proud PGA Professionals" who make up the organization, 167 were Black in 2021—according to the PGA.

At least Monahan made no self-righteous claims in his April 3 statement about diversity, equity, and inclusion. Instead, he went the charity route.

The PGA Tour annually holds its season-ending event in Atlanta at East Lake Country Club, a few miles from downtown Atlanta. Monahan's excuse for not moving the tour was that the local charities that benefit from the event would be damaged if the tournament were to be moved.

In 2020, the tour gave the local charities "a record" (the tour's phrasing) $3.6 million. Given that the tour, flush with a new TV contract that kicks in beginning in 2022, had just started a $40 million program to reward the ten "most popular" players on tour (according to a social media formula it did not make public), one wonders why $3.6 million of that money could not have been diverted to the Atlanta charities. Meanwhile, other charities — those in the city where the tournament was moved — would also benefit.

"We've held the tour championship at East Lake since 1998," Monahan said. "The event is about more than just the $3.6 million. It's about the support we give to everything the East Lake Foundation has done for the golf course and for people who live in the neighborhoods around the golf course.

"The progress that's been made since 1998 because of the work done by Tom and Ann [Cousins, who run the East Lake Foundation] is remarkable. Every year, we get to help tell that story and raise awareness so that they can continue to make an impact. We didn't want to give up that impact."

I asked Monahan if it would have been a bad thing to walk away for just a year to make a statement about the voting rights law. After a long pause, he said, "Yes, it would have been a bad thing. It was pretty clear to us that we would do far more good staying in Atlanta than not staying in Atlanta."

Fair enough.

It is now up to Monahan and the tour to back up what he said in his tour championship press conference in 2020 — with money and actions — regardless of what some golf fans, players, and sponsors might think.

EPILOGUE

When I began conducting research for this book, I was hoping to get a better understanding of the racial polarization going on in our country.

I'd witnessed it for many years, dating to when I grew up in New York City playing ball with the Black and Hispanic kids in my neighborhood and in my schools. My nickname on my junior high school basketball team was "White Boy," which was a term of endearment and respect. But it also made clear that I was different from the Black and Hispanic kids who made up the rest of the team.

As a reporter, I've witnessed racism through the years, some of it blatant, some of it subtle, but all of it real.

As I wrote in the introduction, the national anthem protests in the NFL in 2017 are what crystallized for me how divided we truly were when it came to race in sports. Week after week, I watched Black players kneeling for the anthem and being booed loudly and angrily by mostly white audiences. Almost none of the players kneeling were white; almost none of the fans booing were Black.

No doubt both sides were egged on by Donald Trump's infamous "Fire the sons of bitches" rant in Alabama. The players weren't going to be told what to do by Trump, and many fans let the players know they agreed with Trump. The week before his rant, a total of six players knelt for the anthem. On the Sunday afterward, more than two hundred players either knelt or stayed in the locker room during the playing of the anthem.

In short, Trump got exactly what he wanted—more proof to his base that Black athletes were "unpatriotic," even though the protests never had anything to do with patriotism.

Many in the right-wing media expressed outrage that Black men, "making millions of dollars," would be so unpatriotic; the pundits ignored the fact that the protests were about white police officers killing Black people and had nothing to do with patriotism or money. The protesters were trying to say they loved their country and wanted to make it better by finding a way to stop—or at least slow down—white police officers running amok and killing Black people.

No one ever said there weren't times when police needed to pull their weapons; the protesters and others were just saying they shouldn't be so quick to do it. And that it seemed as if most unjustified police shootings involved white officers and Black victims.

There was so much anger. Every time I defended the Black protesters, whether in print, on radio, on TV, or on Twitter, I received angry responses. People said—among other things—that the protesters, who were almost always referred to in an angrily pejorative way, were ruining their enjoyment of football.

How were the protests doing that? None of the protests took place during a game or delayed a single kickoff. They were peaceful and nonviolent. After a while, it became clear to me that what upset the white fans so much was that the sight of the protesters forced them to think about something they didn't want to think about—or even admit existed. Their lives were unaffected by racism. They didn't have to fear for their lives during a routine traffic stop, and they didn't have to sit down and give their children The Talk so that they would understand that any interaction with police could quickly become dangerous.

Nor did they have to deal with the three letters — DWB — that almost every Black person, but especially men, knows in the same way that we all know DUI. That is, they didn't have to worry about Driving While Black. Not one Black person who I interviewed for this book had *not* been stopped for DWB at least once; most have dealt with it multiple times.

"And the first question is almost always the same," said Kenny Williams, the executive vice president of the Chicago White Sox. "Where'd you get this car?"

If you combine being Black with driving a nice car in a nice neighborhood, you will almost certainly be pulled over for DWB early and often. When Ed Tapscott was general manager of the New York Knicks and would drive home after games to the tony Riverdale neighborhood where he lived, he was stopped on a regular basis when he got near the apartment he lived in.

"I can tell you, without exaggeration, that it happened about every two weeks," he said. "It was just part of my life."

There are a number of people who I had hoped to talk to for this book but who I didn't get to speak with for various reasons. Notable among them are Harry Edwards, Colin Kaepernick, Kareem Abdul-Jabbar, and Bill Russell. Both Edwards and Kaepernick are under contract to TV networks for documentaries and clearly did not want to give away — literally — anything that might be part of the documentaries. Abdul-Jabbar has always been reticent about interviews, and his longtime gatekeeper made it clear about five minutes after I got on the phone with her that she wasn't even going to take my request to him. Russell, who is eighty-seven, has had some health issues that would have made a lengthy conversation difficult for him.

Fortunately for me, many others were willing to talk at length and, sometimes, on multiple occasions. I did get to talk to Tommie Smith and John Carlos, the Olympic sprinters whose raised gloved fists during the 1968 medal ceremony for the 200 meters in Mexico City may have been the most iconic sports-related moment of the Civil Rights Movement. They were thrown out of the Olympic movement at the time.

Now, fifty-three years later, Smith and Carlos are heroes to most for the courage they showed. They have been inducted into the US Olympic and Paralympic Hall of Fame. Both men believe that Kaepernick, who was blackballed by all thirty-two NFL teams after he began the anthem protests in 2016, will be seen as a hero in the not-too-distant future.

Kaepernick is never going to play in the NFL again. He had just turned twenty-nine when he played his last game for the San Francisco 49ers at the end of the 2016 season. Now, he's thirty-four and hasn't taken a snap for four years. It's clear he'll never get another chance—and wasn't ever going to get another real crack at playing after his protests.

During an August 2020 interview—after the country had been inflamed by the Floyd murder—former NFL player Emmanuel Acho asked NFL commissioner Roger Goodell how Goodell would apologize to Kaepernick.

"The first thing I'd say," Goodell answered, "is, 'I wish we had listened earlier, Kaep, to what you were kneeling about—and what you were trying to bring attention to.' We had invited him in several times, to have the conversation, to have the dialogue. I wish we had the benefit of that. We never did. We would have benefited from that absolutely."

Goodell went on: "It's not about the flag. The message here and what our players are doing is being mischaracterized. These are not people who are being unpatriotic. They're not disloyal; they're not against our military. In fact, many of these guys were in the military and are [from] a military family. What they were doing was trying to bring attention to something that needs to be fixed. That misrepresentation in who they were and what they were doing was a thing that really gnawed at me."

Talking about Floyd's murder and the video of Derek Chauvin's knee on Floyd's throat, Goodell said, "It was horrific to see that play out on the screen. There was a part of me that said, 'I hope people realize that's what the players were protesting.' And that's what's been going on in our communities. You see it now on television, but that's been going on for a long, long time. And that's where we should have listened sooner."

It was an eloquent apology—although it came after Kaepernick had been blackballed for three seasons. There was also the implication that somehow Kaepernick should have come to the league to discuss what he had been trying to do rather than the other way around.

By the time Goodell made his apology, Kaepernick's career was, for all intents and purposes, already over. Goodell's words sounded good, but in reality, they were empty.

The previous November, the NFL had offered Kaepernick a "tryout," contingent on his agreeing to sign a waiver that he would not sue any team or the league if he wasn't signed. What's more, the league wanted the tryout conducted inside the Atlanta Falcons facility with no media present and no one except the Falcons allowed to video the workout—just in case, apparently, he looked really good. A Falcons tape could have been edited quite easily.

The whole thing was a public relations sham.

Kaepernick ended up moving the workout to a high school field about an hour outside Atlanta. Seven teams showed up to watch, and even though from all reports his arm strength and mobility looked good (there's only so much you can prove in one of those workouts), no one so much as invited him to come to their camp for a tryout.

The NFL once again sold the bogus notion to the media that the league had wanted to give Kaepernick a chance, but he wouldn't comply with their rules. Shame on him!

There was never any doubt that the workout wasn't going to result in Kaepernick's getting a job. He went along with the workout to try to quiet all the anonymous voices claiming he didn't want to play football or wasn't good enough to play again in the NFL.

The league had put out all sorts of PR about Kaepernick's chances to sign with a team. Most prominent was the story that Denver Broncos general manager John Elway had offered to make a sign-and-trade deal with the 49ers before the 2016 season — *before* Kaepernick sat or knelt for the anthem. Few of those stories noted this fact or that Elway had gone on to play the immortal Trevor Simien at quarterback instead.

A year later, when Kaepernick was a free agent, Elway signed Case Keenum to a two-year $36 million contract to play quarterback. He lasted one season in Denver and was last seen as Baker Mayfield's backup in Cleveland. Denver's search for a quarterback continues. One wonders what might have been if it had brought in a twenty-eight-year-old who had been to a Super Bowl and still had something to prove.

When Joe Flacco was injured during training camp in 2017, the Baltimore Ravens brought Kaepernick in to discuss a possible deal — or at least a tryout. Nothing happened — he never got on a practice field. People in the Baltimore organization said later that they just didn't feel as if Kaepernick was eager to play football. How one can sense an athlete's competitive drive in a conference room is hard to say. More likely, the angry-fan backlash (when word leaked that the team was talking to Kaepernick) is what ended the dialogue. The Ravens ended up signing a former Arena Football League quarterback instead.

The Seattle Seahawks also considered giving Kaepernick a try-out, but that, too, fizzled—quite possibly for the same reason.

Most fascinating to me about the NFL's sham tryout in November 2019 was the media's reaction to it. I walked into the press box at M&T Bank Stadium in Baltimore the day after Kaepernick's appearance at the Atlanta high school. I was almost instantly attacked by a number of my colleagues—friends—who knew I had supported Kaepernick and had said he had been blackballed from the very beginning.

"What do you think about your guy now?" was the refrain. "The league tried to give him a chance, and he screwed it up."

Those were pretty much the exact words thrown at me. When I argued that the whole thing had been a PR ploy and nothing more and that the NFL had tried to force Kaepernick to work out in a closed environment, I was told that thirty teams had been waiting to watch him at the Falcons facility and that his insistence on moving the workout had cut that number to seven.

"What, none of those guys could have gotten a ride?" I said. "They couldn't afford to rent a car or call an Uber?" (For the record, I doubt NFL scouts travel by Uber very often.) I also said, "If all thirty-two general managers had been there, he still wouldn't get a contract."

Behind me a voice said, "Amen to that." It was one of the handful of Black reporters in the press box.

To some, Kaepernick is now a hero. "The kid was willing to risk his career to do the right thing," John Carlos said. "In the end, people will understand that."

To others, he's still a pariah. They still mention that the socks he wore at the outset of his protests bore pictures of pigs wearing police hats. Kaepernick explained then he was making a point about police who protected *everyone* and those who did not. The socks are brought up constantly by the right wing as proof that he's both un-American and a racist—not to mention a terrible person.

As I talked to people over the last eighteen months, I came to realize that arguing that Black and white people in this country are polarized over the issue of race was a little bit like pointing out that the sun was likely to rise in the east tomorrow morning.

The polarization is, sadly, a given. Some of it is subtle, some not.

The Major League Baseball TV Network, which does superb work covering the sport, likes to run public service announcements in which a player explains his motivation to become a champion. One of those that ran during the 2021 season had Yankees catcher Gary Sanchez speaking in Spanish about the great catchers he had followed behind the plate at Yankee Stadium. Sanchez named Bill Dickey and Yogi Berra—both Hall of Famers—and Thurman Munson and Jorge Posada, both of whom were outstanding players, though not Hall of Famers.

Not mentioned is Elston Howard, who in 1955 was the Yankees first Black player, someone who went on to win an MVP award and to be selected for nine All-Star Games. My guess is there was no malice in leaving Howard out, but, somehow, he was left out.

That sort of thing tends to go unnoticed. Most white people would shrug at that sort of oversight and see it as a mistake, nothing more. They would say that to put any racial implication to it is creating as issue where there's no issue.

Which gets to the crux of the problem. As George Raveling pointed out to me almost at the outset of my research, there was no way — regardless of how many people I interviewed or how sympathetic I might be to the Black experience — that I could truly understand that experience, because I have never lived it.

"You just can't walk in our shoes," he said. "The first breaths of air I took in my life were in a segregated hospital. I grew up knowing there were certain places you did not go as a Black person in Washington, D.C. I knew if I saw a white woman walking in my direction, I dropped my head because I didn't want there to be any misunderstanding or her having any notion that I might be a threat to her in any way."

You might say that the world was a different place when Raveling — born in 1937 — was growing up. And it certainly was. Jim Crow not only existed but also flourished in the South. Ask someone who grew up during those times about "separate but equal," and then wait for the laughter to subside.

"Separate?" longtime basketball coach Tubby Smith said. "Yes, separate. But equal? Are you kidding?"

That was a long time ago in a place far, far away. Or was it?

As I was wrapping up this book, England hosted Italy in the finals of the European Championships, which had been delayed a year by COVID-19. For European countries, the "Euros" rank only behind the World Cup in importance. England had not won either a World Cup or a Euro since the 1966 World Cup.

With fans allowed inside Wembley Stadium, the entire country prepared for a long-awaited celebration. It never happened. England scored early, but Italy tied the score at 1 in the second half. Thirty minutes of overtime failed to produce a goal, meaning the title would be decided by penalty kicks.

Italy won the penalty kick tiebreaker 3–2. The last three Englishmen to attempt penalties were Marcus Rashford, Jadon Sancho, and Bukayo Saka—all Black. All missed.

Within minutes of Saka's miss, the internet was filled with racist bleatings directed at the three players. A mural of Rashford in Manchester—where he plays for Manchester United—was defaced with racial slurs in what police described as a hate crime. The mural had been placed there to honor Rashford for the work he has done dealing with poverty and hunger among children.

The Football Association of England denounced the racist rants, as did Prime Minister Boris Johnson, who called them "appalling."

The incident reinforced what we all already knew: racism is an issue well beyond the shores of the United States.

The more I talked to Black people in the last eighteen months, the more I came to understand that their day-to-day lives are always colored (no pun intended) by the fact that so many white people look at them with suspicion for the simple reason that they're Black.

"When I wake up in the morning, I have to think, 'Where am I going today?'" Olympic swimmer Cullen Jones said. "Do I have to be careful to dress in a way that will be nonthreatening to white people I may encounter? If it's cold, can I wear a hoodie, or will that scare people? It's something I have to think about every day."

If I get pulled over by a police officer, it is almost certainly because I've done something wrong: speeding, running a light, having a taillight out. I feel fear when I see flashing lights behind me because I don't want a ticket and certainly don't want a lecture. But those are my greatest fears. I was once issued a warning late at night because it took me a couple of minutes to find my registration in a cluttered glove compartment. The warning was for potentially endangering the cop by making him stand and wait for me to find the registration.

But that's about as close as I've ever been to being given a hard time that I probably didn't deserve. I'm polite to police, but I can't ever remember putting my hands on the dashboard when the cop approached the car. Never occurred to me.

Being pulled over if you are Black is a completely different experience: hands on the dashboard, don't make a move without permission, and know that much of the time, you've been pulled over for doing one thing wrong: DWB.

No wonder Black people are suspicious of white cops. Tony Dungy, the Hall of Fame football coach and one of the most reasonable people I know, made this point: "I imagine when a police officer walks up to a car, he's nervous too. He has no way of knowing what he's going to encounter when he gets there."

There's no doubt about that. But then, as Dungy points out, "If you don't stop someone for the crimes of being Black and driving a nice car, you don't have to deal with that issue."

Some of the numbers that Richard Lapchick has compiled through the years are scary. For all the talk about getting more people of color into positions of authority, the progress continues to be slow. When Derek Jeter selected Kim Ng to be general manager of the Miami Marlins last winter, it was certainly a breakthrough.

But Ng's hiring was treated as if Jeter had issued a second Emancipation Proclamation. "What I want to see," said Chicago White Sox executive vice president Kenny Williams, "is a time when hiring someone of color or hiring a woman for an important position *isn't* news. We've got a long way to travel before we get there."

As Florida State basketball coach Leonard Hamilton points out, the progress made in this country in the area of race is hard to grasp.

Most kids today don't even know what Jim Crow means unless they pay close attention in history class.

And yet, what has happened since the George Floyd murder is both encouraging and discouraging. "The encouraging part is that I think it woke a lot of white people up," Duke coach Mike Krzyzewski said. "Not that any of us can completely understand it—we can't—but at least we understand *that*. The notion that because things have slowly gotten better over the years does not mean we're anywhere close to the answers that we need.

"I mean, we're still so far away. The fact that there are still white people who honestly believe that Black people should somehow be grateful that there's been progress is ludicrous. Well, how the hell did we get into a position where we had so far to go to begin with? You can't just say, 'Okay, we'll start with square one and go from there.' That's not good enough. We have to *get* to square one. You can't just wipe the slate clean because it's more comfortable to do that."

Or as John Thompson said in our last interview, "I get pretty damn sick and tired of being told I should be grateful for all that I have and for all that I was *allowed* to accomplish. Allowed? Yes, I'm grateful that Georgetown hired me when it did and allowed me to run the basketball program I wanted to run. But grateful? You think they hired me as an act of charity, or do you think it was because there weren't a hell of a lot of people lining up to coach a team that had just gone three and twenty-three? You think they'd have let me do the things the way I wanted to if we weren't winning a lot of games and making the school a hell of a lot of money?"

There is one number that Lapchick doesn't track but probably should: white men in the sports media. Just as Ozzie Newsome correctly says things have improved for Black quarterbacks, since he *knew*, in 1970, that he wouldn't be given a chance to play quarterback at Pop Warner tryouts, things have improved in sports journalism.

Men like Michael Wilbon and Stephen A. Smith are stars on television, and their voices are important ones. But Jemele Hill was forced to leave ESPN because she (correctly) called Donald Trump a white supremacist on her twitter feed. ESPN employs a plethora of women—Black and white—to anchor *SportsCenter,* but most of them damn well better look good in a dress and high heels.

The top five NFL TV analysts are Fox's Troy Aikman, CBS's Tony Romo, NBC's Cris Collinsworth, and ESPN's Monday night duo of Brian Griese and Louis Riddick. The top play-by-play men for NFL broadcasts are CBS's Jim Nantz, NBC's Al Michaels (although Mike Tirico is being groomed to replace Michaels), Fox's Joe Buck, and ESPN's Steve Levy. The only Black analyst in that group is Riddick—who shares top billing with Griese. Tirico, still waiting in the wings for Michaels to retire sometime around 2050, is also Black.

Three years ago, when Dan Patrick left the anchor desk on NBC's Sunday Night pregame show, *Football Night in America,* and was replaced by Tirico, NBC had an all-Black anchor desk of Tirico, Tony Dungy, and former Patriots defensive back Rodney Harrison. The following season, Chris Simms, who is white, was moved into Harrison's spot on the desk and Harrison became a floater, frequently sharing the second desk with *Pro Football Report*'s Mike Florio.

Notably, the NBC show is by far the best of the network pregame shows. Even so, I asked Dungy why he thought the network felt the need to move Simms to the anchor desk.

"You know it's something we [he, Tirico, and Harrison]

discussed," Dungy said. "But I've never been given a reason why they did it. Chris is very good. But so is Rodney."

Simms is good. But Harrison was far more willing to disagree with Dungy, which made for better television.

The top college football analysts are ESPN's Kirk Herbstreit and CBS's Gary Danielson. Their play-by-play partners are Chris Fowler at ESPN and Brad Nessler at CBS. All are white. When it comes to network number one broadcast teams, only Fox's Gus Johnson, who is its number one college football play-by-play man, is Black.

This is not meant to demean any of those men, all of whom are talented, but it does make you wonder. As with team owners and athletic directors, the ultimate sports decision makers at networks are white men.

The numbers in basketball are little different. Dick Vitale was replaced as ESPN's number one analyst by Jay Bilas. CBS's top analysts are seventy-eight-year-old Bill Raftery and Grant Hill, who is Black. ESPN's number one college play-by-play man is Dan Shulman; CBS's lead guy is Nantz, backed up by Ian Eagle and Andrew Catalon when Nantz is unavailable. All are white.

Those who work in television — Black, white, or anything else — are under what amounts to a gag order on air. Never is to be heard a discouraging word other than perhaps questioning an official's call or a time-out. Every coach is a wonderful person, all the players are "student-athletes," and just about anyone who makes a jump shot in a college game is a potential lottery pick. On TV, all is well in jock world.

This rah-rah spirit means the real reporting still must be done in the print world. And the majority of those working there — myself included — are white men. That helps explain why so many writers were pro-NFL and anti-Kaepernick when the quarterback was blackballed. It also helps explain why so few — if any — have wondered publicly how in the hell any self-respecting NFL scout or general manager could possibly look at Mitchell Trubisky, Patrick Mahomes, and Deshaun Watson in 2017 and say, "Trubisky, that's my guy."

Many in the media have called this simply a scouting mistake. A scouting mistake? Seriously? Or did Trubisky merely look the way so many still think an NFL quarterback is supposed to look.

The media, the scouts, the coaches, the owners — collectively — help define consensus views about players. They all should share the blame when the consensus is wrong. Why did so many in the NFL want to make Lamar Jackson a running back or a wide receiver? I've read countless stories comparing Robert Griffin III to Jackson. Griffin might very well have been on his way to a Hall of Fame career in Washington until he badly injured his knee in a playoff game in 2012.

More important, though, is this: Jackson plays nothing like Griffin. Griffin was fast; Jackson is faster. Beyond that, Griffin, at six feet three and 215 pounds, constantly tried to run through people. Jackson, not quite as big — six two and 210 — constantly and consistently makes people miss him. Unlike Griffin, he is elusive. He rarely takes a hard hit and has missed only one game since becoming the Ravens starter halfway through the 2018 season: he missed the game because of COVID-19, not because of any hard hit that he took.

As his fellow MVP quarterback Mahomes says, "I really believe so many people focused on Lamar's running at Louisville, they never noticed how well he passed the ball."

Certainly possible. But did anyone ever suggest Fran Tarkenton, who both ran and passed his way to the Hall of Fame, or Steve Young — same thing — should switch positions? Even for a second?

Tim Tebow switched positions—and was brought back by the Jacksonville Jaguars as a tight end in the summer of 2021. But there was a difference: he couldn't throw the ball at an NFL level. Period.

So why were Griffin and Jackson compared? The answer is easy: both are Black. If Jackson had the exact same skill set coming out of college and if he had been white, changing positions would never have been mentioned. Never.

That's why Newsome says there has been plenty of progress since his Pop Warner tryouts fifty-one years ago but there is still a long way to go before a quarterback's race—or a coach's or general manager's race—is no longer an issue.

"I hope I live to see it," he said with a laugh, "But I'm not counting on it."

Although this book is largely about what it was like to be Black fifty-plus years ago and what it's like to be Black now, I did get the answer to the question I first asked John Thompson in that first meeting I had with him more than four years ago.

"Why does this issue scare so many white people?" I asked, in March 2020.

Thompson laughed. "What is it that people fear the most?" he asked rhetorically. "The unknown. We all fear the unknown, and the idea that the time has come when what's been done so unfairly to Black people in this country for so many years has to be recognized scares a lot of white people because it's been unknown to them. As far as they were concerned, it didn't exist. Never happened. Or if it did, it's been fixed. Why has it been fixed? Because they *say* it's been fixed.

"We're a hell of a long way from that happening. But the more people who are willing to discuss it and admit to it, the better off we'll all be. I won't be alive to see it, but the very fact that more people are willing to start asking the questions means we're going in the right direction."

Less than three months after Thompson spoke those words, George Floyd was murdered. I never did get to talk to Thompson about Floyd's death or the aftermath. I know the sight of Black people and white people marching together would have made him happy. I know the responses that so many white people—led by the president of the United States—had to those marches would have been heartbreaking for him, as it was for so many of us.

It has been more than fifty-eight years since George Raveling stood directly behind Martin Luther King as he said repeatedly, "I have a dream, yes, I have a dream!"

The dream lives. But we have yet to actually live it.

ACKNOWLEDGMENTS

When Patrick Ewing was playing center for Georgetown in the 1980s, his coach, John Thompson, was often asked why Ewing didn't score more often.

"Center," he answered, "is a dependent position. You can't score if your guards don't get you the basketball."

In a different context, I could be Ewing. And in a twist, Thompson was my coach on this book.

Writing—reporting—is a dependent position. Ewing needed his guards; I need my sources. Never was that more true than in the creation of this book.

Unlike many of my other books, I was dealing with many people whom I didn't know at all or—more important—who didn't know me at all. And yet, as I think the book reflects, they were remarkably generous with their time and extremely willing to tell me exactly what they thought about what remains arguably the most sensitive subject in this country: race.

It is difficult to know where to start in saying thank you. Thompson is obvious; just read the book's dedication. So is Doug Williams, who not only gave me lengthy interview time but also wrote the book's foreword.

One of my first interviews was with Tony Dungy—one of those people who I didn't know before starting this book. Fortunately,

349

Tony was familiar with my work and was extraordinarily generous and forthcoming with his thoughts on many questions. Every time I talked to him, I came away feeling smarter.

That was true of a long list of people: Marlin Briscoe, James Harris, Warren Moon, Jimmy Raye, Ozzie Newsome (who has been teaching me about football and life for eighteen years now), Eric DeCosta, Donovan McNabb, Mike Tomlin, Marvin Lewis, Jim Caldwell, Lovie Smith, Jimmy Raye, Eric Bieniemy, Patrick Mahomes, Ed Tapscott, George Raveling, Nolan Richardson, Tubby Smith, Gary Williams, Shaka Smart, Tommy Amaker, Sam Jones, Doc Rivers, Steve Kerr, Gregg Popovich, Mike Krzyzewski, Willie Randolph, Dave Stewart, Kenny Williams, Joel Ward, Cullen Jones, Adam Silver, baseball commissioner Rob Manfred, and PGA Tour commissioner Jay Monahan. It was an honor for me to talk to Tommie Smith and to John Carlos. I'm grateful to Dr. Smith's wife, Delois—who didn't know me from Adam when I first contacted her—for setting me up to talk with her husband. Extra thanks to Marlin Briscoe for convincing John Carlos to speak to me.

And special thanks to Michael Wilbon and Kevin Blackistone, longtime colleagues and friends, who helped me in multiple ways on multiple occasions.

The list of those I interviewed just once and used limited material from is lengthy, and I'm grateful to all of them.

In many cases, I needed help to track down and connect with some of the people I mentioned but did not know well. So thanks also to Ted Crews, Burt Lauten, Mike Bass, Tim Frank (a wonderful person in spite of his lack of any formal higher education), Pat Courtney, Brian McCarthy, Laura Neal, Tony La Russa, Mike Unger, George McPhee, Kevin Byrne, Ken Rosenthal, Richard

Justice, and Chad Steele (who gets extra credit for being the son of one of my heroes, Gary Steele—Army's first Black football player).

Special thanks to three men from Hachette Book Group. First, Michael Pietsch, who was my editor for many years at Little, Brown and is now the CEO of Hachette Book Group. Michael was open to this idea and believed in it after five editors at other publishing houses turned it down. One publisher said, "How can you write a book on race when you're white?" My response: by listening to Black athletes, coaches, and others. The intent of this book was to *report.* I think all those I spoke with did an eloquent job of explaining the challenges they have faced and still face.

Michael, who doesn't edit books anymore, passed me on to a very good young editor named Phil Marino, who also saw potential in the book and eventually bought it for Little, Brown. Turns out you can go home again. When Phil left the company, Bruce Nichols stepped in and was remarkably patient working on a book he was literally handed on the fly.

Thanks, as always, to my agent Esther Newberg, who has now put up with me for thirty-six years, and even though we often disagree—frequently on the Mets and Red Sox—her loyalty to me through good times and bad has been unflagging. Esther's greatest strength—other than scaring the hell out of publishers—might be her ability to select assistants. Hell, I married one of them. Her current assistant, Estie Berkowitz, is another in a long line of very patient people who have put up with me and several other high-maintenance clients.

John Delaney has lawyered most of my book contracts and has done so with great patience and an eye for every possible detail.

Then, as always, there are my friends, many of whom encouraged me to continue pursuing this book when many folks in publishing were saying, "John, we love you, but how about a different idea?"

As usual, in no special order, that group includes Keith and Barbie Drum, Dave Kindred, Jackson Diehl and Jean Halperin, Linda Maraniss, Matt Vita, Matt Rennie and Dan Steinberg (Steinberg has proven to be a wonderful editor to work with since taking over for Rennie on what was no doubt the happiest day of Rennie's life). More *Post* folks: Matt Bonesteel, Sally Jenkins, Marty Weil, Lexie Verdon and Steve Barr (Posties forever), Mark Maske, Gene Wang, Micah Pollack, and Kathy Orton.

Longtime friends: Terry and Patti Hanson, Doug and Beth Doughty, Bob DeStefano, Wes Seeley, Lefty and Joyce Driesell, Mike and Mickie Krzyzewski, Roy Williams, Tony Bennett, Seth and Brad Greenberg, Dan Bonner, Jim Calhoun, Fran Dunphy, Jay Wright, Steve Donahue, Phil Martelli, Mike Brey, Bobby Cremins, Dave and Lynne Odom, Ryan Odom, Pat Skerry, Pat Flannery, Zach Spiker, Tom Brennan, Fran O'Hanlon, Matt Langel, Nathan Davis, Mike Rhoades, Ed McLaughlin, Robby Robinson, Jimmy Allen, Ed DeChellis, Kenny Niumatalolo, Chet Gladchuck, Mack McCarthy, Emmett Davis, Andy Dolich, Rick Brewer, Steve Kirschner, Pete Alfano, Lesley Visser, Gary Cohen, Beth Shumway-Brown, Beth Sherry-Downes, Pete Van Poppel, Phil Hoffmann, Joe Speed, Andrew Thompson, Dicky Hall, Tim Kelly, Gordon Austin, Rich DeMarco, Dean Darling, Joe Beckerle, Tony Marino, John Minko, Jim Cantelupe, Derek Klein, Anthony and Kristen Noto, Chris Knoche, Mike Werteen (still the best TV producer I ever worked with), Bob Zurfluh, Vivian Thompson-Goldstein, Mike and David Sanders, Tony and Karril Kornheiser, Nancy Denlinger, General Steve Sachs, Tim Maloney, Harry Kantarian, Jim Rome, Dick and Joanie "Hoops" Weiss, Mike Purkey, Bob Edwards, Tom and

Jane Goldman, Holland and Jill Mickle, Bob Costas, Larry Dorman, Jerry Tarde, Mike O'Malley, Ryan Herrington, Sam Weinman, Jay Edwards, Chris Edwards and John Cutcher, Len and Gwyn Edwards-Dieterle, Bill Leahey, Andy North, Paul Goydos, David Duval, Steve Flesch, Billy Andrade, Jeff Sluman, Gary "Grits" Crandall, Drew Miceli, Brian Henninger, and Tom Watson—our virulently different politics aside. Wait, there's more: former radio colleagues Andrew "Arnold" Bogusch, Max Herman, Peter Bellotti, Anthony Pierno, Mike Diaz, and Billy Giacalone.

Special thanks to Chris Ryan for his superb work launching my podcast *Storytime*. And to Tom Stathakes, who has been a great boss and a better friend in many roles in the last dozen years. And to Frank Mastrandrea, whose advice is so smart it is almost as smart as he knows it to be. (Just joking, Frank...sort of.)

Thanks also to many others in golf I have worked with through the years: Courtney Holt, Frank Nobilo, Kristi Setaro, Eric Rutledge, David Gross, Adam Hertzog, Jon Steele, Tony Grbac, Brandel Chamblee, Rich Lerner, Kelly Tilghman, Whit Watson, Mark Rolfing, Notah Begay, Lisa Cornwell, Gary Williams (the non-coach), Damon Hack, Tripp Isenhour, Jay Coffin, John Feyko, Todd Lewis, Jeremy Davis, and Jon Albanese.

Thanks also to two retired United States Golf Association executive directors—David Fay and Mike Davis—and to USGA stars Mike Butz, Mary Lopuszynski, and Greg Midland. Mark Russell and Slugger White will be retiring at the end of 2021 after being the PGA Tour's two primary tournament directors for more than thirty years. They have been my friends for almost that long, and I can tell you from watching them work from close-up, they and their colleagues may be the most underappreciated people in golf—perhaps in sports. The same can be said about my favorite Oregon Duck,

Steve Rintoul; Jon Brendle; Robby Ware; Dillard Pruitt; and the one and only John Paramor. I have missed seeing Mark Russell's wife, Laura, and daughter, Alex, during the pandemic. At the PGA of America, thanks go to Julius Mason, John Dever, and Joe Steranka (an emeritus member). Others in golf are also due my thanks: the great Marty Caffey, Sid Wilson, Henry Hughes (sigh), Guy Scheipers, Frank and Jaymie Bussey, Dave Lancer, John Bush, and the very-much-missed Denise Taylor.

Several years ago, I dedicated a young adult book I wrote about basketball recruiting (*Foul Trouble*) to two of the best people I've ever met in the sport: Tom Konchalski and Frank Sullivan. The basketball world lost Tom in January, a massive hit to all of us who loved him. Frank and his wife, Susan, remain among my dearest friends.

With Bud Collins gone, I have few friends left in tennis, but I do still have Mark Preston, Patrick McEnroe, and Mary Carillo. No one makes me laugh more often or think more often than Mary does.

My swimming pals and I haven't been together for a while, but we are all planning postpandemic comebacks: Jeff Roddin, Jason Crist, Wally Dicks, Clay F. Britt, Mark Pugliese, Paul Doremus, Mike Fell, Danny Pick, Erik "Dr. Post" Osbourne, John Craig, Doug Chestnut, Penny Bates, Carole Kammel, Peter Ward, Tom Denes, A. J. Block, Mary Dowling, and Peter Lawler. No athlete in any sport has ever inspired me more than my late teammate Margot Pettijohn.

Obviously, the Red Auerbach lunch group didn't meet for fourteen months during the pandemic, but we are up and running again. It includes Aubre Jones, Murray Lieberman, Harry Huang, Geoff Kaplan, Jeff Gemunder, Stanley Copeland, Mark Hughes, Steve Polakoff, and Lew Flashenberg and, in absentia, Jack Kvancz, Joe

McKeown, Pete Dowling, and Bob Campbell. Missed always: Red, Zang, Hymie, Reed, Rob, Arnie, and Morgan.

I thank the Rio Gang: Tate Armstrong, Mark Alarie, Clay Buckley, and, on occasion, Mike Gminski.

I'm still here in large part because I have great doctors who happen to be good friends: Eddie McDevitt, Dean and Ann Taylor, Bob Arciero, Gus Mazzocca, Murray Lieberman, and the two men who probably saved my life twelve years ago: Joe Vassallo and Steve Boyce.

Last—never least—my family. My brother, Bobby, and sister, Margaret. Bobby's ever-patient wife, Jennifer, has clearly done remarkable work raising Matthew and Brian. Margaret lost her husband, my brother-in-law David, three years ago, and she and her sons, Ethan and Ben, have shown remarkable courage dealing with David's death.

I also have to mention my in-laws, Cheryl and Marlynn Bauch, who put up with all the various eccentricities of their son-in-law because they know that—for some strange reason—their daughter loves him.

That daughter is Christine, and I am so fortunate to be married to her and to be the father of three remarkable people: Danny, Brigid, and Jane. It is Jane, now eleven, who keeps me in line better than anyone. No one can roll her eyes at her father like Jane can.

—John Feinstein
Potomac, Maryland
June 2021

INDEX

ABOUT THE AUTHOR

John Feinstein is the author of forty-five books, including two #1 *New York Times* bestsellers: *A Season on the Brink* and *A Good Walk Spoiled*. Fourteen of his books are young adult mysteries. One of them, *Last Shot*, won the Edgar Allan Poe Award for mystery writing in the Young Adult category. He is a member of five Halls of Fame and currently contributes to the *Washington Post, Golf Digest, Golf World*, and the Black News Channel. Feinstein is also the TV color analyst for UMBC basketball.